D1690899

H. A. Sigg

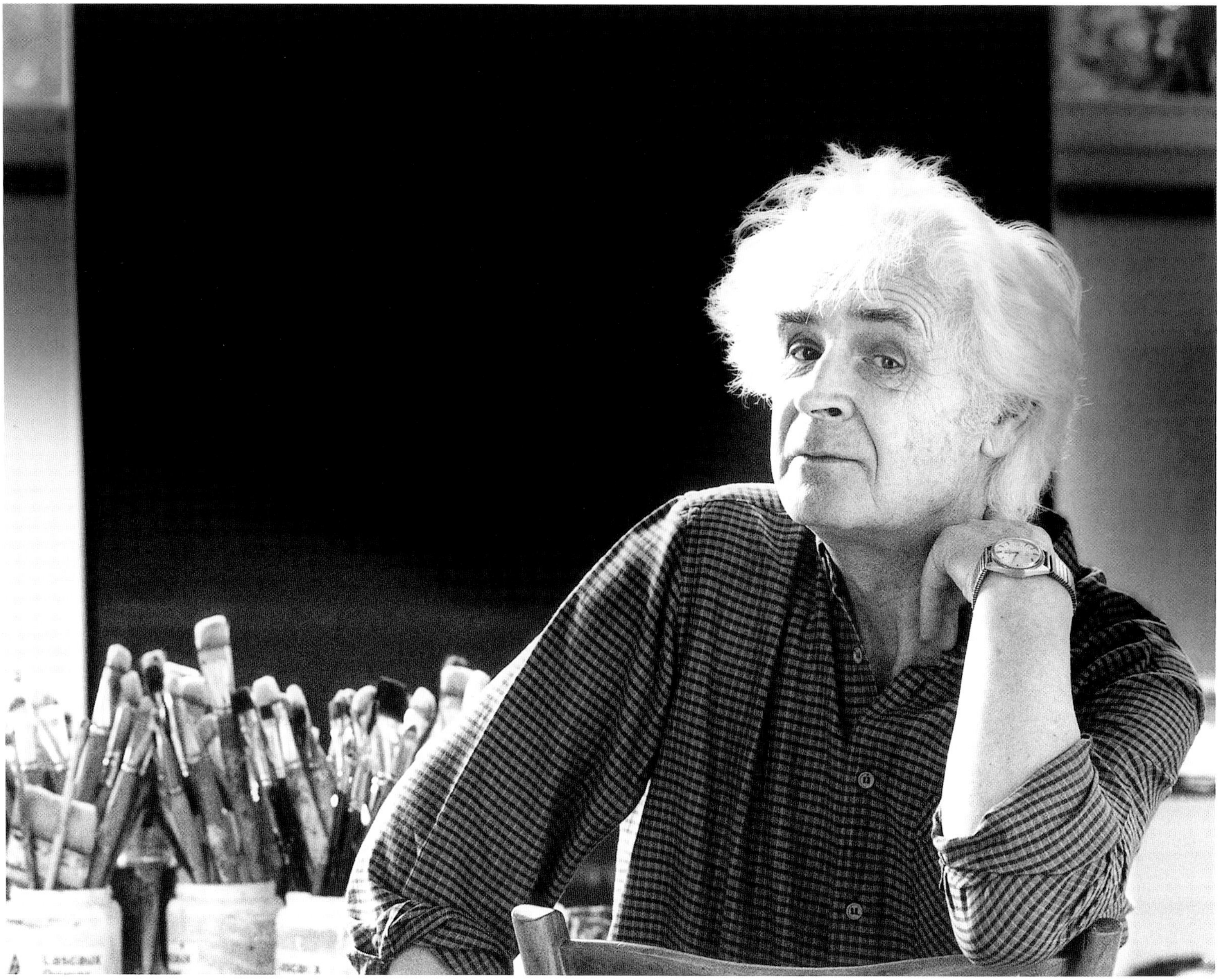

H. A. SIGG

MONOGRAPHIE
MONOGRAPH

Mit Texten von/With texts by
Fritz Billeter, Guido Magnaguagno, Karl Ruhrberg

Benteli Verlag Bern
Benteli Publishers Berne

Der Künstler, die Autoren und der Verlag danken folgenden
Institutionen für ihre finanzielle Unterstützung:
The artist, the authors and the publishers would like to thank
the following institutions for their financial support:

Julius Bär Stiftung, Zürich
Cassinelli-Vogel-Stiftung, Zürich
Schweizerischer Bankverein, Zürich
Crédit Suisse, Zürich
J. Henry Schroder Bank AG, Zürich

sowie all jenen, die nicht genannt sein wollen.
as well as all those who wish to remain anonymous.

Inhaltsverzeichnis

Contents

Fritz Billeter	**Hermann Alfred Sigg**	13
	Vorspiel/Die Anfänge/Erste Reife/Blick auf die Menschenfigur/Zum Gipfel, zur Mitte/ Der Grundton/Bemerkungen zur Kunst am Bau	
	Hermann Alfred Sigg	63
	Prelude/First Steps/First Bloom/A Glance at the Human Figure/To the Peak, to the Centre/ The Ground Shade/Remarks on Construction-Related Art	
Guido Magnaguagno	**Ein Hohes Lied**	143
	Song of Songs	147
Karl Ruhrberg	**Malerische Meditationen**	167
	Zu den Arbeiten von Hermann Alfred Sigg	
	Artistic Meditations	171
	Hermann Alfred Sigg's Works	
	Kunst am Bau	228
	Construction-Related Art	
	Biographische Notizen	241
	Biographical Notes	
	Werkverzeichnis	257
	Catalogue of Works	
	Anhang	260
	Appendix	
	Einzelausstellungen/One-man Exhibitions	260
	Auswahl Gruppenausstellungen/Selected Group Exhibitions	261
	Ausgewählte öffentliche Arbeiten/Selected Public Projects	262
	Radio und Television	263
	Ausgewählte Bibliographie/Selected Bibliography	263
	Zu den Autoren	264
	The Authors	265
	Photonachweis/Photocredits	266

Selbstbildnis/Self-Portrait, 1946/47, Ei-Öltempera/egg-oil tempera, 34×25,5 cm

Mutter/Mother, 1945, Öl/oil, 66×49 cm

Am Tisch/At the Table, 1946, Ei-Öltempera/egg-oil tempera, 130×80,5 cm

Die Entscheidung/The Decision, 1946, Ei-Öltempera/egg-oil tempera, 90×61 cm

Fritz Billeter — Hermann Alfred Sigg

Vorspiel

Ort der Handlung

Oberhasli im Zürcher Unterland: das 1951/52 erbaute Haus von Hilda und H. A. Sigg liegt an einer wenig befahrenen Strasse. Schon sein Eingang sagt etwas über seine Bewohner aus: kein feierliches Portal, das stolzen Besitz oder den Übergang von aussen ins Innere zelebrieren will, sondern eine schlichte Holztür, die man auf den ersten Blick leicht übersieht. Dahinter, ahnt man, beginnt eine eigene Welt mit ihrer besonderen Intimität.

Durch einen gedeckten, zum Sitzplatz erweiterten Korridor erreicht der Gast einen Wohnraum. Die Tür zur Rechten würde in die beiden rückwärts gelegenen, geräumighohen Ateliers führen. Aber es ist vorläufig nicht nötig, so weit vorzudringen. Die Vorhalle verrät schon viel von einem entfalteten Künstlerleben; die Faktoren und Mächte, die dieses ermöglicht und bestimmt haben, sind gleichsam verdinglicht an Einrichtung und Hausrat ablesbar. Vieles hat sich hier angesammelt und ist doch zu einer unaufdringlichen Harmonie zusammengewachsen. Die überall verteilten Kleinplastiken von Schweizer Künstlern wie Hildi Hess, Ellen Weyl und Charles Otto Bänninger, ein Metallrelief von Silvio Mattioli, ein eindrückliches Frauenkopffragment von Paul Speck, Werke der Zürcher Konkreten Camille Graeser und Richard Paul Lohse streifen wir mit einem Blick. Das alles sind Freundesgaben, meist im Austausch mit eigenen Arbeiten erworben, oder Reverenzen gegenüber Kollegen, deren Schaffensweise einem vielleicht sogar fern liegt, denen man aber die Hochachtung nicht versagt.

Auch Arbeiten einiger moderner Klassiker – Braque, Matisse, Picasso – seien im Vorbeigehen wahrgenommen. Sie hängen hier nicht unbedingt deswegen, weil sie Sigg menschlich oder künstlerisch eng verwandt wären, sondern sie verkörpern gleichsam einen nie mehr verlierbaren, unverbrüchlichen Massstab.

All das notiert der schweifend-musternde Blick wohl; aber erst an fünf schwarzafrikanischen Holzmasken bleibt er haften. Eine der fünf, etwas kleiner und unauffälliger, ist Sigg als Erinnerungsstück an seinen ersten Förderer Josef Müller teuer; die andern vier, von seltener Qualität und wahrscheinlich alle von den im Nordwesten der Elfenbeinküste siedelnden Senufos, erwarb er selbst. Sie bieten dem Eintretenden an der gegenüberliegenden Wand gleichsam die Stirn. Es sind gehörnte Tiere, finster blickend, aufgeladen mit Magie. Tragisch verdüstert wirken sie, und eigentlich müssten sie in ihrer heftigen Expressivität als Fremdkörper erscheinen, wären sie nicht auf unerklärliche Weise in eine Gesamtharmonie der ganzen Wohn- und Lebenslandschaft eingebettet. Dennoch, an der hinteren Seite des Raumes angebracht, sind sie gleichsam zurückgedrängt. Sie vertreten, könnte man sagen, Siggs Schatten, seine Gegenwelt, Möglichkeiten, die er als Künstler gemieden hat: eben Unruhe und Tragik, das Dunkle und Dämonische.

Wendet sich hingegen der Blick des eintretenden Gastes nach rechts, dann erfährt er auf konzentriertem Raum, welche Kräfte diesen Künstler tragen, welche Stimmungen und

Seelenlagen er in seinem eigenen Werk ausdrückt. Da hängt nämlich ein Bild grossen Formats von Sigg selbst mit dem Titel «Inselformen III», und davor steht aufgesockelt der Kopf eines Buddha.

Immer wieder begegnet der Gast auch sonst im Haus der Siggs Reliefs und Statuen aus Indien, Kambodscha und Indonesien.

1968 unternahm Sigg seine erste grosse Studienreise durch diese und andere Länder des fernen Ostens. Sie bewirkte keinen Bruch in seinem Schaffen, wohl aber eine Verdeutlichung. Von jetzt an ist der Künstler bei sich selbst angelangt, zu seiner Reife gekommen. Er ist zu einer «innerlich längst vorbereiteten» persönlichen lyrischen Abstraktion vorgestossen, wie sie heute allgemein mit seinem Namen verbunden wird.

«Inselformen III» von 1975 bezeugen Siggs reifen Stil. In der Tat evoziert das Bild Landschaftliches: Mosaikartig sind die «Inseln» in Ocker, Orange bis Gelb und einzelnen Grünspuren in einen braunoliven Hintergrund, wenn man will, in ein «Meer» oder auch in einen stofflich dichten «Himmel», eingesenkt. Diese Paysage d'âme atmet Sammlung, Stille, Entrückung. Ein gleiches drückt sich in den aus dunklem Lavagestein gehauenen Gesichtszügen des erwähnten Buddhakopfes aus.

Die geistige Verwandtschaft zwischen dieser Skulptur und Siggs Bild ist offensichtlich. Der Künstler hatte die Gelegenheit, diese innere Beziehung auch einem grösseren Publikum nahezubringen. Eine vom Direktor des Kunsthauses Zürich, Felix A. Baumann, konzipierte Ausstellung konfrontierte 1976 im Helmhaus Bilder von Sigg, die von der erwähnten Südostasienreise inspiriert waren, mit originalen Skulpturen desselben Kulturraumes aus dem Besitz des Museums Rietberg und des Künstlers. Diese Konfrontation wurde von den Ausstellungsbesuchern nicht immer richtig verstanden. Stimmen wurden laut, die Sigg ein Qualitäts- und Kräftemessen mit der «klassischen» ostasiatischen Kunst unterstellten. Dabei sollte, am modischen Umgang mit Zen, Kamasutra und anderen fernöstlichen Kulturfetischen anknüpfend, lediglich gezeigt werden, dass ein Europäer jenseits solcher Moden sein tiefinneres «Indien» in sich tragen konnte.[1]

Damit ist Wesentliches von Siggs geistiger Haltung vorweggenommen. Doch der Gast erfährt, wenn er dieses Haus betritt, auch Hinweise auf dessen familiäres Herkommen. Zur Linken weitet sich ihm das Entrée zu einem Sitzraum mit Cheminée, und durch die grossen, nach Südwesten gerichteten Fenster erblickt er das sich öffnende Wehntal, eine unspektakuläre, befreiende, leicht hüglige Landschaft in sattem Grün. Doch zuerst wird der Ausblick, bevor er ungehindert in die Weite dringen kann, nach wenigen hundert Metern durch eine Tannenzeile gebremst. Dahinter verbirgt sich der elterliche Bauernhof, ein ehrwürdiger Fachwerkbau, der bis heute von Siggs jüngerem Bruder bewirtschaftet wird.

[1] «H. A. Sigg Bilder 1968–1976, Skulpturen aus Indien und Südostasien», Katalog, Zürcher Kunstgesellschaft, 1976, Vorwort von Felix A. Baumann.

I. Die Anfänge

Frühe Schwierigkeiten

Kaum ein Kritiker oder Kunsthistoriker, der Siggs bäuerliches Herkommen nicht mindestens erwähnt. Dieses erweist sich in der Tat als eine soziologische Ausnahme – wie andererseits ein Arbeitermilieu ebenfalls recht selten einen künstlerisch Gestaltenden hervorbringt. Beschränkt man sich auf die Schweiz der Neuzeit (deren Beginn in diesem Fall etwa mit 1848, mit der Gründung unseres Bundesstaates, anzusetzen wäre), dann fällt auf, dass selbst die grossen Bauernschriftsteller unseres Landes, etwa Gotthelf und Ch.-F. Ramuz, keineswegs aus bäuerlichen Familien stammten. Aber auch bildende Künstler, die ländlich-alpine Motive vorziehen – ich erwähne nur etwa Cuno Amiet, Albert Anker, Giovanni Giacometti, René Auberjonois, Alois Carigiet, Edouard Vallet – gingen nicht aus einem Elternhaus hervor, dessen Vater den Bauernberuf ausgeübt hatte.[2]

Es genügt mir, diese auffällige Tatsache hervorgehoben zu haben; eine rasche Erklärung dafür zu geben, sehe ich mich ausserstande. Was nun Sigg betrifft, so hatte er seine Berufsentscheidung zum Künstler zäh zu erstreiten. Als der 14jährige Sohn solche Zukunftsvorstellungen bekanntgab, behandelte ihn der Vater, den Sigg einmal als «bewussten, hervorragenden Bauern» bezeichnet hat, wie einen Abtrünnigen. Denn gerade ihn, der mit Tieren so gut umzugehen wusste, hatte er als seinen «Kronprinzen» ausersehen, als denjenigen, der den Hof weiterführen sollte.

Die Mutter stammte aus einer in Säckingen beheimateten Familie von Seidenband-Fabrikanten. Sie brachte kultivierte Sensibilität in den Haushalt. Dieser sei zwar sozusagen bilderlos gewesen; aber die literarisch gebildete Mutter gab Hermann anstelle von Kinderbüchern Goethe, Schiller, Lessing und Uhland zu lesen. Sie verstand den Entschluss ihres Sohnes; doch es bedurfte darüber hinaus der Fürsprache einer Lehrerin, dass Hermann die Kunstgewerbeschule Zürich besuchen durfte – aber vorerst nur für einige Monate. Erst als er in der Rekrutenschule an Herzbeschwerden zu leiden begann, vermochte er sich endgültig von der schweren Arbeit auf dem Hof zu befreien, und der Besuch der Kunstgewerbeschule (1944–1947) war nun gesichert.

Was hat sich in der Tat zugetragen, als der Sohn, mit der Mutter verbündet, seinen Berufswunsch gegenüber dem Vater durchzusetzen vermochte? Warum hat sich diesmal die Kunst gegenüber der patriarchalischen Norm behauptet? Dasselbe hat sich im Haus Goethe modellhaft ereignet. Auch da liess sich die mütterliche «Lust am Fabulieren» von «des Lebens ernstem Führen» nicht einfach verdrängen. Es wäre falsch, bei solchen Austragungen einen einfachen Dualismus zwischen dem Weiblichen (zum Beispiel der Kunst) und dem Männlichen (der Ratio) anzunehmen. Man könnte im Fall von Sigg genausogut behaupten, dass der Bauernstand ebenfalls im Zeichen des Weiblichen stehe, entspreche er doch einem Dienst an der Erde, an der Grossen Mutter. Vielleicht kam Meret Oppenheim der Wahrheit am nächsten, als sie 1970 anlässlich der Verleihung des Basler Kunst-

---

[2] Es gibt in der modernen Schweizer Kunst eine bedeutende Ausnahme: Augusto Giacometti. Giovanni Giacometti verbrachte zwar sein Leben in ländlich-alpinen Verhältnissen wie schon sein Vater, der sich aber, ähnlich wie der Vater von Frank Buchser, als Gastwirt schon einen Schritt vom Bauerntum entfernt hatte. Meines Wissens ist noch nie eine Untersuchung über diesen Fragenkomplex geschrieben worden.

preises in ihrer Ansprache Kunst und Künstler als androgyn erklärte. Tatsächlich hat sich Sigg später, mindestens symbolisch auf der Ebene des Werkes, mit dem Vater versöhnt, als er nämlich auf hoher Abstraktionsstufe das Motiv von Feld und Acker in ihrer Parzellenform als Bildstruktur aufnahm.

Ernst Gubler, Ernst Georg Rüegg, Johannes Itten, Otto Morach und Heinrich Müller waren Siggs wichtigste Lehrer. Am meisten verdankt er dem Letztgenannten. Müller (1903–1978) sei ihm vor allem behilflich gewesen, die Kunstgewerbeschule für seinen persönlichen Gebrauch zur «Akademie umzufunktionieren», das heisst nur Fächer zu belegen im Hinblick auf ein Leben als freier Künstler. Sigg ging also voll auf Risiko: er war nie darauf bedacht, die Unterrichtsfächer so zu wählen, dass er mit einem Diplom für die Ausübung eines gestalterischen Berufs hätte abschliessen können. Schliesslich ermutigte ihn Heinrich Müller, schon während der Ausbildungszeit auszustellen, was die anderen Lehrer weniger gern sahen.

Nach Beendigung seiner Zeit an der Kunstgewerbeschule hat Sigg ein weiteres, allerdings weniger tief verwurzeltes gesellschaftliches Grundmuster nachvollzogen. In den vierziger Jahren herrschte in der Schweiz noch immer die Überzeugung vor, wer als Künstler ernst zu nehmen sei, müsse seine Feuertaufe in Paris holen. Erst zwei Generationen später sollte New York der Hauptstadt Frankreichs den Rang ablaufen. Doch bevor ich mich diesem Abschnitt in Siggs Entwicklung zuwende, möchte ich einen Blick auf die wichtigsten Bilder seiner Frühzeit werfen.

Der Aufbruch

Das 1945 entstandene Bildnis von Siggs Mutter zeigt eine alte, abgearbeitete Frau. Entspannt, aber auch erschöpft lehnt sie im Sessel zurück, liegen die Hände im Schoss. Die Augen sind geschlossen, im Schlummer, oder als ob die Frau in sich hineinblickte. Sigg präsentiert die von ihm dargestellten Menschen meistens frontal; da er dieses Portrait im Profil angelegt hat, gelingt es ihm, den in keiner Weise bäuerlichen, verfeinerten Gesichtsschnitt gut zur Geltung zu bringen, die leicht geschwungene Adlernase, den hohen schlanken Hals. Die Profilansicht verstärkt auch den Eindruck, die herabgleitenden Arme seien überlang. Gerade dadurch wird der erwähnte Zustand der Entspannung und Entkräftung betont. Das im Bild vorherrschende gedämpfte und wie abgeschossene Rot und Braunrosa vertiefen noch einmal den Gesamteindruck, dass wir auf das erfüllte Leben einer Ruhe suchenden Frau blicken.

Auf dem «Selbstbildnis», das 1946 entstanden ist, blickt der Jüngling skeptisch und melancholisch in die Welt. Der düstere, leicht weltschmerzähnliche Gesichtsausdruck ist typisch für das Selbstportrait eines jungen Menschen, der die Wirklichkeit noch nicht in tätiger Auseinandersetzung kennengelernt hat, sondern erst in ihren Möglichkeiten, in ihren Gefahren und Versprechen erahnt. Zwei weitere, im selben Jahr wie das «Selbstbildnis» gemalte Werke enthalten motivisch und stimmungsmässig eine ähnliche Latenz,

Le lit, Paris 1947, Öl/oil, 41,5×22,5 cm

das ähnliche Erahnen eines Kommenden. Schon im Bildtitel «Die Entscheidung» ist diese Situation ausgesprochen; im Bild «Am Tisch» wird sie vor allem an zwei Motivzusammenhängen anschaulich. Im Vordergrund sitzt ein junger Mensch an einem Tisch in der Pose des Nachdenkens. Er ist an den rechten Bildrand in den Schatten gerückt und befindet sich in einem Raum, der in einen zweiten übergeht. Dieser zweite Raum ist in die Helle getaucht und mündet in ein Fenster, in dem ein Zipfel Aussenwelt aufscheint.

Eine ähnliche Raumschluchtung weist «Die Entscheidung» auf, und auch hier hält sich, an den rechten Bildrand gedrängt, ein junger Mann auf, wiederum sinnend und den Kopf in die Hand gestützt, doch diesmal steht er aufrecht. Hier öffnet sich ebenfalls der verschattete, vordere Raum zu einem hinteren und helleren. Was sich dort abspielt – drei weibliche Figuren sind um einen Tisch gruppiert und scheinen sich zu beraten – bleibt einigermassen ungeklärt. Aber gerade diese Unbestimmtheit steigert die Intimität der Szene, und der Umstand, dass die Frauen im Hellen eine Gruppe bilden, betont die Isolierung des Jünglings im Schatten.

Alle drei eben besprochenen Bilder stehen im Zeichen von Siggs damaliger kritischer Lebenssituation. Noch hat er die bergende Häuslichkeit nicht verlassen; aber schon hat sich über sie der Abschied, ein Unbekanntes und Ungewisses gesenkt; der Schritt in die Welt, der lange Weg mit dem Ziel, sich als Künstler zu behaupten, steht bevor.

Unter diesen vier frühen Bilder sticht die nichtnaturalistische Farbigkeit der «Entscheidung» heraus. Hier beginnt sich die Farbe in aufleuchtenden Komplementärkontrasten zu strukturieren – das Blau und Türkis der Lichtreflexe an den Frauenfiguren stehen im Gegensatz zu den Senfgrau und Rotbraunflächen des Bodens –, während die anderen drei Bilder dunkler und eher tonig gehalten sind. Sigg lehnt sich wohl in der «Entscheidung» an die von den Fauves übernommene Farbskala des verehrten Lehrers Heinrich Müller an. Um so auffälliger erscheint dagegen, dass er in der Gestaltung des Raumes seinem Lehrer nicht gefolgt ist. Dieser neigte dazu, auch eine Tiefenräumlichkeit im Bild auf die Fläche zu bringen, wogegen Sigg den Raum gerade in die Tiefe getrieben und auf diese Weise mit zur oben beschriebenen Stimmung beigetragen hat, in der sich Geborgenheit und das unmittelbar bevorstehende Heraustreten aus ihr die Waage halten.

Intermezzo Paris

Zieht man die Bilder heran, die im zeitlichen Umfeld von Siggs Pariser Aufenthalt (1947) entstanden sind, also etwa «Café Select», «Nachtcafé Paris III» oder noch «Hilda mit Hund», kommt man zum Schluss, dass er sie so auch hätte malen können, wenn er zu Hause geblieben wäre.

Im Sinn einer Horizonterweiterung hat ihm diese Stadt zwar viel gegeben; aber zum Schicksal wie für andere Schweizer – ich erwähne nur Alice Bailly, Serge Brignoni, Wilfrid Moser und Robert Müller – ist sie ihm nicht geworden. Für Sigg bewahrheitet sich in Paris zum ersten Mal in seinem Leben ein Grundsatz, wie er schon von Heinrich Müller überliefert ist: «Man sieht nur, was man in sich hat», und «nur was man kennt, kann man darstellen».[3]

Dazu ist zu sagen, dass Paris durch den Zweiten Weltkrieg viel von seinem Glanz eingebüsst hatte. Wohl gab es noch Picasso, Braque und Léger in der Stadt; aber die Provokationen der Surrealisten waren verstummt; die meisten von ihnen waren vor den Nationalsozialisten in die USA ausgewichen. Das vor der Tür stehende Neue, das was der Kunstkritiker Charles Estienne 1951 «Tachisme» nennen sollte, keimte erst im dunklen und konnte von einem unerfahrenen Jüngling, der Sigg damals war, unmöglich wahrgenommen werden.

Er besuchte die Akademie von André Lhote (1885–1962). Dieser vertrat einen gemässigten, den sogenannten Sekundären Kubismus ähnlich wie das Gespann Albert Gleizes und Jean Metzinger. Lhotes Fähigkeit als Lehrer strahlte weltweit aus – auch Schweizer wie Serge Brignoni und Heiny Widmer (später als Museumsleiter bekannter denn als Maler) rühmten sie. Hermann Sigg konnte sich dieser Wertschätzung anschliessen, und doch profitierte er vom Unterricht nicht allzu viel – einmal davon abgesehen, dass er unter den Studierenden die Churerin Hilda Jörger, seine spätere Frau, kennenlernte. Lhotes Ausführungen kamen ihm zu kopflastig vor, zumal er sich schon an der Kunstgewerbeschule Zürich mit den Farbtheorien von Johannes Itten hatte auseinandersetzen müssen. So lernte er am meisten vom reichen Angebot der Museen und Galerien; insbesondere berührte ihn die Farbsinnlichkeit von Pierre Bonnard.

Zwar hat Sigg auch nach Paris immer wieder Metropolen besucht: Singapur, Hongkong, New York; aber heimisch fühlte er sich als Landmensch in ihnen nie. Bemerkenswert, wie er Paris als Künstler erlebte – etwa im Gegensatz zu einem anderen Schweizer, Wilfrid Moser, der sich seit 1945 in dieser Stadt niedergelassen hatte. Während Moser vor allem in die Unterwelt, in die Schächte der Métro mit ihren schreienden und zerfetzten Plakaten stieg, während er sich wie ein von van Gogh und Ensor herkommender nordischer Visionär verhielt, blieb Sigg im oberen, zivilisatorischen Bereich. Eines seiner bevorzugten Motive während der Pariser Zeit war das Caféhaus, von dem der Kunsttheoretiker George Steiner sagt, in ihm lägen die Quellen für die Kultur des Westens. Wohl tritt im Bild «Nachtcafé» in der Pinselführung eine nervöse Handschrift hervor, und die Gestalt eines Blinden im Vordergrund, mit dunkler Brille und weissem Stock, tönt die Unerbittlichkeit der Grossstadt diskret an. Im «Café Select» hingegen ist alles Beunruhigende ausgeschieden, oder besser: Es erscheint hier sublimiert als lichte, glitzernde Verlockung in der Gestalt einer jungen Frau im perlmutternen, weit ausgeschnittenen Kleid. Auch im ganz unnaturalistisch apfelgrünen Kopf eines hinter ihr sitzenden Gastes teilt sich etwas vom Aufregenden dieser einmaligen Nacht mit.

[3] Herbert Gröger, «Heinrich Müller», Vontobel-Druck AG, Feldmeilen, 1973, S. 111, 116 (Beitrag von Paul Honegger)

Brotberufe

Hermann Alfred Sigg hatte ein grosses Ziel vor Augen: als freier Künstler ein hinreichendes Auskommen zu verdienen; aber von Paris zurückgekehrt, galt es zunächst einmal zu überleben, galt es zuzugreifen, wo ihm etwas angeboten wurde. Er schlug sich als Illustrator von Büchern und Zeitschriften durch, als Schaufenstergestalter für Jelmoli und Globus. Er unterrichtete auch als Zeichenlehrer und schuf bis 1960 Bühnenbilder zuerst für die von Hans Schaub gegründete, poetisch-satirische «Laterne», aus der sich die «Zeitbühne» in der Nachfolge des legendären «Cornichon» entwickelte. Schliesslich war er auch zeitweise ein Mitarbeiter des Graphikers, Designers und Architekten Fritz Keller.

Sigg hat sich solcher Aufgaben gewiss mit Bravour und dem nötigen Ernst entledigt; aber wirklich am Herzen lagen sie ihm nicht. Es bedeutete ihm beispielsweise nichts, neben der eigentlichen künstlerischen Arbeit eine zweite Karriere als Plakatgestalter anzustreben, wie sie Maler wie Alois Carigiet, Hans Erni, Hans Falk, Niklaus Stöcklin unternahmen. Sigg hat zwar in seinen Plakaten eine Poesie entfaltet, die sich etwa neben der von Falk oder Leupin durchaus sehen lassen konnte; aber es kam ihm nicht darauf an, unter diejenigen gerechnet zu werden, die das goldene Zeitalter des Schweizer Plakats (ca. 1940 bis 1965) herbeigeführt haben.

Allmählich ging es aufwärts. 1949 wurde Sigg der Conrad-Ferdinand-Meyer-Preis für Malerei und zweimal ein Beitrag der Kiefer-Hablitzel-Stiftung zugesprochen. 1952 kaufte das Sammlerehepaar Nelly und Werner Bär die ersten Werke von ihm, und 1953 stellte sich der erste grosse Erfolg ein. Sigg gewann den vom Kantonsspital Schaffhausen ausgeschriebenen Wettbewerb für die Gestaltung von drei Farbfenstern, einer Wandmalerei und von Sgraffiti. Von da an wurde er bei «Kunst-am-Bau»-Aufgaben immer wieder berücksichtigt, so dass er nun endlich in der Lage war, sich ausschliesslich seiner Malerei zu widmen. Parallel dazu festigte sich auch sein ziviler Status: 1949 heiratete er Hilda Jörger, 1951 entwarf Hannes Trösch, damals Mitarbeiter im Architekturbüro von Max Frisch, das Atelierwohnhaus in Oberhasli, das mit viel eigener Arbeit erbaut wurde, und 1956 kam Sohn Daniel auf die Welt.

II. Erste Reife

1950 reiste Hermann Alfred Sigg erstmals in den Mittelmeerraum, nach Italien, Sizilien, auf die Liparischen Inseln. Solche Reisen wurden bis 1966 fast jährlich fortgesetzt; der Radius weitete sich: nach Griechenland und Spanien, Nordafrika (Marokko, Tunesien), in den Vorderen Orient (Libanon, Syrien, Jordanien, Israel).

Das Fenster/The Window 1948, Ei-Öltempera/egg-oil tempera, 105×146 cm

Auf dem Balkon I/On the Balcony I, Paris 1947, Öl/oil, 40×22,5 cm

Nacht-Café III/Night-Café III, Paris 1947, Öl/oil, 49×34 cm

Hilda mit Hund/Hilda with Dog, 1954, Öl/oil, 92×65 cm

Café Select/Café Select, 1946/47, Öl/oil, 90×70 cm

Reisen in die Welt und nach innen

Warum hat es Sigg in diese südlichen Länder gezogen? Rief ihn das berühmte mittelmeerische Licht?

Zeitlich parallel zu diesen Reisen ergeht an den Künstler eine ganze Reihe von Aufträgen für Kirchenfenster: etwa von Männedorf, Sternenberg, Lichtensteig. Nach eigener Aussage hat Sigg im Zusammenhang solcher baugebundener Tätigkeit für Kirchen im «Morgenland» nach irgendwelchen christlichen Symbolen geforscht, die ihm für seine Farbfenster hätten dienlich sein können; er ist nicht fündig geworden.

1964/65 entstand eine Bildnisserie von Josef Müller, und von Dr. Walter Bechtler erhielt der Künstler den Auftrag, ihn inmitten seiner Familie zu malen. Müller und Bechtler waren beide Kunstsammler und gehörten zu Siggs ersten Förderern. Das Portrait von Müller ist «klassischer», herkömmlicher gehalten als das weit kühnere Familienbild der Bechtler. Doch wird es nicht überraschen, dass Sigg in denjenigen Bildern der sechziger Jahre sich noch weiter vorgewagt hat, die im «eigenen» Auftrag entstehen konnten, also ohne dass er mit Wünschen oder der Erwartungshaltung eines Auftraggebers, beziehungsweise eines zu Portraitierenden rechnen musste. Siggs Darstellungen von Pferderennen und vor allem seine Landschaftsbilder aus dieser Zeit sind nun in dem Sinn «modern», dass der Künstler sich anschickt, seine Werke aus der Eigengesetzlichkeit des Bildes heraus zu entfalten.

Neben dieser angestrebten Bildautonomie bewahrheitet sich gleichzeitig ein Gesetz, in dem Sigg als Künstlerpersönlichkeit gründet. So wie er nicht nach Paris reisen musste, um dann die Bilder zu malen, die er dort wirklich gemalt hat, so wie er später nicht notwendig Indien und Indonesien kennenlernen musste, um die lyrische Abstraktion der Fluss- und Küstenbilder hervorzubringen, so bedurfte es auch nicht der zahlreichen Reisen im Mittelmeerraum, dass die Landschaftsvisionen der sechziger Jahre entstehen konnten. Wohl gibt es darunter einige, etwa den «Apulischen Frühling» von 1967, in denen eine südliche, fast «schwarze» Helle, eine gezähmt-subtropische Üppigkeit eingefangen scheint; wohl mag man die kubisch-weissen, eng zusammengerückten Häusergruppen in «Stadt im Süden» mit Mittelmeer oder Magna Graecia in Verbindung bringen; dennoch könnte man solche Häusergruppen auch im Engadin oder Tessin antreffen, und jener apulische Blütenzweig könnte auch im Zürcher Unterland oder in Japan blühen. Auch die Bilder, in denen Weiss oder Silbergrau Schnee evoziert, in denen zarte Verschränkungen rechteckiger Elemente an Äcker denken lassen, darf man ebenso gut im Fernen Osten wie in der schweizerischen Heimat ansiedeln. Mit anderen Worten: Siggs Landschaften der sechziger Jahre sind nicht in einem genau bestimmbaren geographischen Raum, sondern in der Seele des Künstlers zu verankern. Um sie zu malen, brauchte er sich nicht unbedingt vom Zürcher Unterland wegzubegeben; er musste den Blick nur nach innen richten. Der Aussenwelt mag allerdings die Rolle eines Katalysators zukommen. Das heisst, das «Inbild» – soll ich gar sagen der Archetyp? – wird durch die Begegnung mit einer realen Entsprechung ins Bewusstsein gehoben und drängt nun danach, Bild zu werden.

Stadt im Süden/Town in the South, 1965, Öl/oil, 65×92 cm

Die Sonnenstreifen/Sun Streaks, 1964, Öl/oil, 116×162 cm

Wege zur Bildautonomie

Den Anlauf zur Eigengesetzlichkeit der Farbe nahm Sigg schon vor seinem Pariser Aufenthalt, etwa mit dem Frühwerk «Die Entscheidung» oder in Paris selbst mit «Nachtcafé – Paris III» und «Café Select». Er bewegte sich da, wohl von seinem Lehrer Heinrich Müller angeregt, im Bereich der Fauves und der Nabis. Sigg selbst erwähnt immer wieder, dass ihn die Farbsinnlichkeit von Pierre Bonnard (1867–1947) nachhaltig berührt habe. In den Landschaftsbildern der sechziger Jahre entfernte er sich eher wieder von einer solchen expressiv-spätimpressionistischen Farbgebung. Im Bild «Das schwarze Feld» von 1961 finden sich beispielsweise Konraste, welche die Nabis nicht ausgelotet haben: Hier stossen in den Farbparzellen, die man als Äcker identifizieren darf, Ziegelrosa, Orangegelb, Violett und Schwarz zusammen; im Bild «Im Lichte des Winters» von 1971/72 treten Ocker, Oliv, tiefes Orange und wiederum Schwarz gemeinsam auf, das heisst, die von den Nabis – Bonnard allerdings ausgenommen – wenig geliebten Erdfarben sind zurückgekehrt. Darüber hinaus sind die von Sigg naturgemäss in den Winterbildern bevorzugten Grautöne, die von Perltönen über Silber bis zu bläulich-milchigen Nuancen reichen, ganz Hermann Sigg eigen. Er setzt in diese Grau-Verhangenheit mit geradezu japanischer Delikatesse belebende Farbtupfer und -flecken, die je nachdem als Pferderücken, als die bunten Leibchen der Jockeys (im Aquarell «Pferderennen» von 1961), als Äcker oder als Tierherden zu erkennen sind.

Während Sigg in der Farbgebung sich Schritt für Schritt zu jener Bildautonomie, die allgemein als ein Grundmerkmal von Modernität gilt, herangetastet hat, erfolgten die Veränderungen der Bildstruktur in Richtung auf eine solche Eigengesetzlichkeit auffälliger, weniger gleitend.

Zeichen und «Gesellschaftung»

Diese neue Bildstruktur ergibt sich beispielsweise, indem Sigg die wenigen immer gleichen Motive, aus denen er seine Landschaften erstehen lässt, in einen ebenfalls stark eingeschränkten Zeichenvorrat fasst.

Das Besondere eines Zeichens besteht darin, dass in ihm ein Abbild zum äussersten vereinfacht, auf sein Wesentliches reduziert wird. Schon Siggs Pferde auf den Rennbildern sind stark typisiert; aber die Pferde sind als solche ohne weiteres zu erkennen – wäre es anders, hätte Sigg für diese Bilderserie gewiss nicht 1965 eine Goldmedaille der Schweizer Sportjournalisten entgegennehmen können.

Noch mehr vereinfacht sind die Zeichen für Kühe und Schafe auf den Landschaftsbildern – nämlich so weit, dass sie weitgehend austauschbar geworden sind. Nicht nur Kühe und Schafe, sondern auch Ackerparzellen und kubisch-mittelmeerische Häuser stellt Sigg mit einem nur ganz leicht variierten Rechteckzeichen dar. Für Gestrüpp oder Vögel setzt er ein anderes Kürzel: locker über das Bildfeld verteilte, fast winzige schwarze Markierun-

Schafe/Sheep, 1962, Öl/oil, 73×175 cm

Schafe im Schnee/Sheep in the Snow, 1962, Öl/oil, 65×116 cm

Herde unterwegs/Roving Herds, 1965, Öl/oil, 114×162 cm

Das schwarze Feld/The Black Field, 1961, Öl/oil, 81×162 cm

Das Rennen/The Race, 1961/68, Acryl/acrylic, 81×130 cm

Pferderennen/The Horse Race, 1961, 45×65 cm, Aquarell/water-colour

Familie des Sammlers Dr. W. A. Bechtler/The Family of the Collector Dr. W. A. Bechtler, 1964/65, Öl/oil, 81×175 cm

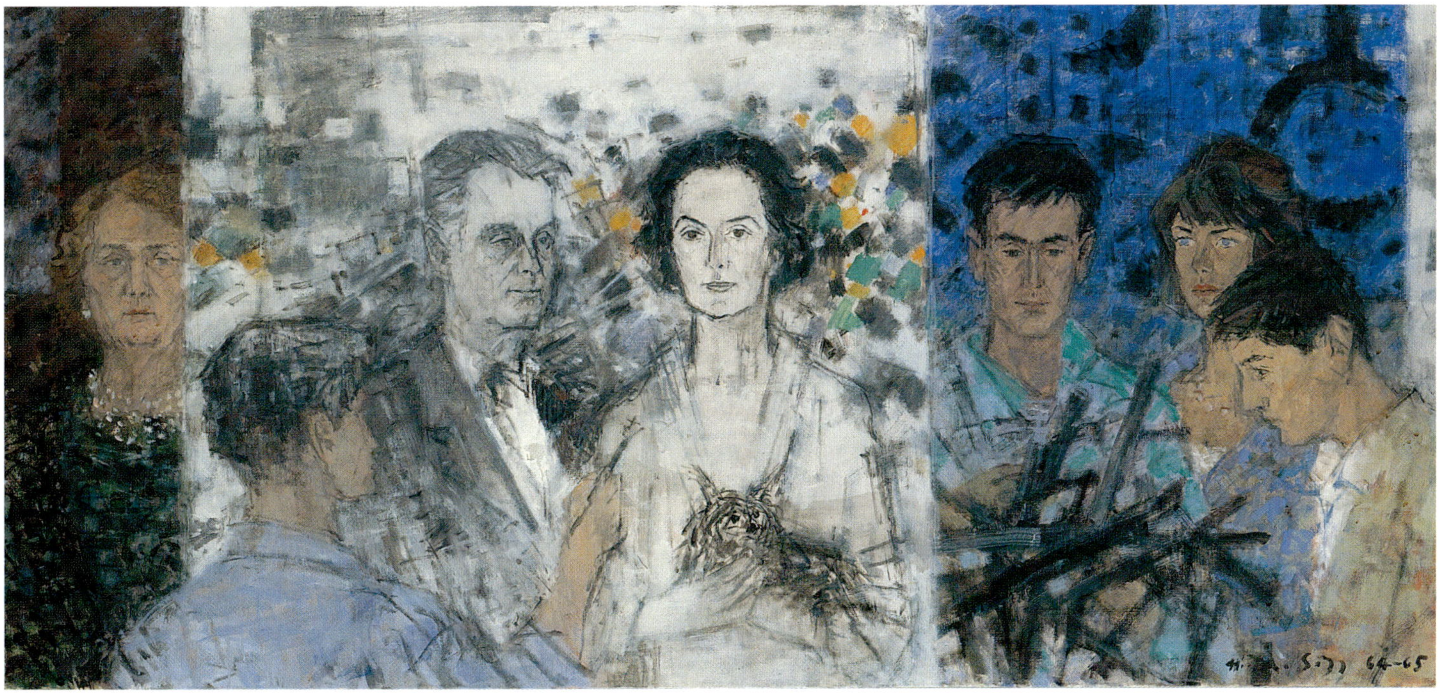

Der Sammler Josef Müller I/The Collector Josef Müller I, 1964/65, Öl/oil, 130×65 cm

Im Atelier/At the Studio, 1965, Photo/photograph by Robert Gnant gen. Auf dem Bild «Das schwarze Feld» erscheinen Vogel- und Gestrüppmotiv zugleich und vermischen sich fast – ganz ähnlich wie auch Schaf, Kuh, Acker und Haus. In der Tat geht es Sigg nicht mehr um das je einzelne Schaf oder Haus, sondern um die Group form, oder, nach einer glücklichen Bezeichnung von Paul Weder, um «Gesellschaftung»: Nicht das als einzelnes Auffällige zählt, sondern die Herde, die Vogelschar, das gewachsene Dorf, das Netzwerk, welches alle Äcker zusammen bilden, also auf abstrakt struktureller Ebene Homogenität und Formähnlichkeit, Formverdichtung, Lockerung, Zerstreuung, Ballung von Dunklem, Vereinzelung, sichtbar gemacht durch ein aus dunkler Umgebung plötzlich aufleuchtendes Weiss.

Paul Weder hat sich als Kunstkritiker häufig mit diesen Landschaften befasst, hat für ihre Eigenart sowohl treffend genaue als auch poetisch-evozierende Worte gefunden. Anlässlich einer Ausstellungseröffnung in Zofingen im Oktober 1968 hat er sie folgendermassen charakterisiert: «Hermann Alfred Sigg sucht eine Landschaft zur Hauptsache als gedehnte, aber geordnete Fläche, als etwas sich Ausbreitendes, das sich zum Grenzenlosen weitet (...). Von links nach rechts scheint, in keiner Weise behindert, Bewegung in den Landschaftsraum einzuströmen, zum Beispiel ein langsames, stetiges Wandern einer Herde. Nur um ein Geringes schreitet die Bewegung vor; sie tastet sich weiter, ähnlich wie die Zeit durch das Dasein rinnt, wie die Körner in einer Sanduhr fallen.» Dieses schön beobachtete, «sanfte Ziehen» (der Herde, also der durch eine Formstruktur sichtbar gemachten Zeit) wird zuweilen angehalten, etwa in einem Bild von 1962, wo die Schafe sich nicht durchs Bildfeld bewegen, sondern für einmal frontal gestellt sind. Dazu kommt, dass die einzelnen Tiere voneinander recht deutlich abgesetzt wurden. Frontalität und Abgrenzung des je einzelnen Tiers, verbunden mit deren schwarzen, aus der hellen Wolle hervortretenden Gesichtsmasken, führen dazu, dass trotz Herdenbildung das Charakteristische des Schafes wieder stark wahrgenommen werden kann.

Offen ins Unbegrenzte

Einen besonderen Hinweis verdienen die gleichzeitig nebeneinander durchprobierten Raumgestaltungen in diesen Bildern der sechziger Jahre. «Stadt im Süden» von 1965 schliesst traditionell den Horizont durch ein fast nächtlich schwarzes Himmelsband ab. Andere Bilder wie «Die Sonnenstreifen» oder «Schafe im Schnee» führen die Landschaft über den oberen Bildrand hinaus, ein Ende ist nicht zu bestimmen. Diese vage Offenheit wird in Bildern wie «Das schwarze Feld» und «Im Lichte des Winters» noch betont: In ihnen geht die feste Erde in einen nicht mehr begrenzbaren Graubereich über. Das sich Ausbreitende, zum Grenzenlosen Weitende der Siggschen Landschaft, wie es auch Weder bemerkt hat, ist damit erreicht.

Der Eindruck solcher Unbegrenztheit wird durch eine ungewöhnliche perspektivische Konstruktion noch verstärkt. Nicht etwa indem diese das Auge in unergründliche Tiefen risse, so etwas ist nicht angestrebt. Der Betrachter blickt vielmehr in leichter Aufsicht

Harlekin vor dunklem Bild/Harlequin by a Dark Picture, 1965, Öl/oil, 116×65 cm

Harlekin/Harlequin, 1957, Öl/oil, 100×50 cm

auf eine nur wenig zurückgeklappte Landschaft. Die Ahnung von «Unendlichkeit», besser «Unbegrenztheit» tritt dadurch ein, dass sich die Fluchtlinien, welche durch die Begrenzungen links und rechts der Felder gebildet sind, in einem Fluchtpunkt treffen, der weit ausserhalb der oberen Bildkante angenommen werden muss. Eine solche offene, gleichsam ins Unendliche verlaufende Bildperspektive hat Sigg auch in späteren Landschaftsdarstellungen fortgesetzt, etwa in «Wintertag» von 1976 oder im noch einmal zehn Jahre später entstandenen Werk «Es hellt auf».

III. Blick auf die Menschenfigur

Akt und Erotik

Selbstverständlich ist auch in der Schweizer Kunst des 20. Jahrhunderts die Aktmalerei häufig vertreten – wobei auch bei uns wie überall im Westen die Frauenakte weit überwiegen. Bedenkenswert aber ist beim näheren Hinsehen, dass solche Darstellungen selten die Frau als erotisches Wesen feiern. So eignen etwa die Akte von Max Kämpf (Kunstmuseum Olten, 1984 gemalt) etwas Frierendes, Ausgesetztes, gar Mitleiderregendes; in ähnliche Richtung, aber ganz ohne Sentimentalität und fast mystisch vertieft, weisen die überlängten Frauenfiguren von Alberto Giacometti. Wilhelm Gimmis Aktmalereien verleihen der Frau oft Erdhaftigkeit oder Monumentalität; Vallottons Frauen wirken immer wieder nicht einfach nackt, sondern entblösst; die «Fille dans la chambre rouge» (1948, Museum zu Allerheiligen) von René Auberjonois, an sich ein bedeutendes Bild, scheint sich ihrer Blösse zu schämen, genauer, diese Blösse sich sogar hartnäckig verhehlen zu wollen. Will man innerhalb neuerer Schweizer Kunst einen unverkrampften Erotiker nennen, muss man auf Böcklin zurückgreifen.[4]

Gibt man sich über diesen Umstand Rechenschaft, dass Nacktheit auch in der modernen Kunst keineswegs notwendig mit Erotik (mit befreiter Erotik) verbunden ist, dann muss man die Unbefangenheit, mit der Sigg in den 1964 und 1966 entstandenen Frauenakten weibliche Körperschönheit und Anziehungskraft erlebbar macht, geradezu als einen Glücksfall werten. Gewiss handelt es sich um Aktbilder traditionellen Zuschnitts, die aber schon deswegen alle Beachtung verdienen, weil Sigg die Mittel, welche ihnen erotischen Zauber einhauchten, mit Meisterschaft und Diskretion eingesetzt hat. Da wäre zuerst das geradezu kostbare Inkarnat zu erwähnen, das den einen Körper mehr ins Perlmutt, den andern mehr ins Elfenbein spielen lässt. Beiden Körpern ist etwas Schimmerndes, eine zarte, vom Betrachter her grundsätzlich überbrückbare Entrücktheit verliehen; das heisst auch, die Sublimierung ist nicht bis zur Entsinnlichung getrieben, nicht bis dahin, wo Kants interesseloses Wohlgefallen eintreten könnte. Das Bild von 1964 ist ein Rückenakt; da auf diese Weise der Gesichtsausdruck wegfällt, damit auch Individualität, das Sichtbarmachen eines Charakters und eines Bewusstseins, nicht ins Spiel kommen kann, tritt das

[4] Zu Arnold Böcklins Neuinterpretation vgl. «Arnold Böcklin, Gorgio de Chirico, Max Ernst. Eine Reise ins Ungewisse», Katalog, Kunsthaus Zürich, 1998, Herausgeber Guido Magnaguagno und Juri Steiner.

Rückenakt/Rear-View Nude, 1964, Öl/oil, 130×65 cm

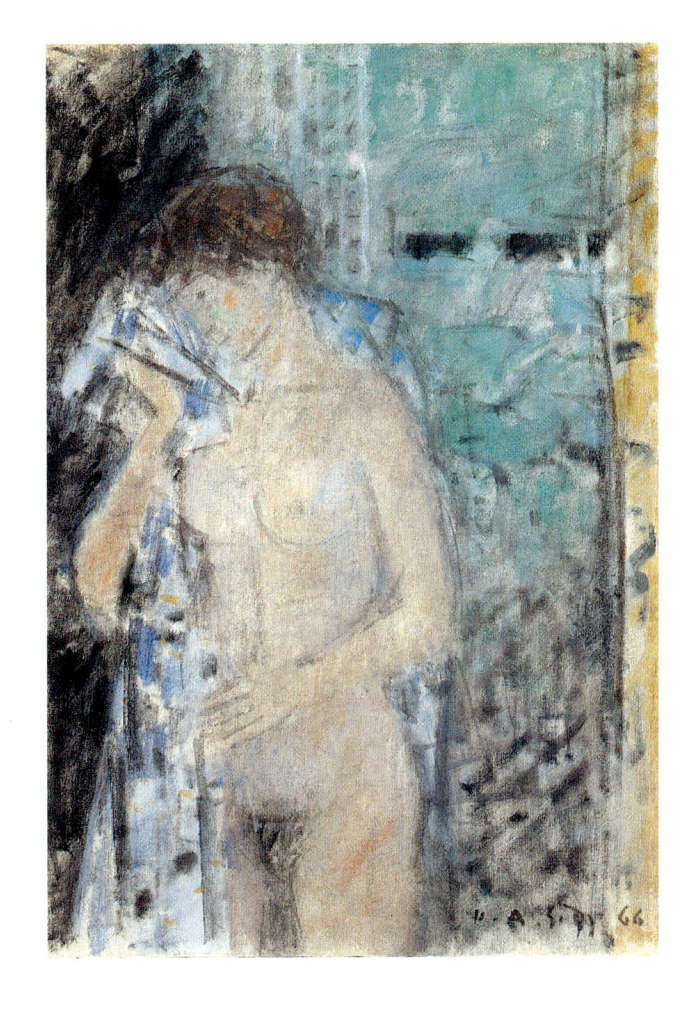

Nach dem Bade/After the Bath, 1966, Öl/oil, 92×65 cm

Apulischer Frühling/Apulian Spring, 1967, Öl/oil, 210×114 cm

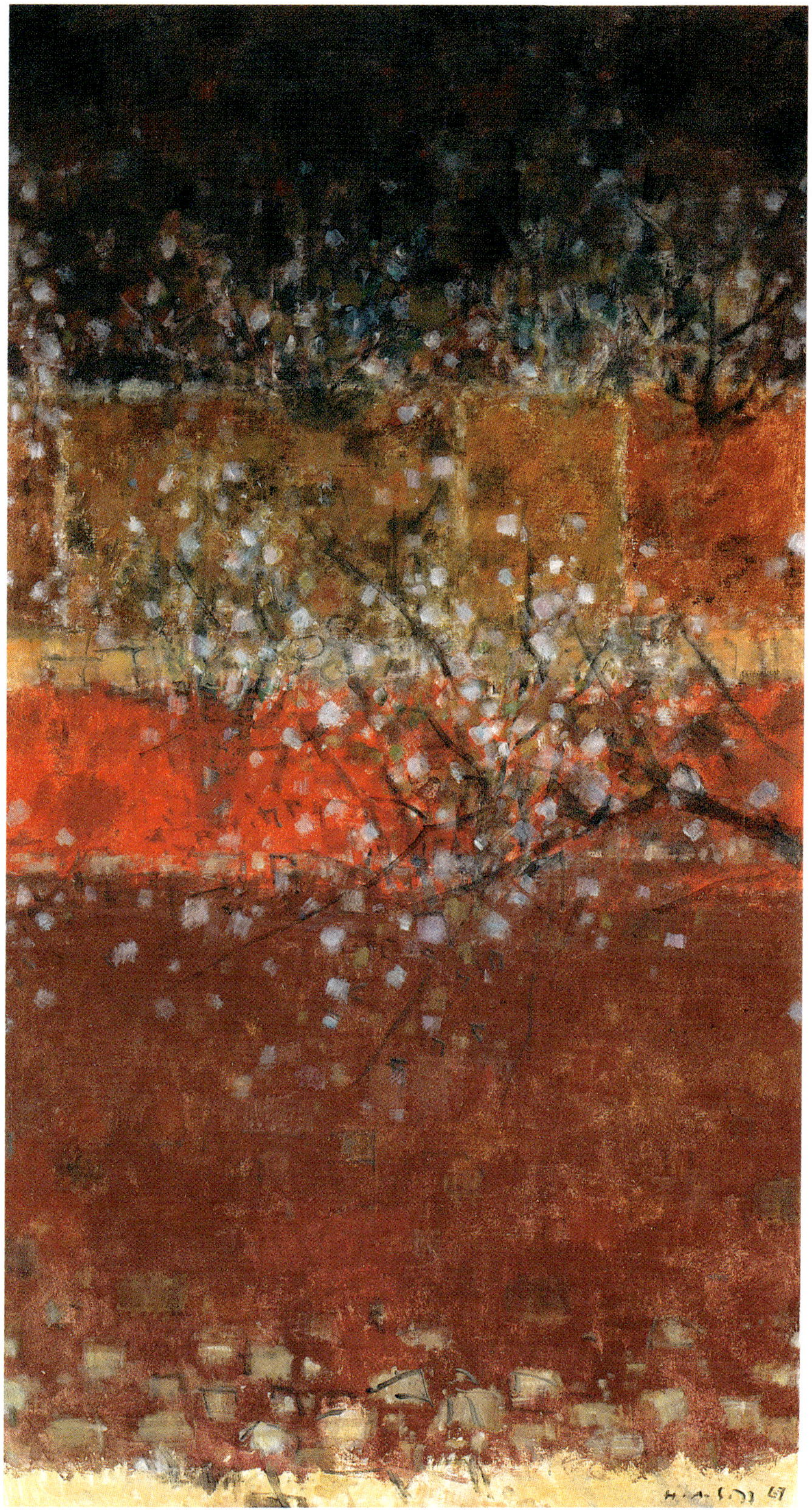

In den Gärten Salomos/In Solomon's Gardens, 1971, Litho/lithograph, 60×46 cm.
In diesem Zusammenhang erschien 1968 ein bibliophiles Buch «Das Hohe Lied von Salomo» in der ARTA, Zürich.
In this connection, a bibliophile edition of «Das Hohe Lied von Salomo» (Solomon's Song of Songs)
was published by ARTA in 1968

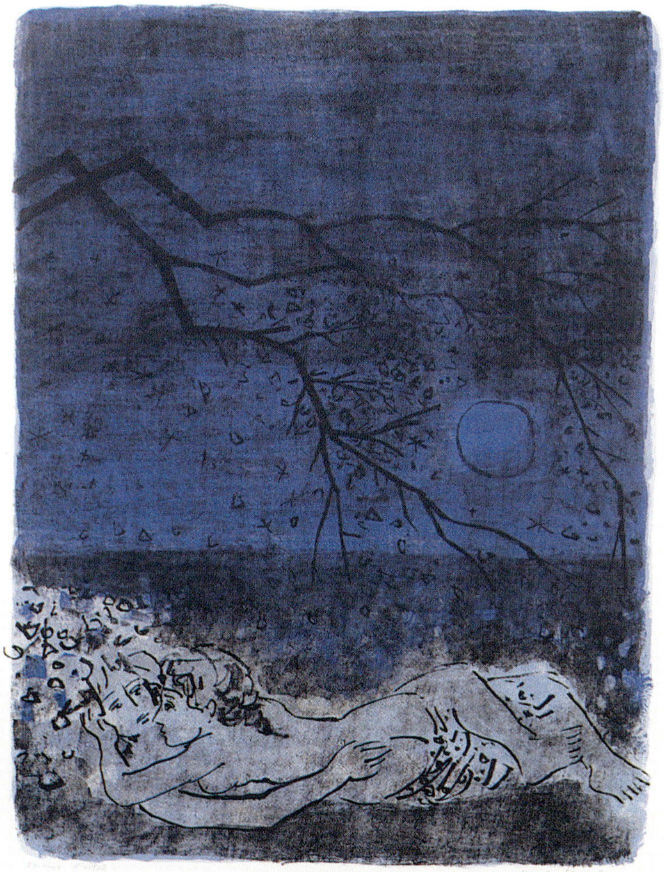

rein Körperhafte, Gattungsmässige in den Vordergrund. Dem Akt von 1966 ist zwar ein Gesichtsausdruck mitgegeben; aber dieser ist ganz allgemein, in sich gekehrt gehalten. Derart wird die Sinnlichkeit des Betrachters stark angeregt; sie darf sich ungehindert von intellektueller Kontrolle entfalten, da die gemalte Figur ihr auch keinen Intellekt entgegensetzt. Andererseits aber sind beide Akte wie traumumfangen; ihr Ich ist noch nichterwacht; also können sie in einer Art Unschuld, in einem fast pflanzenhaften Dasein verharren.

Blicklosigkeit – ausser verständlicherweise in den Portraitaufträgen – hat Sigg in den meisten seiner Menschendarstellungen bevorzugt. Es kann zwar durchaus vorkommen, dass er ihnen Augen einsetzt. Aber auch dann suchen sie kaum je den Blick des Betrachters; dieser kann daher nie zum Komplizen des dargestellten Menschen werden. Das Selbstbildnis von 1946 blickt uns zwar durchaus entgegen; doch diese Ausnahme erscheint logisch, da es sich ja um das Selbstbildnis eines Jünglings handelt, der die Existenz von Aussenwelt eben entdeckt hat. Auch wird hier gerade nicht um unser Einverständnis geworben; hier wird im Gegenteil das Gegenüber, der Betrachter auf den Prüfstand geschickt.

Verhüllen und in Erscheinung treten

Es ist mehr als ein poetisches Reden im Gleichnis, wenn ich zu sagen versucht bin, die Akte von 1964 und 1966 seien mit ihrer Nacktheit bekleidet. Später, zum Beispiel in «Kimono I» (1985) und «Kimono III» (1986), wird Sigg seine Menschen nicht nur bekleiden, sondern geradezu in kostbar wirkende Mäntel einhüllen.

Bei diesen Beispielen brauche ich nicht lange zu verweilen; Guido Magnaguagno hat in seinem Textbeitrag zu diesem Buch auf dieses Gestaltungsmittel des Bergens und Verbergens durch Mantel, Decke oder Tuch (erstmals 1947 im Bild «Le Lit» angewandt) nachhaltig aufmerksam gemacht.

«Der Traum» und «Die Träumende», beide 1986 entstanden, zeigen die Menschenfigur teilweise verhüllt. Hier ruht die Figur entspannt auf einer Decke, sie ist förmlich in sie eingeschmiegt. Der Gegensatz zwischen deren üppiger Blumenornamentik und der glatten, rosigen Haut des oder der Ruhenden steigert noch die sublim erotische Stimmung. Ein horizontales Farbband am unteren Rand beider Bilder und parallel dazu mehrere geschichtete Bänder oberhalb der Figur bilden für sie eine Art Lager, jedenfalls eine geschützte Zone. Auf dem Bild «Der Traum» breitet sich über den Bandschichtungen so etwas wie Aussenwelt aus, die man als bewegtes Meer unter einem tiefdunkelblauen Nachthimmel deuten könnte.

Das Blatt «In den Gärten Salomos», 1971 im Zusammenhang mit dem lithographischen Zyklus «Das Hohe Lied Salomos» entstanden, zeigt ein Liebespaar auf einem angedeuteten Blumenteppich (der formal von den reich ornamentierten Decken der Bilder von 1986 nicht weit entfernt ist). Doch sind es auf der Lithographie vor allem die Körper des Paares selbst, welche, umschlungen übereinander liegend, sich Geborgenheit geben. Auch

Im Lichte des Winters/In the Light of Winter, 1971/72, Acryl/acrylic, 210×310 cm die Nacht mit dem grossen Mond und das über den Liebenden aufgefächerte Geäst eines Baumes sind dazu bestellt, über dem Paar Wache zu halten.

In Siggs 1968 einsetzender und bisher letzter Entwicklungsphase der lyrischen Abstraktion vermag sich das Erotische als Fluidum zu erhalten. Nun nicht mehr an eine Menschenfigur gebunden, ist es auch nicht mehr so leicht haftbar zu machen. Ob man die in den siebziger, achtziger und zum Teil noch in den neunziger Jahren entstandenen Kompositionen mit Landschaften und dann etwa Küstenstriche mit weiblichen Formen assoziieren will, bleibt der Vorstellungskraft des einzelnen Betrachters überlassen.

Geheimnisvoll, entrückt wie die Schlummernden und Liegenden wirken auch Siggs Bilder von indischen Tempelfiguren aus den Jahren 1973 bis 1975. «Die grosse Tempelfigur» (195 × 116 cm) hebt sich von ihrer Tempelwand kaum ab. Sinkt sie in das Gemäuer zurück, oder aber bringt diese umgekehrt, mit einer Projektionsleinwand vergleichbar, die Göttin gerade zur Erscheinung? In Erscheinung treten oder aber Entschwinden – beides Momente, da ein Wesen sich nicht in ruhiger, plastischer Erscheinung darbietet, sondern, wie noch nicht ganz materialisiert, sich auf der Grenze zwischen Traum und Wirklichkeit hält.

Die Epiphanie, das plötzliche Erscheinen der Gottheit, spielt in vielen Religionen, auch in der christlichen, eine wichtige Rolle. Sigg hat sich als Maler indischer Götterskulpturen an sie herangetastet.

IV. Zum Gipfel, zur Mitte

Von 1968 an dringt Sigg mit seinen Reisen über den Mittelmeerraum, die Alte Welt hinaus; er gelangt nach Indien und Indonesien, in den Fernen Osten. Wiederholt zieht es ihn auch nach 1968 dorthin: 1972, 1975, 1982. Wer die genaueren Destinationen erfahren möchte, orientiere sich in den «Biographischen Notizen» in diesem Buch.

Vom Reisen und Ankommen

Am Beginn stand ein Zufall, und das erzählt die Anekdote: Die Swissair erwarb von Sigg einige Gemälde für ihre Büroräumlichkeiten, wobei sie einen Teil der Bezahlung mit Flugzeugkarten beglich. Nur, warum ist Sigg immer wieder nach diesen östlichen Horizonten aufgebrochen? Sollte er in dieser fernen Fremde endlich bei sich, in «seinem» Land angekommen sein?

Bedurfte es des typischen romantischen Umwegs, wie ihn ein bekanntes Wort von Novalis bezeichnet hat: «Wo gehen wir hin? – Immer nach Hause.» Oder in den Worten von Walter Bernet: «Er lässt sich auf seinen Reisen nirgends nieder. Ja man könnte fast sagen, er ist auf allen seinen Reisen ständig auf dem Rückflug (…). Er ist ein Bauernsohn, ja in gewisser Weise ein Bauer geblieben. Er ist da, wo er herkommt.».[5]

[5] «H.A. Sigg, Bilder und Zeichnungen aus Südostasien», Orell Füssli Verlag, Zürich, 1976, S. 97 (Beitrag Walter Bernet)

1993 machte sich der Künstler nach Taiwan, Hongkong und in die Volksrepublik China auf. Auch diese Reise gab seinem Schaffen neue Impulse. Andererseits besuchte Sigg von 1986 an Nord- und Südamerika und Mexiko, vor allem Städte wie New York, Chicago, Mexico City. Was ihm aber hier auffiel, hatte für seine Kunst keine unmittelbaren Folgen. Und zwar ist es nicht einfach die «Neue Welt» mit High Tech, Drive und Optimismus, was alles er zwar mit Neugier aufnehmen, aber nicht in sein Schaffen einbringen kann. Auch für die präkolumbische Kunst Mexikos bringt er lediglich eine abstrakte Bewunderung auf.

Doch auch die Horizonterweiterung in Richtung Ferner Osten hat seine bisherige Schaffensweise nicht etwa umgekrempelt. Das ist und war (wir wissen es inzwischen) nie seine Art: Seine Entwicklung als Künstler schreitet langsam fort, wobei Altes oft auf höherer Stufe gewandelt wiederkehrt. Der Grundgestus von Siggs künstlerischer Entfaltung könnte mit einer aufsteigenden Spirale verglichen werden.

In seinen durch Asien- und Indienreisen inspirierten Bildern hat Hermann Alfred Sigg seine Reife erreicht. Wer sich «einen Sigg» vorstellt, wird in erster Linie an ein Werk der letzten dreissig Jahre denken. Das hier folgende Grobschema verschafft einen Überblick über diese bis heute anhaltende Werkphase:

1968 – 1993: Bilder von Fluss- und Erdformationen und Küstenlandschaften; vornehmlich Breitformat;
ab 1973: Meeres- und Himmelsbilder; vornehmlich Hochformat;
ab 1993: Skulpturen und Bilder, in denen die Mitte thematisiert wird.

Diese Angaben, als Schema zwar tauglich, müssen in mancher Hinsicht modifiziert werden. So überlappen sich die zeitlichen Ränder der einzelnen Abschnitte. Sigg nimmt zum Beispiel nur zögernd von seinen vor allem in den sechziger Jahren entstandenen «winterlichen» Bildern Abschied: «Im Lichte des Winters» wurde 1971/72, «Wintertag» 1976, und «Es hellt auf» gar erst 1986 gemalt. Aber auch die motivischen Bestimmungen der seit 1968 entstandenen Werke sollen im folgenden verfeinert werden.

Gewiss vernimmt man in diesen «fernöstlichen» Bildern einen Nachhall von Abbildlichkeit; man wird Küstenlandschaften, Ebenen mit Feldparzellen und Flussläufen begegnen, in denen Inselchen schwimmen können, wie sie ähnlich auch den Küstenstrichen vorgelagert sind, und man wird solchen Motiven darüber hinaus einen symbolischen Sinn abgewinnen. Andererseits muss sofort wieder festgehalten werden: Siggs fernöstliche Landschaftsvisionen sind wie die früher beschriebenen Landschaftsbilder der sechziger Jahre geographisch nicht genau bestimmbar; sie entsprechen dem, was die Jahrhundertwende unter «Paysages d'âmes» verstand. Doch obwohl sich das Betrachterauge lange an den blossen Struk-turen, am Rhythmus der Form und Zusammenklang der Farben weiden kann, so wird doch niemand Siggs Malerei der reinen Nichtfiguration zurechnen. Dieser Künstler hält sich auf der schmalen Grenzlinie zwischen «Gegenständlichkeit» und «Ungegenständlichkeit»; ich bezeichne seine Gratwanderung als «lyrische Abstraktion».

Der Reichtum des Flusses

Sigg breite, wird häufig geschrieben, die indisch-ostasiatische Landschaft aus, wie sie sich ihm aus der Vogelschau, vom Flugzeug aus dargeboten habe. Doch das stimmt nur annähernd; denn er lässt beispielsweise alle diese zerrissenen Küsten und Flussebenen mit oder ohne Reisfelder nicht als flüchtige Erscheinung im Bildgeviert vorbeistreichen, sondern er hält sie eher wie etwas Wohlgefügtes, wie aus Mosaiksteinen zusammengesetzt, fest. Die Welt vom Flugzeug aus, gestaltet im «kartographischen Verfahren» – Eduard Hüttinger hat dieses Vorgehen von Sigg in grossen Zügen kunsthistorisch hergeleitet.[6] Nachzutragen wäre noch, dass Sam Francis (1923–1994) ebenfalls durch das Erlebnis des Fliegens zu seinem persönlichen Malstil entscheidend angeregt wurde. Interessant ist, dass die Flugerfahrung der beiden zu je anderen Resultaten geführt hat. Nur selten, wie etwa im Bild «Im Reich des Herbstes» (1994/95), hat sich Sigg dem Tachismus von Sam Francis angenähert.

Die Gliederung der Gestaltungsfläche in einen freien Raster verschiedenfarbiger Rechtecke, wie sie sich erstmals in den Landschaftsbildern der sechziger Jahre als ein Netzwerk von Äckern identifizieren lässt, wird in den Landschaften Asiens weitergeführt; Fluss und Meer kommen als neue Hauptmotive ins Bild. Vor allem dem Fluss gewinnt Sigg nahezu unerschöpfliche Möglichkeiten des Erscheinens ab: er windet sich in majestätischen Bögen durch das Bildfeld, verzweigt sich zum silberblinkenden Delta, scheint zu versikkern und wieder aufzutauchen, bildet weitschweifige Mäander, blitzt auf wie ein Peitschenhieb, erstarrt zum Ornament, verfestigt sich zum Schriftzeichen und wird in dieser kalligraphischen Form von 1993 an in die nächste Phase, in der Sigg sich mit dem Thema der Mitte befasst, mit hinübergenommen.

Der Fluss bringt in diese Bilder der Festgefügtheit den Faktor Zeit – nicht als Fortriss und Hinfliehen, sondern als jenes ganz sanfte Ziehen, das schon die Kuh- und Schafherden in die Werke der sechziger Jahre gebracht haben.

Um die dreissig Jahre und darüber hinaus hält bei Sigg die Flussmetapher vor. Gleichbleibend hat sie sich ständig verändert, und schon diese Wandlungsfähigkeit müsste von vornherein jede Kritik, welche die Einseitigkeit oder Einfallslosigkeit dieses Künstlers beklagen wollte, im Keim ersticken. Sigg sagt wohl *dasselbe*, aber nie das gleiche. Für «dasselbe sagen» ist uns bei Künstlern oder Philosophen eine pathetische Umschreibung geläufiger: sie heisst «Vision». Siggs Bestehen auf *einem* Formzug, auf *einem* Motiv hat er mit vielen anderen gemeinsam, etwa mit Capogrossi und seinen Kamm-Elementen, mit Lucio Fontana und seinen Schlitzen in die Leinwand, mit Horst Antes und seinen Kopffüsslern, mit Alberto Giacometti, dessen ausgezehrte, hochgeschossene Figuren fast immer aus klumpigen Riesenfüssen wachsen.

Gerade auch die anhaltende Wiederholung und Abwandlung bestätigt die Symbolhaltigkeit der Flussform. Der Künstler selbst hat deren Symbolik in Notizen angesprochen, aus denen hier beispielsweise folgendes zitiert sei:

[6] Ebenda, S. 21 ff. (Beitrag Eduard Hüttinger)

«Der Fluss bedeutet mir mehr als nur eine bewegte farbige Form. Er ist für mich etwas Existentielles, etwas, das mit meiner inneren Haltung zu tun hat.»

Sigg setzt ihn als Bild «des Verströmens, der sanften oder raschen Bewegung, nicht stille stehend, sondern sich bewegend, auf ein Ziel: das grosse Wasser.» Der Fluss sei für die Inder ein Zeichen für Kreativität, hält Sigg ein andermal fest. So kann man dieses Motiv auch in seinen Bildern verstehen: indem er die Ur-Figur des Flusses stetig abwandelt, bestätigt sich sein Künstlertum.

Kommen wir zur Farbe der fernöstlichen Bilder: Breite Skalen von Grün und von Gelb zieht er vor: von Smaragd bis zu Oliv, von Safrangelb über Orangegelb bis zu hellem Ocker. Dazu treten gern ein tiefes, fast nächtliches Blau und ein sattes Bordeauxrot, das ich mit der Farbe von Zimt vergleichen möchte. Es ist, als strömten alle Gewürze und Wohlgerüche Asiens aus Siggs Farben. Das Winterliche, die zarte Verhangenheit in den Landschaften der sechziger Jahre ist mit wenigen Ausnahmen («Le Fleuve» von 1969 zum Beispiel erinnert noch daran) der Sonnensattheit, dem Urwalddunkel, der Erdhaftigkeit gewichen.

Diese neuen Wirkungen erzielt Sigg nicht allein durch die Farbwahl, sondern auch durch den Farbauftrag. Er verwendet kaum Öl, sondern Acryl, wobei er die Gefahr der Stumpfheit, die diesem Malstoff anhaftet, stets zu vermeiden weiss. Er vermag das Acryl so aufzutragen, dass die Farboberfläche eine ungemeine Dichte, eine sozusagen murale Qualität gewinnt.

Meer geht in Himmel über

Die 1973 begonnenen Himmels- und Meerbilder, die dann mit den fernöstlichen Landschaften gleichzeitig nebeneinander geführt werden, unterscheiden sich von diesen in Materialität, Farbigkeit, Struktur und Ausdruck. Schon in etwas scheinbar Äusserlichem, dem Bildformat, weichen die beiden Bildreihen voneinander ab. Die Formate der fernöstlichen Bilder sind meist breitgelagerte Rechtecke, was mit ihrer erwähnten Erdhaftigkeit und mit dem sich oft weithinziehenden Flussverlauf übereinstimmt. Die Formate der Himmels- und Meerbilder dagegen entsprechen meist einem Hochrechteck, was wiederum die ihnen eigene Struktur und Geistigkeit betont. Die Himmels- und Meerbilder erstehen aus horizontal geschichteten Farbbändern verschiedener Breite, wobei da und dort ein schmaler, scharf durchgezogener Farblauf in Weiss die vorherrschenden, ruhig gedehnten Blauflächen belebt. Eine solche Dreiheit – Hochformat, überwiegend geistig-ferne Blautöne und deren horizontale, über das ganze Gestaltungsfeld gelegte Schichtung – verleiht diesen Werken, verglichen mit den fernöstlichen Landschaften, gesteigerte Entmaterialisierung und gesteigerte Spiritualität. Sie sind fast nur noch Struktur, Motive klingen kaum mehr an; ihr hoher Abstraktionsgrad, ihre Entstofflichung zu Wolke und Dunst hin gestatten den Vergleich mit Rothkos Bildern der vierziger Jahre, in denen Landschaftliches zur reinen Essenz verdichtet wurde. Vielleicht aber liegt für einen Schweizer Künstler noch näher der Vergleich mit den «Paysages planétaires» des späten Hodler.

Die Landschaftstektonik hat sich bei Sigg fast verflüchtigt: «Festland» (im doppelten Wortsinn) gibt es kaum mehr, und oft ist nicht mehr zu unterscheiden, wo das Meer endet und der Himmel beginnt.

Und doch gehören die Landschaften mit den Flussebenen und den Küsten und die Himmels- und Meer-Bilder einander ergänzend innerlich zusammen. Zum Beispiel kombiniert Sigg die beiden Bildtypen, indem etwa in «Flusslauf – Erde – Himmel» von 1988/89 der Fluss wie ein helles Geschmeide in einer zimtfarbenen unteren Bildzone schimmert, über der sich die den Himmel-Meer-Bildern eigenen horizontalen Farbbänder aufschichten. In solchen Kombinationen wird offensichtlich, dass der Fluss nach dem «grossen Wasser» strebt. Oder, angesichts von Siggs Zurückhaltung gegenüber jeglicher Buddha- und Indienmode schon fast zu deutlich: Der Fluss führt in die Unendlichkeit (ins Nirwana). Und diesen Sinnzusammenhang weiterspinnend: Der Himmel geht am Horizont ins Meer über oder berührt da die Erde; seine Wolken nähren die Quellen der Flüsse, deren Wasser sich wieder dem Meer hinwendet. So wird das Ganze erahnbar: Samsara, der ewige Kreislauf.

Kräfte im Gleichgewicht

1993 hat Sigg in seiner Kunst noch einmal die Akzente verschoben. Von einem Neuansatz wie Ende der sechziger Jahre kann zwar nicht gesprochen werden – wohl aber von einer unvorhersehbaren Ausprägung der fernöstlichen Vision. Vieles, was schon früher erarbeitet wurde, bleibt auch jetzt weiter bestehen: etwa das zum schriftzeichenartigen Emblem gewandelte Flussmotiv, der satte, materiell dichte, «freskale» Farbauftrag, die vollen Farbklänge, die Verwendung tiefer Rottöne, darunter jenes von mir als Zimtfarbe bezeichnete Bordeaux. Dagegen hat die Bildstruktur, in die Sigg die Betonung der Mittelachse eingeführt hat, eine entscheidende Wendung erfahren. Diese Betonung der Mitte kann als bloss gedachte Symmetrieachse in Erscheinung treten, in den Skulpturen auch als vertikale Nische oder als Schlitz, in den Bildern als Öffnung, begrenzt und hervorgebracht durch zwei zu beiden Seiten des Bildfelds über die ganze Gestaltungsfläche ausgebreitete Grossformen.

In zwei erst kürzlich entstandenen Bildern könnte man bei solchen, übrigens in Zimtfarbe gehaltenen Grossformen an einen nicht ganz gezogenen Vorhang denken, der einen Durchblick offen lässt, in dem das Flusszeichen schwarz und auf blauem Grund wie eine erstarrte Blitzform aufscheint. Aber kaum hat man, diese beiden Bilder umschreibend, auf derartige Gegenstandsmotive hingewiesen, möchte man solche Anspielungen auch wieder zurücknehmen. Der Künstler hält in seinen Bildern der Mitte eben auch eine Balance zwischen reiner Form und Motiv, zwischen Figuration und Nichtfiguration.

Zu Siggs erneuertem Bildaufbau um 1993 trugen auch Impulse bei, die der Künstler im Zusammenhang mit einer Reise in die Volksrepublik China empfing. Aber diesmal ist er

Weit verzweigter Strom/Ramified River, 1971, Acryl/acrylic, 210×310 cm

Fleuve, 1969, Acryl/acrylic, 146×400 cm

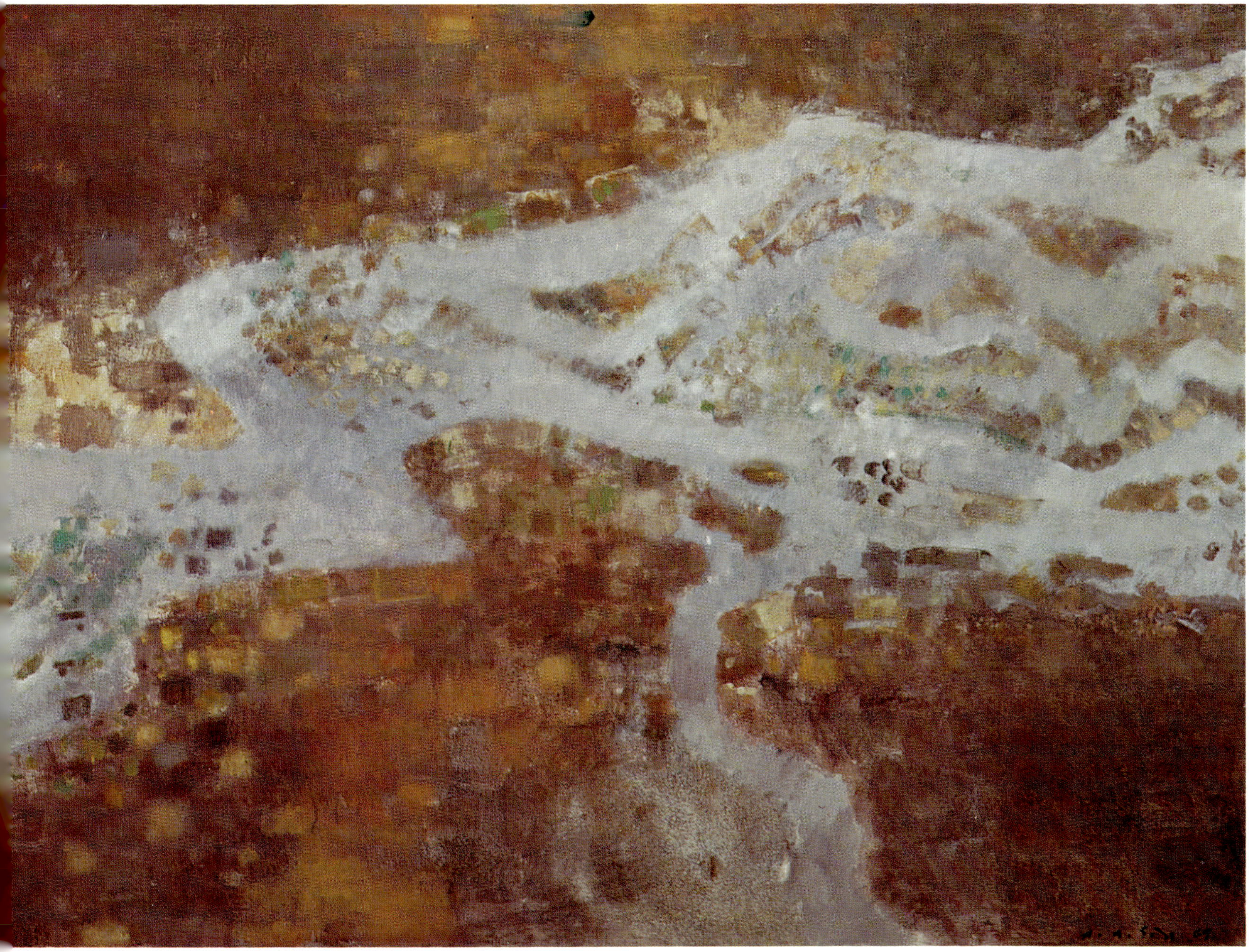

nicht in dem Mass «nach Hause» zurückgekehrt wie 1968, als er das erste Mal nach Indien und Indonesien gelangte. Er habe China und seine Kultur immer aus einer (zwar bewundernden) Distanz betrachtet. Auf seiner Reise sei ihm nun aufgefallen, was für eine wichtige Rolle in China die Mittelachse in Architektur und Städtebau bis heute spiele. Wobei aber eine derartige Zuordnung zur Zentralachse anders als in den westeuropäischen Kulturen nie dazu diene, eine eigentlich autoritäre Architektur, gar eine der Einschüchterung aufzurichten.

Diese letztere Beobachtung in China scheint mir nicht nur objektiv zutreffend, sie gilt auch in bezug auf Siggs eigene Werke, die, von der Chinareise angestossen, die Mitte thematisieren. Gewiss strahlen derart zentrierte Bilder eine gewisse Kraft und Ruhe aus, mitunter sogar eine hoheitsvolle Ruhe, aber nie pervertiert sie zu einem eisernen Schweigen, und nie zeigen sie ihre Kraft ungebändigt. Mit andern Worten: Stets liegt es Sigg fern, den Betrachter zu umgarnen oder zu überwältigen.

Von seiner Chinareise zurückgekehrt, brauchte es Zeit, bis Sigg in der Lage war, seine Erfahrungen in Kunst umzusetzen. Er begann mit plastischen Gebilden zu experimentieren – etwas, das er früher in dieser spielerischen Art kaum versucht hatte. Darum fühlte er sich wenigstens vorläufig nicht dazu gedrängt, sich an seinen eigenen, anspruchsvollen Massstäben zu messen. Es fiel ihm daher leichter, Materialien wie Holz (Rahmenteile) Kunststoffe und Metall, wie sie sich in einem Atelier mit der Zeit ansammeln, unbefangen-spontan zusammenzufügen.

Es kamen Aufbauten zustande, die an kleine Altäre, Schreine oder geheimnisvolle Architekturen erinnern, denen manchmal etwas Idolhaftes eignet. Sigg hat sie differenziert schwarz bemalt, was eine gewisse Nähe zu den Plastiken von Louise Nevelson noch betont, wie dies Robert M. Murdock richtig bemerkt hat.[7]

Die Heraushebung der zentralen Achse erreicht Sigg etwa dadurch, dass er ein oder mehrere hochrechteckige und flache Elemente über die links und rechts angefügten Teile hinausragen lässt. Ein schmaler, schlitzförmiger Durchbruch oder eng geführte Raumkanäle können, wie schon kurz erwähnt, die Vertikallinie noch zusätzlich betonen. Wie man sich eine entsprechende, auf Mitte und Mittelachse zentrierte Strukturierung in den Bildern vorzustellen hat, ist oben bereits beschrieben worden.

Im Fortschreiten der Arbeit ist es Sigg bewusst geworden, dass er nicht nur eine Mitte der Form thematisiert. Form-, Farb- und Strukturanordnung als Mittelachse oder auf eine Mitte hin erscheinen vielmehr als Äquivalenzen zu einer inneren Haltung. Sie drücken ein seelisches Gleichgewicht aus, in dem sich die Gegensätze nicht etwa aufheben (so etwas führte geradewegs in die Langeweile), sondern in dem sie ausgewogen in der Schwebe gehalten werden.

Diese Ausgewogenheit erreicht Sigg in seinen besten Bildern in vierfacher Hinsicht. Um mit dem Allgemeinsten, wiederholt Festgestellten zu beginnen: Weder ist Siggs Kunst abbildhaft, noch strikt auf sich selbst bezogen, also nicht, wie es in der üblichen Sprache der Kunstbetrachtung heisst, «ungegenständlich»; sie ist vielmehr auf eine übersetzte

[7] «H. A. Sigg, Recent Work», Katalog, Margaret Mathews · Berenson Fine Arts, New York, 1997 (ohne Jahr)

Weise welthaltig, was hier auch schon als «lyrische Abstraktion» bezeichnet wurde. Die Farbkontraste sind zweitens weder bis zum Verdampfen und Verdunsten vergeistigt, noch sind sie zum Grobmateriellen verklebt und verdumpft, sondern sie erscheinen volltönend und vital. Die Bildkomposition ist drittens weder erstarrt noch explodierend, sondern ausbalanciert. Was schliesslich den Ausdruck der Bilder betrifft: er schreit und eifert nicht, er erreicht den Betrachter als beredte Stille.

Der Grundton

Im Überblick zeigt es sich als ein Grundgesetz, dass der Künstler Hermann Alfred Sigg immer wieder ausgezogen ist, um sich selbst zu finden. Nicht immer brachten solche Auszüge das Erhoffte. Sigg selbst: «Es fällt dir nichts zu, wenn du keine Vergangenheit, keine Bilder in dir trägst.» Als der Sesshafte, der von sich selbst behauptet, nicht gern zu reisen, sich nach Indien und Ostasien aufmachte, da fand er dort die Bilder, die in seinem Innern ihm zwar noch verborgen, aber schon vorbereitet vorlagen. Andererseits vermochten Reisen im Vorderen Orient (1965) wenig in seiner Seele zu wecken. Zu Beginn der neunziger Jahre – der Künstler spürt es selbst – ist er in einem «Reich der Mitte» angelangt – so der Titel einer grösseren Anzahl kürzlich entstandener Bilder. Jedoch: eine solche Mitte ist nie ein für allemal gewonnen; sie muss bei jedem frisch begonnenen Werk neu erarbeitet werden.

Selbst der zutiefst in sich selbst versunkene Künstler will sich mitteilen. Einige wollen die Wahrheit, nichts als die Wahrheit, einige andere die Schönheit, nichts als die Schönheit Gestalt werden lassen, es gibt solche, die wollen sich und/oder die Welt heilen; noch andere wollen diese verändern, und wieder andere errichten für sich und die Betrachter Gegenwelten, Fluchtwelten. Was eigentlich will Sigg mit seiner Kunst bewirken? Hin und wieder, verdeckt oder geradezu habe ich ihn darum gefragt, und immer lautete die Antwort in diese Richtung:

«Ich glaube, dass in der Stille, im Meditativen auch eine vitale Kraft liegt, die Kraft der Ausstrahlung.»[8]

Anhang: Bemerkungen zur Kunst am Bau

Hermann Alfred Sigg ist ein vielseitiger Künstler. Dieses Buch aber ist auf seine freie Kunst hin konzentriert; die im Auftrag entstandene – Illustration, Portraits und vor allem Kunst-am-Bau, darunter zahlreiche Farbfenster für sakrale und profane Räume – verdienten eine eigene, umfassende Darstellung. Hier seien lediglich einige Bemerkungen zu Siggs letzten wichtigen Auftragsarbeiten angefügt.

[8] Im Gespräch mit Sigg von mir notiert am 17. Dezember 1997

Mit wachsender Berühmtheit des Künstlers nahmen die Aufträge zu – auch an innerem Gewicht und äusserem Umfang. So entstanden 1978 für die protestantische Kirche in Fribourg acht Farbfenster; 1985 fand die Raumgestaltung des Langhauses mit einem Chorwandbild ihren Abschluss.[9] 1981 malte Sigg für die Universität Zürich-Irchel ein Wandbild (3,5 × 6 m) und ein weiteres für das Hotel Mariott (ehemals Hotel Zürich, 2,2 × 12 m) in Zürich. 1995/96 entstand das Farbfenster für den Aufnahmeraum der Notfallstation im Zürcher Universitätsspital.

Für die kleine, 200 Jahre alte Kirche von Davos-Laret hat der Künstler 1993 sechs Farbfenster gestaltet. Das vorher nicht existierende, zentrale Rundfenster im Chor liess er zusätzlich einsetzen, um dank der so errichteten Mittelachse dem Kirchenraum eine klare Ausrichtung zu geben.

Die beiden erwähnten Wandbilder für die Universität Zürich-Irchel und das Hotel Mariott sind ganz aus Siggs Gesamtschaffen herausgewachsen, wie es seit 1968 immer vielfältiger Gestalt gewonnen hat. Sie entsprechen dem, was in diesem Buch als Siggs fernöstliche Landschaftsvision dargelegt wurde.

Im Fall der Farbfenster von Fribourg, von Davos-Laret und des Universitätsspitals hat Sigg den Abstraktionsprozess über die auftragslos entstandenen Südostasienbilder hinausgetrieben. Zwar ist von theologischer Seite versucht worden, den Fenstern in Fribourg dennoch gewisse motivisch-ikonographische Anklänge zu unterlegen.[10] Der Künstler selbst hat seine Aufgabe vor allem so verstanden, dass er den Gottesdienstbesucher mit seinen Form- und Farbrhythmen auf die Verkündigung einstimmen will. Bei den Farbfenstern im Universitätsspital ging es Sigg nach eigener Aussage darum, «die emotionellen Belastungen und Ängste der Patienten zu mildern.» Dazu diente ihm eine Komposition, die sich in wogenartigen Auf- und Abschwüngen entfaltet. Sie sind hauptsächlich auf Blau- und Grüntöne in einem hellen Umfeld gestimmt; der letzte Abschwung erglüht kräftig-sanft in einem Zyklamrot. Sigg vergleicht diese Farb-Formkomposition mit Musik: «Im Orchester klingen einzelne Stimmen stärker, heller oder dunkler auf, tauchen wieder in den Orchesterklang ein, und andere Stimmen treten hervor.»

[9] «H. A. Sigg, Farbfenster und Malerei. Reformierte Kirche Freiburg», Benteli Verlag, Bern, 1994 (Beitrag Margrit Hahnloser-Ingold)

[10] Ebenda S. 38 f. (Beitrag Matthias Thurneysen)

Reisfelder/Rice Fields, 1969, Acryl/acrylic, 116×175 cm

Prelude

Scene of the Action

Oberhasli in the Zurich *Unterland*: Hilda and Hermann Alfred Sigg's house built in 1951/52 is located at the side of a quiet road. The entrance reveals interesting information about its occupants: no solemn portal to celebrate any proud ownership or the transition from the outside to the inside, just a plain wooden door, which at first sight easily passes unnoticed. Behind it, one suspects, begins a world of its own, a world of special intimacy.

At the end of a unobtrusive corridor turned into a sitting corner the visitor enters a living room. The door on the right would take him into the two spacious, lofty studios at the rear. But no need to go so far into the house just now. The entrance hall reveals many signs of an artistic career in full bloom; the features, the forces contributing to and paving this road have assumed here concrete, visible forms in the furniture and fittings. A wealth of various items has accumulated here, yet blending together into an atmosphere of discreet harmony. The small sculptures scattered everywhere by Swiss artists such as Hildi Hess, Ellen Weyl and Charles Otto Bänninger, a metal relief by Silvio Mattioli, an impressive woman's head fragment by Paul Speck, works by members of the Zurich concrete school, Camille Graeser and Richard Paul Lohse, are taken in by our cursory glance. These are all gifts from friends, usually the result of an exchange for his own works, or tributes to colleagues whose creative approach may be far removed from his own but who nevertheless remain in his high esteem.

Passing through, the visitor also spies some works by modern classical artists – Braque, Matisse and Picasso. They hang here not necessarily because they are closely related to Sigg from a human or artistic point of view, but because, in a manner of speaking, they embody an everlasting, infrangible standard.

Indeed, all this is taken in by the sweep of the visitor's scrutinising glance, which is then suddenly arrested by five black-African wooden masks. One of the five, somewhat smaller and less conspicuous, is for Sigg a precious memory of his first sponsor, Josef Müller; the other four, of a rare quality and probably all from the Senufos living in the north-west of the Ivory Coast were acquired by himself. On the wall opposite they glare boldly at the visitor entering the room. Horned animals, they glower at him, charged with magic. They seem tragically sombre, in fact their violent expressiveness would normally seem totally out of place, were they not inexplicably embedded in the overall harmony of the living environment. And yet, as they are hanging at the rear end of the room, they are repelled, figuratively speaking. One possible interpretation is that they represent Sigg's shadow: his antipodal world, the possibilities he shunned as an artist; realms restless and tragic, dark and demonic.

Turning his gaze to the right, the visitor experiences in a condensed space the strength sustaining the artist, the moods and the emotions he expresses in his oeuvre. It is there that one sees a large-format painting by Sigg himself, titled 'Inselformen III' (Island Forms III), behind the head of a Buddha on a pedestal.

The visitor constantly encounters reliefs and statues from India, Cambodia and Indonesia in other corners of Sigg's house. In 1968 Sigg undertook his first extensive study trip through these countries and others in the Far East. They did not lead to a rupture in his oeuvre, but to an accentuation. The artist has now arrived at his interior self, he has matured. He has advanced to (inwardly prepared long before) lyrical abstraction, the concept generally associated with his name today.

In 1975, 'Inselformen III' (Island Forms III) bears testimony to Sigg's mature style. The painting does indeed evoke a landscape dimension: in mosaic-like fashion the 'islands' are painted in shades ranging from ochre to orange and yellow and individual traces of green plunged into a brown-olive background (a 'sea', if one wishes, or even a materially dense 'sky'). This *paysage d'âme* exudes composure, tranquillity, detachment. The same is expressed in the physiognomy, sculpted from dark lava stone, of the above-mentioned Buddha.

The spiritual relationship between this sculpture and Sigg's painting is clear. The artist took the opportunity to present this inner relationship to a larger audience. At the *Helmhaus* in 1976 an exhibition based on an idea by the director of the gallery Kunsthaus Zürich, Felix A. Baumann, contrasted Sigg's paintings, inspired by the Southeast Asia trip mentioned above, with original sculptures from this cultural area on loan from Museum Rietberg and the artist himself. This contrast was not always correctly interpreted by the visitors to the exhibition. Some even accused Sigg of competing in quality and strength with 'classical' East Asian art. And yet the real aim of the exhibition was merely to demonstrate, in view of the widespread interest in Zen, Kamasutra and other culture fetishes from the Far East, that a European was able to nurture deep-down within his own 'India', irrespective of all the whims of contemporary fashion.[1]

This would largely explain Sigg's spiritual disposition. But the visitor also perceives on entering the house allusions to his family origins. On the left, the hall widens out into a sitting corner with a fireplace, and through the large window facing south-west he has a view of the opening valley of the Wehn, an unspectacular, relaxing, slightly hilly landscape in luxuriant green. Initially the view is interrupted by a row of fir trees a few hundred metres away before it is permitted to continue into the distance. Behind it, hidden from view, lies his parents' farm, a time-honoured half-timbered house, still run by Sigg's younger brother.

[1] 'H. A. Sigg, Bilder 1968–1976. Skulpturen aus Indien und Südostasien' (H. A. Sigg, Paintings 1968–1976. Sculptures from India and Southeast Asia), catalogue, Zürcher Kunstgesellschaft, 1976, Foreword by Felix A. Baumann

Nachklänge, Zyklus indische Figurationen/Echoes, Cycle of Indian Figurations, 1974/82,
Tusche laviert/ink wash drawing, 33,5×26 cm

Die grosse Tempelfigur/The Large Temple Figure, 1973, Acryl/acrylic, 195×116 cm

Der Eingang zum Tempel/The Entrance to the Temple, 1971/72, Acryl/acrylic, 175×125 cm

Indische Tempelfigur I/Indian Temple Figure I, 1973, Acryl/acrylic, 175×81 cm

Die Tempelwand/The Temple Wall, 1973/74, Acryl/acrylic, 210×310 cm

Geburtstagsblatt/Birthday Drawing, 1975, Tusche laviert/ink wash drawing, 33×25 cm

Indische Tempelfigur II/Indian Temple Figure II, 1975, Acryl/acrylic, 175×81 cm

I. First Steps

A Difficult Start

Nearly all the critics and art historians at least briefly refer to Sigg's farming background, which, sociologically, does constitute an exception – just as the working class has seldom produced an artist. In terms of modern Switzerland, beginning in around 1848 with the founding of our Federal State, it is clear that even the great farmer writers in our country, for example Gotthelf and Ch.-F. Ramuz, did not at all originate from farming families. Neither did any visual artists who prefer rural-alpine motifs – Cuno Amiet, Albert Anker, Giovanni Giacometti, René Aberjonois, Alois Carigiet and Edouard Vallet, just to name a few – come from a family whose father was a farmer.[2]

My reference to this remarkable fact must suffice; I am unable to provide a ready explanation. As far as Sigg is concerned, he had to struggle very hard before being able to realise his decision to become an artist. After announcing his plans at the age of fourteen, he was treated by his father, once described by Sigg as an 'aware, outstanding' farmer, as if he were a deserter. For he, an excellent friend and custodian of animals, was the one his father had chosen as his heir, as the one who was to continue running the farm.

His mother came from a family of silk-ribbon manufacturers in Säckingen. She brought a cultivated, sensitive hand into the home. Admittedly, there were no paintings hanging on the walls, but his mother who had enjoyed a literary education gave Hermann the works of Goethe, Schiller, Lessing and Uhland instead of children's books. She well understood her son's decision, but Hermann also required a word of support from one of his teachers before being permitted to attend the College of Commercial Art in Zurich, initially only for a few months. Not until he was beset by the first signs of a heart complaint at recruit school was he finally exempted from the heavy labour on the farm and allowed to continue his studies at the College of Commercial Art (1944–1947).

What actually happened when the son, with his mother's support, managed to assert his career wishes against the will of his father? How did it come about that on this occasion art prevailed over the patriarchal norm? A classic example of the same constellation also won the day in Goethe's family. There, too, the maternal 'joy in telling stories' was not to be suppressed by 'life's first responsible conduct'. It would be wrong, in the ensuing disputes, to presume a straightforward clash of beliefs between the female side (for example, art) and the male side (reason). It could equally be upheld, in Sigg's case, that farming also falls under the female aspect, after all it corresponds to a service administered on behalf of the Earth, the Mother of us all. Perhaps Meret Oppenheim came closest to the truth when she proclaimed in her address on the occasion of the award of the Basel Art Prize in 1970 that art and artists are androgynous. Sigg was in fact reconciled with his father later on, at least symbolically on the level of his oeuvre,

[2] In modern Switzerland there is one significant exception: Augusto Giacometti. Giovanni Giacometti spent his life in a rural-alpine environment as had his father before him, who, like Frank Buchser's father, was an innkeeper, having moved away from the land. To my knowledge a study has never been written on this topic.

when he adopted the motif of fields and farmland as a structure for his paintings at a high level of abstraction.

Ernst Gubler, Ernst Georg Rüegg, Johannes Itten, Otto Morach and Heinrich Müller were Sigg's most important teachers. He owes most to the last, Müller (1903–1978), who was of particular assistance to him in 'remodelling...' for his special purposes the College of Commercial Art '...into an Academy', i.e. enrolment solely in courses relevant to his career as an autonomous artist. Sigg risked everything: he never intended to select the subjects he studied so that he should later obtain a diploma for a career in design. Müller did in fact encourage him to exhibit his works during his studies, a practice frowned upon by the other members of the teaching staff.

After completing his studies at the College of Commercial Art, Sigg opted for another, albeit less deeply rooted social convention. In the forties the general belief in Switzerland was that an artist of any merit had to receive his baptism of fire in Paris. It was not until two generations later that New York took over from the French capital. But before I actually turn to this phase in Sigg's development, I would like to review briefly the most important paintings in his early period.

Sigg's Early Period

The portrait of Sigg's mother painted in 1945 reveals an old, worn woman. Relaxed, and yet weary, she is leaning back in her armchair with her hands in her lap. Her eyes are closed, in slumber, as if contemplating inwardly. Sigg usually portrays the people he chooses as his subjects from the front; having adopted the profile approach for this portrait, he succeeds in showing to its advantage this refined, by no means peasant-like face, the accentuated aquiline nose, the high, slim neck. The profile also intensifies the impression that the arms flowing downwards are exceptionally long, thus emphasising the above mentioned state of relaxation and exhaustion. The subdued, paled red and brownish pink again strengthens the overall impression that we are witnessing the fulfilled life of a woman in search of peace.

In 'Selbstbildnis' (Self-Portrait) painted in 1946, the young man gazes sceptically and melancholically into the world. The gloomy expression on his face revealing a touch of *weltschmerz* is typical for the self-portrait of a young man who has not yet been actively confronted with everyday reality, but only suspects its opportunities, dangers and promises.

Two further works painted in the same year as a 'Self-Portrait' feature a similar latency regarding the motif and the atmosphere, a similar anticipation of something coming. The very title of the painting, 'Die Entscheidung' (The Decision), suggests this situation; in the painting, 'Am Tisch' (At Table), it is primarily conveyed by two motif connections. In the foreground a young person is sitting at a table in a state of contemplation. He has entered the shadow at the right edge of the painting in a room that leads off into another.

Die grosse Biegung/The Large Bend, 1975, Acryl/acrylic, 125×175 cm

The second room is plunged in brightness, ending at a window revealing a corner of the outside world.

'The Decision' features a similar protracted perspective. On the right edge there is also a young man deep in thought, his head leaning on his hand, but on this occasion he is standing. Again the shadowy room at the front leads off to another brighter room at the rear. What is actually going on there – three female figures are grouped around a table, apparently engrossed in a discussion – is hardly clear. But this lack of clarity raises the level of intimacy in the scene; the grouping of the women in the bright part highlights the isolation of the youth in the shadows.

All of these three paintings depict the critical situation in Sigg's life at the time. He has not yet left the shelter of his home, but the moment of parting, an unfamiliar and uncertain quantity has already come over it; the step out into the world outside, the long road towards establishing himself as an artist lie ahead.

The non-naturalistic colourfulness of 'The Decision' stands out among these four early paintings. Here the colour features bright complementary contrasts – the blue and the turquoise of the light reflections in the women figures contrast with the mustard grey and reddish brown areas of the floor – whereas the other three paintings are darker, adopting clayish shades. In 'The Decision' Sigg probably imitates the Fauves' colour scale of his revered teacher Heinrich Müller. What is most striking, however, is his decision not to follow his teacher with regard to spatial structure. The latter tended to raise the spatial depth of the painting to the surface, while Sigg pushed the spatiality back into the depths, thus enhancing the atmosphere described above of the balance between the security of the home and imminent departure.

Intermezzo Paris

Reviewing the works Sigg painted during his stay in Paris (1947), for example 'Café Select', 'Nachtcafé Paris III' (Café de Nuit – Paris III) or 'Hilda mit Hund' (Hilda with Dog), one cannot help feeling that he could have painted like this if he had stayed at home.

Paris certainly broadened his horizons, but did not determine Sigg's fate as it did in the case of several other Swiss artists – Alice Bailly, Serge Brignoni, Wilfrid Moser and Robert Müller, to name a few. In Paris a fundamental principle in his life materialises for the first time, as handed down by Heinrich Müller: 'One only sees what one has inside' and 'One can only portray what one knows'.[3]

It should be added that Paris had lost much of its glamour as a result of World War II. It is true that Picasso, Braque and Léger were still in the city, but the provocations instigated by the surrealists had ebbed, most having shunned the Nazi regime and emigrated to the USA. The imminent new style, later termed 'tachisme' by the art critic Charles Estienne in 1951, was still germinating in the dark and could not possibly have been perceived by an inexperienced youth such as Sigg.

[3] Herbert Gröger, 'Heinrich Müller', Vontobel-Druck AG, Feldmeilen, 1973, p. 111, 116 (contributed by Paul Honegger)

Die Flusswindungen III/River Meanders III, 1976/84, Acryl/acrylic, 210×81 cm, 210×310 cm, 210×81 cm

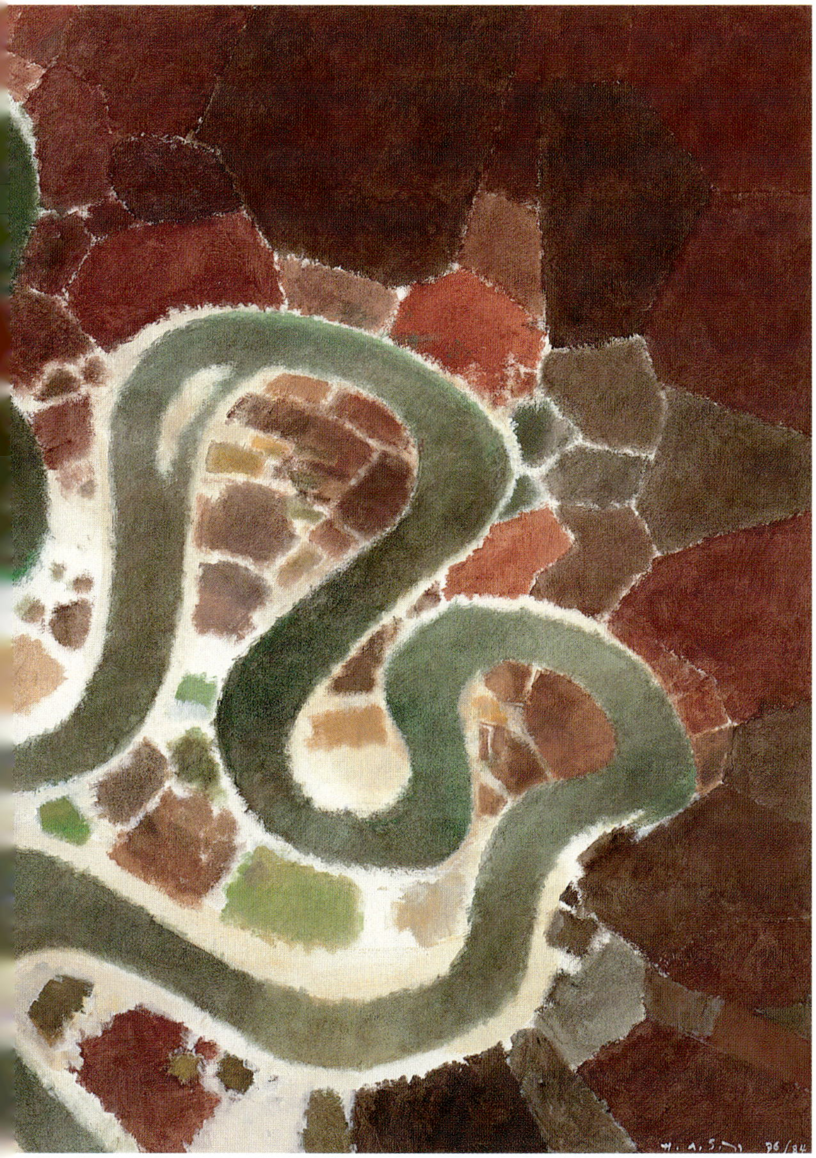

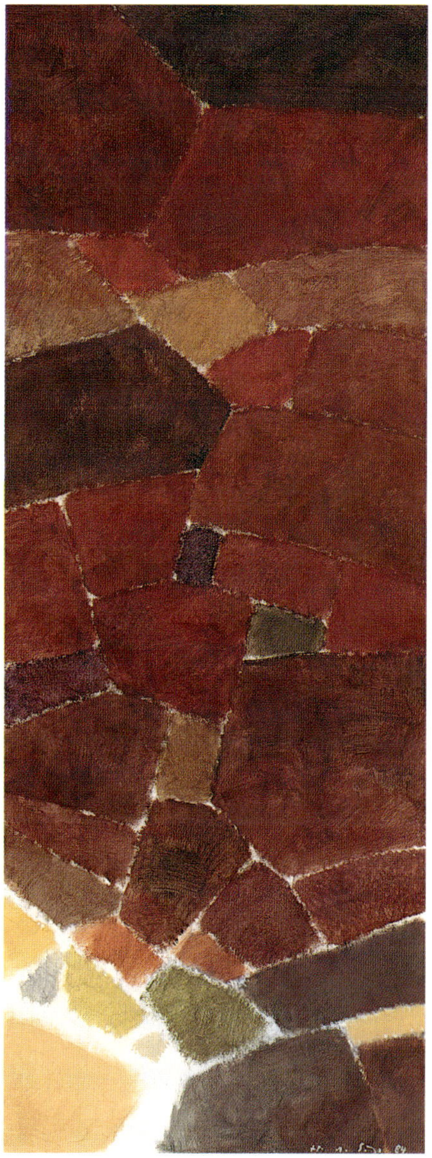

He attended the Académie André Lhote (1885–1962), who advocated moderate, so-called secondary Cubism, like the team Albert Gleizes and Jean Metzinger. Lhote's teaching talent was famous world-wide, extolled by other Swiss artists such as Serge Brignoni and Heiny Widmer (better known as a museum curator than as a painter). Hermann Sigg also had the same esteem for Lhote but did not benefit greatly from the tuition. On the other hand, he did meet a certain young lady from Chur in Switzerland, Hilda Jörger, who was later to become his wife. Lhote's lectures seemed too intellectual to him, especially after his experience of grappling with the colour theories of Johannes Itten at the Zurich College of Commercial Art. He gained most from his visits to the wide and varied range of museums and galleries, Pierre Bonnard's colour sensuousness impressing him immensely.

After Paris Sigg went on to visit many other great cities: Singapore, Hong Kong, New York. But being a country person, he never really felt at home there. It is quite remarkable how he experienced Paris as an artist, not at all like another Swiss, Wilfrid Moser, who had been living there since 1945. While Moser went down to the Underworld, to the tunnels in the métro with their garish torn posters, while he behaved like a Nordic visionary following in the footsteps of van Gogh and Ensor, Sigg remained on the surface of civilised society. One of his favourite motifs during his Paris period was the café, the cradle of Western culture, according to the art theoretician George Steiner. The brushwork in 'Café de Nuit' indicates a nervous hand, the figure of the blind man in the foreground with his dark glasses and white stick discreetly alluding to the harshness of city life. In 'Café Select', on the other hand, there is no trace of comfort or reassurance. On the contrary, here the sublimation of bright, glittering temptation appears in the figure of a young woman wearing a very low-cut, mother-of-pearl dress. The totally non-naturalistic, apple-green head of the guest sitting behind her conveys some of the excitement of this unique night.

Bread-and-Butter Jobs

Hermann Alfred Sigg had one great aim, namely to earn his way as an autonomous artist. But on his return from Paris, his first battle was one for survival. He took what was offered to him. He made both ends meet as an illustrator of books and magazines, as a window designer for Jelmoli and Globus. He also gave drawing lessons and right up to 1960 he designed stage sets, initially for the poetic-satirical theatre, 'Laterne', founded by Hans Schaub, which eventually led on to the 'Zeitbühne' theatre, the successor of the legendary 'Cornichon'. Finally, from time to time he worked for the graphic artist, designer and architect Fritz Keller.

Sigg certainly accomplished such tasks with spirit and the necessary application, but his heart was not completely in them. He had no desire, alongside his work as an artist, to take up a second profession as a poster designer like the painters Alois Carigiet, Hans Erni, Hans Falk and Niklaus Stöcklin. Sigg developed poetry in his posters, on a par with

Inselformen II/Island Forms II, 1975, Acryl/acrylic, 162×125 cm

Zwischen Tag und Traum II/Between Day and Dream II, 1990, Acryl/acrylic, 130×92 cm

Licht über dunklem Wasser/Light above Dark Water, 1986, Acryl/acrylic, 116×81 cm

Inselformen I/Island Forms I, 1975, Acryl/acrylic, 125×162 cm

Die Inseln im Strom/Islands in the River, 1980, Acryl/acrylic, 81×130 cm

Inselreich/Island Kingdom, 1991, Acryl auf Holz/acrylic on wood, 200×200 cm

Falk's or Leupin's. However, he attached no importance to becoming one of the great contributors to the Golden Age of the Swiss poster (about 1940 to 1965).

Slowly things improved. In 1949 Sigg was awarded the Conrad Ferdinand Meyer Prize for Painting and twice a bursary from the Kiefer-Hablitzel Foundation. In 1952 the art collector couple Nelly and Werner Bär purchased the first works from him, and in 1953 came the first great competition success. He won the competition for three stained-glass windows, a mural and sgraffiti at Schaffhausen Canton Hospital. Subsequently, he regularly received commissions for 'Kunst am Bau' (Art in Building Projects), which at last enabled him to devote himself to his painting. His private life also became more settled: in 1949, he married Hilda Jörger; in 1951, Hannes Trösch, then working for Max Frisch the architect, designed the couple's studio house in Oberhasli, which Sigg actively helped to build; in 1956, his son Daniel was born.

II. First Bloom

In 1950 Hermann Alfred Sigg travelled to the Mediterranean for the first time, to Italy, to Sicily, to the Aeolian Islands. He went on such journeys almost every year until 1966, going further afield to Greece and Spain, North Africa (Morocco, Tunisia), to the Near East (Lebanon, Syria, Jordan and Israel).

Journeys to the World Without and the World Within

What is it that attracted Sigg to these southern countries? The call of the famous Mediterranean light?

While venturing on these journeys, the artist receives a series of commissions for stained-glass windows: from Männedorf, Sternenberg, Lichtensteig. In conjunction with these church building projects, Sigg reports having researched in the 'Orient' for certain Christian symbols which he could use in his stained-glass windows. He was not successful.

In 1964/65 the artist painted a series of portraits of Josef Müller; Dr. Walter Bechtler commissioned Sigg to paint him surrounded by his family. Müller and Bechtler, both art collectors, were among Sigg's first sponsors. The portrait of Müller is more 'classical', more traditional than the far bolder family painting of the Bechtlers. But it will hardly come as a surprise that Sigg was more audacious during the sixties in the paintings he painted for 'himself', having no obligation to comply with the wishes or expectations of a client, the subject of a portrait. Sigg's portrayals of horse races and particularly his landscape paintings during this period are now 'modern' in the sense that the artist aims to develop his works on the basis of the painting's own autonomy.

Not only is his goal of painting autonomy achieved but a principle also materialises that provides the basis for Sigg's personality as an artist. Just as he need not have gone to Paris to do the paintings he painted there, just as he need not have become acquainted with India and Indonesia to create the lyrical abstraction of the river and coast scenes, he did not actually require the numerous trips to the Mediterranean to produce the landscape visions of the sixties. There are indeed a few, for instance 'Apulischer Frühling' (Apulian Spring) in 1967, in which a southern, almost 'black' bright light, a restrained, subtropical luxuriance appears to be captured. The cubic-white, huddled clusters of houses in 'Stadt im Süden' (Town in the South) are easily associated with the Mediterranean or Magna Grecia, and yet such clusters of houses could also be encountered in the Engadin or in Ticino, and the Apulian blossoms in the Zurich *Unterland* or in Japan. The paintings, too, in which white and silver-grey evoke the idea of snow, in which gentle overlapping rectangular elements remind the observer of ploughed fields, could equally be attributed to the Far East and to the artist's Swiss homeland. In other words, Sigg's landscapes in the sixties are not to be ascribed to a clearly defined geographical area but to the artist's soul. To paint them he does not need to leave the Zurich *Unterland*; he only needs to look inwards. The world outside may however be seen as a catalyst. This means that the paragon – or must I say archetype? – is raised to the level of consciousness by the encounter with its counterpart in reality, urging to become an image.

Roads towards Painting Autonomy

Sigg started out on the road towards the autonomy of colour before his stay in Paris, in his early work 'The Decision', for example, or in Paris itself in his 'Café de Nuit-Paris III' and 'Café Select'. Here he found himself, probably inspired by his teacher Heinrich Müller, in the realm of the Fauves and the Nabis. Sigg himself remarks time and again that the colour sensuousness of Pierre Bonnard (1867–1947) had an enduring impression on him. In the landscape paintings of the sixties he again withdrew from this expressive, late-impressionist colour environment. The painting 'Das schwarze Feld' (The Black Field) of 1961 features contrasts, for example, that the Nabis had not fathomed: here brick-pink, orange-yellow, violet and black clash in the plots of colour identifiable as ploughed land. In the painting 'Im Lichte des Winters' (In the Light of Winter) of 1971 1972 ochre, olive, deep orange and again black put in a joint appearance, meaning that the less favoured earthy colours of the Nabis – with the exception of Bonnard – have returned. Moreover, the greys that the artist by nature prefers in his wintry scenes, ranging from pearly shades to silver and bluish-milky hues are Hermann Sigg's personal speciality. He applies refreshing spots and dashes to the grey haze with virtually Japanese delicacy, identifiable as horses' backs, jockeys' colourful waistcoats in the watercolour 'Pferderennen' (The Horse Race) and from 1961 as ploughed fields or herds of animals.

Whereas Sigg gradually advanced to painting autonomy in his colour application, generally considered a fundamental feature of modern art, the development of the painting structure towards a similar autonomy was more striking and certainly less gradual.

Symbols and 'Gesellschaftung'

To achieve this new painting structure Sigg sets the few, invariably identical motifs he adopts to create his landscapes in a similarly restricted stock of symbols.

The symbol has one particularity: it is an extreme simplification, reducing the portrayal to its essence. Even Sigg's horses in his paintings at the races are the result of intense typification, but they are easy to identify. If this had not been the case, Sigg would definitely not have received a Gold Medal for this series of paintings from the association of Swiss sports journalists in 1965.

The symbols for cows and sheep in his landscape paintings are simplified even further, to such an extent that they are largely interchangeable. Not only cows and sheep but also ploughed fields and cubic, Mediterranean houses are represented by Sigg as rectangles with little variation. He uses another symbol for thickets or birds: initially, tiny black markings, gently scattered all over the picture. In his painting 'The Black Field' bird and thicket motifs appear both at the same time, virtually intermingling with each other, similar to the portrayal of sheep, cows, ploughed fields and houses. Sigg's concern is no longer the individual sheep or house, but the group form or *'Gesellschaftung'*, to adopt Paul Weber's apt term. Individual striking features are insignificant; what counts is the herd, the flock of birds, the naturally grown village, the network or ensemble of all the ploughed fields, meaning, on the abstractly structural level, homogeneity and similarity of form, intensification of form, loosening, scattering, condensation of dark elements, isolation, revealed by the use of white suddenly rising brightly from its dark surroundings.

Paul Weder, who in his capacity as an art critic often studied these landscapes, found highly accurate, poetic-evocative words to describe their very special nature. On the occasion of the inauguration of an exhibition at Zofingen in October 1968 he portrayed them as follows: "Hermann Alfred Sigg looks for a landscape, the main subject, in the form of a drawn out, but structured area, stretching boundlessly (…). From left to right movement seems to pour into the landscape area, with no impedance or restriction, in the form of the slow, steady roving of the herd, for example. The onward movement is negligible; it gropes slowly forward, similar to time slipping through existence, to the grains of sand trickling to the bottom of a sandglass". This beautifully observed 'gentle roving' (of the herd, i.e. of time demonstrated by a structure of form) is occasionally halted, as in a painting in 1962, where the sheep do not advance across the surface of the painting, but are depicted frontally for once. What is more, the individual animals are distinctly set off against each other. The frontal aspect and the demarcation of each creature, coupled with their black masks or faces rising above their bright wool, mean that in this case, despite the herd formation, the individual traits of the sheep are clearly perceived.

Openness towards Boundlessness

The spatial structures simultaneously experimented on in these paintings during the sixties deserve special reference. 'Town in the South' in 1965 traditionally ends the horizon with an almost nocturnal black band of sky. Other paintings such as 'Die Sonnenstreifen' (Sun Streaks) and 'Schafe im Schnee' (Sheep in the Snow) take the landscape above the upper edge of the painting; no end is discernible. This vague openness is emphasised even further in paintings such as 'The Black Field' and 'In the Light of Winter', where the solid earth passes over to an immeasurable expanse of grey to accomplish the sprawling boundlessness of Sigg's landscapes, referred to by Weder.

The impression of this boundlessness is intensified even further by an unusual perspective construction. Not by the latter luring the observer's gaze down to unfathomable depths; this is not the intention. On the contrary, the observer gently surveys a landscape which has been just slightly folded back. The suspicion of 'infinity', rather 'boundlessness' is created by the fact that the lines formed by the borders left and right of the fields meet at a vanishing point inevitably presumed far above the upper edge of the painting. Such an open perspective heading for infinity, as it were, was continued by Sigg in later landscape paintings, for example 'Wintertag' (Winter Day) in 1976 and ten years later in the work 'Es hellt auf' (Brightening up).

III. A Glance at the Human Figure

The Nude and Eroticism

Naturally, nude painting is also a common feature of Swiss art in the 20th Century, female nude paintings predominating, as in the rest of the western world. On closer scrutiny, such portrayals are rarely seen to celebrate the woman as an erotic being, which is certainly food for thought. The nudes of Max Kämpf (Kunstmuseum Olten, 1984), for example, assume a frosty, exposed, even pitiable aspect; the exceptionally long women figures by Alberto Giacometti follow a similar direction, but without a trace of sentimentality, almost mystically engrossed; Wilhelm Gimmi's nude paintings frequently endow the woman with earthiness or monumentality; Vallotton's women constantly seem not just naked, but exposed; the 'Fille dans la chambre rouge' (Girl in the Red Room) (1948, Museum zu Allerheiligen) by René Auberjonois, itself a significant painting, seems to feel ashamed of her nakedness, to be more exact, she seems to be bent on concealing her nakedness. One example of an uninhibited eroticist in Swiss modern art would be Böcklin.[4]

Bearing in mind the fact that nakedness is by no means necessarily related to eroticism (liberated eroticism) in modern art, the candour with which Sigg conveys the beauty and attraction of the female body in his nude paintings of 1964 and 1966 must be

[4] For Arnold Böcklin's modern interpretation cf. 'Arnold Böcklin, Giorgio de Chirico, Max Ernst. Eine Reise ins Ungewisse', catalogue, Kunsthaus Zürich, 1998, Editors Guido Magnaguagno and Juri Steiner

Rote Erde, dunkler Fluss/Red Earth, Dark River, Acryl/acrylic, 1977/78, 162×125 cm classed as a true stroke of luck. These nude paintings are certainly traditional in approach, but for that precise reason they are all the more meritorious, Sigg having applied true mastery and discretion to inspire them with erotic magic. Firstly, the splendid incarnadine deserves a special mention: it endows one nude with a tint of mother-of-pearl, the other with a hue of ivory. Both nudes feature a slight shimmer, a delicate detachment, in principle accessible from the observer's standpoint: the process of sublimation has not been pursued to the point of desensualisation, to the point where Kant's indifferent pleasure could enter the scene. The 1964 painting is a rear-view nude. As there is no facial expression, preventing any individuality, any expression of character and awareness, the purely corporeal, genre-specific component comes to the fore. The 1966 nude is in fact accompanied by a facial expression, but it is kept quite general and introvert. This serves to stimulate the sensuality of the observer, encouraged to swell without any intellectual control because the painted figure does not confront it with any intellect. On the other hand, both nudes seem as if they are enveloped in a dream; their ego has not yet awakened; they can remain suspended in a kind of innocence, in an almost vegetable state.

Sigg preferred no eye-contact in most of his portrayals of people, with the exception of his portrait commissions, of course. He may happen to give his subjects eyes. But even then they rarely attempt to catch the eye of the observer, who can therefore never become the portrayed person's accomplice. The self-portrait of 1946 does look towards us, but this exception seems logical, as it is the self-portrait of a young man who has just discovered the existence of the outside world. Neither in this painting is there any plea for our approval; on the contrary, here the vis-à-vis, the observer is put to the test.

Concealing and Appearing

It is more than just a literary parable when I am tempted to say that the nudes of 1964 and 1966 are clothed in their own nakedness. At a later date, for instance in 'Kimono I' (1985) and 'Kimono III' (1986) Sigg not only proceeds to clothe his subjects, but to wrap them in what are sumptuous gowns.

It is not necessary to dwell on these examples; in his contribution to this book Guido Magnaguagno has made a lengthy reference to the artistic methods of concealment by way of gowns, blankets and drapes (initially applied in the painting 'Le Lit' (The Bed) in 1947).

'Der Traum' (The Dream) and 'Der Träumer' (The Dreamer), both painted in 1986, reveal the human figure in a state of partial concealment. Here the figure is lying relaxed on a blanket, literally nestled into it. The contrast between the opulent flower ornamentation and the smooth, rosy complexion of the figures at rest enhances the sublimely erotic atmosphere.

A horizontal band of colour at the lower edge of both paintings and several parallel layers above the figure form a kind of bed, in any event a protected zone. In the painting

Heller Fluss im Dunkel der Nacht/Bright River in the Dark of the Night, 1981, Acryl/acrylic, 116×175 cm

'The Dream' the semblance of an outside world spreads out above the bands, which could be interpreted as a rough sea under a deep dark-blue night sky.

The drawing 'In den Gärten Salomos' (In Solomon's Gardens), which goes back to 1971 and the lithographic cycle 'Das Hohe Lied Salomos' (The Song of Solomon), shows a loving couple on what seems to be a carpet of flowers (regarding the form, not unlike the sumptuously ornamental blankets in the paintings of 1986). But in the lithograph particularly the lovers' bodies themselves, lying one above the other entwined in an embrace, give each other a feeling of security. The night harbouring the large moon and the fan-like branches of a tree above the lovers have been appointed to keep guard over them.

In Sigg's last development phase of lyrical abstraction, which began in 1968, the erotic component survives as an atmosphere. No longer attached to a human figure, it is now more difficult to pinpoint. It is up to the imagination of the individual observer whether it wishes to associate the compositions featuring landscapes and stretches of coastline executed in the seventies, eighties and partly in the nineties with female forms.

Similar to the slumbering, lying figures, Sigg's paintings of Indian temple figures from 1973 to 1975 also create a mysterious, detached effect. 'Die grosse Tempelfigur' (The Large Temple Figure), 195 cm by 116 cm, hardly rises above its temple wall. Does the figure recede into the wall, or conversely does the latter project the goddess to the fore? Appearing or disappearing – both important aspects, since a being does not simply assume a calm, plastic appearance; not yet materialised, it hovers above the borderline between dream and reality.

Epiphany, the sudden appearance of deity, plays an important role in many religions, including Christianity. Sigg, a painter of Indian divine sculptures, ventured towards it.

IV. To the Peak, to the Centre

From 1968 Sigg extends his travels beyond the Mediterranean and the Old World to more distant lands; he undertakes several journeys to India, Indonesia and the Far East: in 1972, 1975 and 1982. For more details of his destinations, the 'biographical notes' at the end of this book may be consulted.

On Travelling and Arriving

It all started with a coincidence, as the anecdote goes: Swissair purchased a few paintings from Sigg for its office premises, paying a part of his commission in air tickets. But why did Sigg constantly set out for these oriental lands? Had he perhaps finally arrived home, in 'his' country? Was a typical, romantic detour necessary, or to quote Novalis' famous words: "Where are we going? Always home." Or as Walter Bernet put it: "On his travels he never settles down. In fact, one could almost say that on all his journeys he is always on the plane back (…). He's a farmer's son, and in a certain way has remained a farmer. He is where he comes from".[5]

In 1993 the artist travelled to Taiwan, Hong Kong and the People's Republic of China. This journey also inspired his work. Further trips after 1986 took him to North and South America, Mexico, particularly to towns like New York, Chicago and Mexico City. His observations there did not directly affect his oeuvre. Not just because it is the 'New World' with its high tech, drive and optimism; he takes stock of it all, not without a certain curiosity, but cannot integrate it into his work. Even pre-Columbian art in Mexico only arouses his abstract admiration.

Extending his horizons towards the Far East did not transform the previous approach to his work, either. This never was and still never is, as we now know, his way of doing things: his development as an artist progresses gradually, old elements frequently returning in an transformed way at a higher level. The basis pattern of Sigg's artistic development could be compared to a rising spiral.

In his paintings inspired by the journeys to India and other parts of Asia Hermann Alfred Sigg matures. Anyone thinking of a 'Sigg' will think of a work from the past thirty years. The following provides a general outline of this phase in his oeuvre continuing until today:

1968 – 1993: Paintings of river and earth formations and coastal landscapes; mainly horizontal format;
from 1973: sea and sky paintings; mainly vertical format;
from 1993: sculptures and paintings whose centre is the subject under study.

This information, useful as a general guideline, has to be modified. The beginning and the end of the individual phases overlap. To name one example: Sigg very reluctantly takes his leave of the 'wintry' scenes painted mainly in the sixties: 'In the Light of Winter' in 1971/72, 'Winter Day' in 1976, 'Brightening up' as late as 1986. His motif aspirations in the works after 1968 are later refined, however.

In his 'Far East' paintings an echo of representationalism is certainly perceptible; later one can swim in coastal landscapes, plains featuring fields and rivers with their little islands, such is their similarity to the off-shore coastline. One will also glean a symbolic meaning from such motifs. On the other hand, it must be absolutely clear at this point that Sigg's Far Eastern landscape visions, like the previously described landscape paintings of the sixties, cannot be attributed to exact geographical locations; they correspond to what was understood as paysages d'âme at the turn of the century. Although the observer can feast his eyes on the mere structures, the rhythm, the form and the harmony of the colours, nobody would ascribe Sigg's painting to pure non-figuration. The artist adheres to the narrow borderline between 'representation' and 'non-representation'; my personal term for this tightrope walk is 'lyrical abstraction'.

[5] 'H. A. Sigg, Bilder und Zeichnungen aus Südostasien' (H. A. Sigg, Paintings and Drawings from Southeast Asia), Orell Füssli Verlag, Zurich, 1976, p. 97 (contributed by Walter Bernet)

The Wealth of the River

Sigg is often described as rolling out the Indian-East Asian landscape, seen from the passenger seat in a plane, as a bird's eye view. This is only an approximate evaluation, for he does not have all the fragmented coastlines and river plains with or without rice fields sweep swiftly by in the framework of the painting, but rather captures them in a structure resembling a well-assembled mosaic. The world seen from the aeroplane, created in the 'cartographic process' – Eduard Hüttinger sketchily traced the origins of Sigg's approach in history of art terms.[6] What is more, Sam Francis (1923–1994) also allowed the experience of flying to inspire him to develop his own personal painting style. But their flying experience led to different results. On rare occasions, one being the painting 'Im Reich des Herbstes' (In the Realm of Autumn) (1994/95), does Sigg come close to Sam Francis' tachism.

The structure of the surface in a free grid of rectangles in various colours, first discerned in the landscape paintings of the sixties as a network of ploughed fields, is continued in the landscapes of Asia; the river and the sea are now the new main motifs. The river in particular offers Sigg virtually endless phenomena for his artistic creativity: it winds along majestic loops through the field of vision, branches out into the silvery gleam of the delta, seems to seep away only to reappear further on, forms circuitous meanders, flashes like the crack of a whip, freezes into an ornament, solidifies into a character, to be then transferred in this calligraphic form from 1993 to the next phase, when Sigg deals with the theme of the centre.

The river implants in these paintings of a firmly-established order the factor of time – not by dramatically sweeping and flying past, but applying the same gentle tug effected by the herds of cattle and sheep in the works back in the sixties.

The metaphor of the river in Sigg's oeuvre endures for over thirty years. Despite this consistency it constantly altered, nipping in the bud any reproach of one-sidedness or lack of imagination on the part of the artist. Sigg may say the same thing, but what he says is never identical. In the case of artists or philosophers we are more accustomed to hearing a certain poignant locution for the idea of 'saying the same': that of a 'vision'. Sigg's dogged adhesion to one form feature, to one motif is shared by many, for instance Capogrossi and his comb elements, Lucio Fontana and his slits in the canvas, Horst Antes and his cuttlefish, Alberto Giacometti, whose emaciated, lofty figures almost always grow out of giant lumpy feet.

Precisely the constant repetition and transformation confirm the symbolic nature of the river form. The artist himself has referred to its symbolism in his notes, from which I quote the following:

"The river means to me more than just a moving coloured form. It is for me something existential, something to do with my own inner posture."

[6] Ibid., p. 21 ff (contributed by Eduard Hüttinger)

Der geheimnisvolle Fluss/Secret River, 1990, Acryl/acrylic, 81×130 cm

Die Spur des Flusses/The Course of the River V, 1985, Acryl/acrylic, 210×125 cm

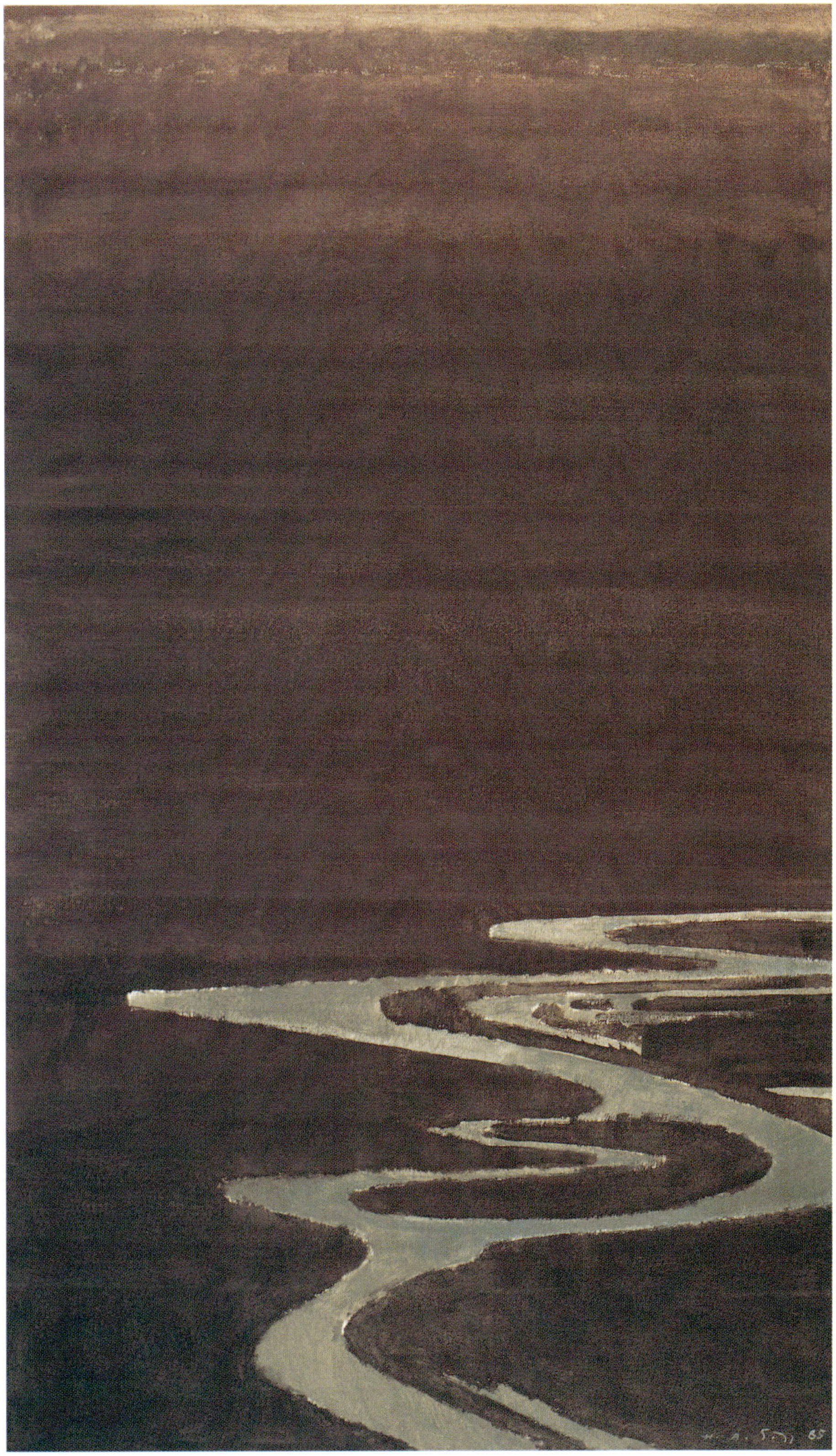

Nacht über der Küste/Night over the Coast, 1975, Acryl/acrylic, 125×210 cm

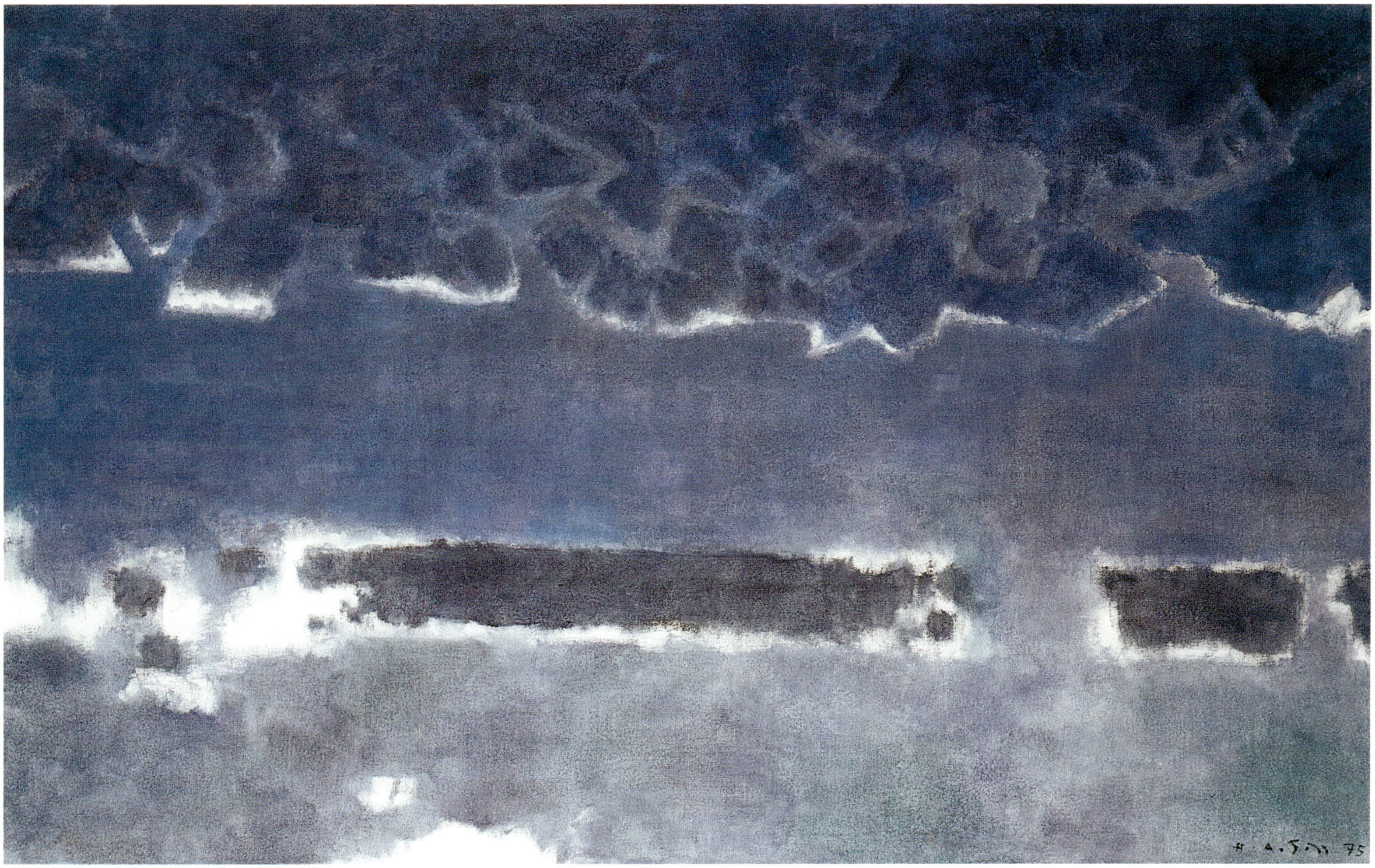

Sigg applies the river as an image "of effusion, of gentle or swift movement, not stagnant, but in motion, towards a destination: the big water". The river is a symbol of creativity for the Indians, Sigg writes elsewhere. This is also a possible interpretation of the motif in his paintings: by persistently transforming the primordial figure of the river, he corroborates his artistry.

Let us pass on to the colour in his Far Eastern paintings: he prefers wide ranges of green and yellow, varying from emerald to olive, from saffron yellow to orange yellow and bright ochre. This is often accompanied by a deep, almost nocturnal blue and a rich bordeaux red, which I would relate to the colour of cinnamon. All the spices and fragrances of Asia seem to be emitted by Sigg's colours. The wintry element, the gentle haze in the landscapes of the sixties has now given way, with a few exceptions ('Le Fleuve' [The River] painted in 1969 is still a reminder), to an earthy nature, the richness of the sun, and the darkness of the primeval forest.

Sigg does not achieve these new effects solely by his choice of colour, but also by the colour application. He uses hardly any oils, but acrylic, always knowing how to avoid the danger of dullness, characteristic of this material. His knowledge of applying acrylic ensures that the colour surface will assume an outstanding intensity, a mural quality, as it were.

The Sea Blends into the Sky

The sky and sea paintings, initiated in 1973 and continued later alongside the Far Eastern landscapes, differ from the latter in terms of materiality, colourfulness, structure and expression. The two series of paintings even reveal differences in what would appear to be a superficial feature, the painting format. The formats of the Far Eastern paintings usually constitute horizontal rectangles in accordance with their above-mentioned earthy nature and the frequently far-stretching course of a river. The formats of the sky and sea paintings, on the other hand, are mostly a vertical rectangle, which correspondingly emphasises their own particular structure and spirituality.

The sky and sea paintings are composed of horizontal bands of colour varying in width, with a narrow, sharp passage of white despatched here and there to vivify the predominant, serene expanses of blue. This trinity – the vertical, predominantly spiritual format, the distant blue and its horizontal bands across the whole of the painting surface – endow these works, compared to the Far Eastern landscapes, with an enhanced level of dematerialisation and spirituality. They consist almost only of structure, motifs are hardly suggested any more; their high level of abstraction, their dematerialising into cloud and haze can be compared to Rothko's paintings in the forties, in which the landscape element was intensified to the point of pure essence. But perhaps in the case of a Swiss artist the comparison with the *Paysages planétaires* of Hodler's later period is less remote.

Die Wasserstellen/The Watering Places, 1973, Acryl/acrylic, 116×81 cm

The landscape tectonics have almost disappeared from Sigg's work: 'Terra firma', in both senses, hardly plays an important role any more, and it is often impossible to tell where the sea ends and the sky begins.

And yet the landscapes featuring river plains and coastlines and the sky-and-sea paintings belong inwardly side by side. Sigg combines the two types of painting: for example, in 'Flusslauf-Erde-Himmel' (River course-Earth-Sky) dated 1988/89, the river gleams like a bright jewel against a lower cinnamon-coloured zone, above which the horizontal bands of colour characteristic of sky-and-sea paintings are stratified. In such combinations there is clear evidence that the river is pressing towards the 'big water'. Considering Sigg's reserve concerning any Buddha and India fashion, the evidence is almost too clear: the river leads to infinity (to Nirvana). Developing this association even further: the sky merges with the sea on the horizon or comes into contact with the earth; its clouds nourish the sources of the rivers, whose water turns back into the sea again. The whole is divinable; samsara, the eternal cycle.

Forces in Equilibrium

In 1993 Sigg shifted his emphasis once again, not meaning a new approach as in the late sixties but an unpredictable development of the Far Eastern vision. Much of what was achieved earlier is still continued: for example the river motif transformed into a character-like emblem; the rich, materially thick 'frescal' colour application; the full colour tones; the use of deep red, including the bordeaux I previously described as cinnamon. On the other hand, the structure of the painting experienced a decisive change, with Sigg's accentuation of the central axis. This emphasis of the centre may appear as a merely conceived axis of symmetry, in his sculptures as a vertical niche or a slit, in his paintings as an aperture, contained and produced by two large forms on either side of the picture, spreading across the entire surface.

In two of his recent paintings such large forms – executed in cinnamon, incidentally – could conjure up the notion of a curtain, not quite completely drawn across, allowing a peep at the river symbol, black against a blue background, shining like a frozen flash of lightning. But no sooner has one referred to these subject motifs while describing the two paintings than one is impelled to withdraw such allusions. The artist also maintains in his centre paintings an equilibrium between pure form and motif, between figuration and nonfiguration.

Around 1993 Sigg's renewed painting structure was also influenced by ideas the artist had received in connection with a visit to the People's Republic of China. But on this occasion he did not return 'home' to the same extent as in 1968, when he first visited India and Indonesia. He had always viewed China and its culture from a distance, albeit with admiration. On his journey he was struck by the importance of the central axis in Chinese architecture and town planning today. But it must be said that this emphasis on the central axis, unlike the situation in West European civilisations, was never used to impose an authoritarian style of architecture, let alone one of intimidation.

This observation about China seems to me not only objectively correct, but also applies to Sigg's own works, which, encouraged by the journey to China, set out to make the centre the theme of his works. Such centred paintings radiate a certain strength and tranquillity, even majestic serenity, but never pervert to stony silence, never resort to an unrestrained display of force. In other words, Sigg always refrains from ensnaring or overpowering the observer.

On his return from China, Sigg needed some time before he could translate his experiences into the art form. He began experimenting with sculptures – a form he had hardly ever experimented with in this playful way. This explains why, for the time being at least, he did not feel any compulsion to subject himself to his own high standards. So it was easier for him to assemble spontaneously and at his ease materials such as pieces of wood (parts of frames), plastic and metal that naturally tend to accumulate in an artist's studio.

Structures emerged that resembled small altars, shrines and mysterious styles of architecture, occasionally reminiscent of idols. Sigg painted them in different shades of black, accentuating a certain proximity to Louise Nevelson's sculptures, as Robert M. Murdock correctly observed.[7]

Sigg accentuates the central axis by raising one or several vertical rectangles and flat elements above the parts attached right and left. A thin slit-shaped aperture or narrow channels, as briefly mentioned above, can further emphasise the vertical line. How to imagine the corresponding structure focusing on the centre and the central axis in the paintings has also been described.

As the work progressed, Sigg realised that he was not only making the centre of the form his theme. In fact, the form, the colour and the arrangement of the structure as the central axis or centre all appear to correspond to his inner posture. They express a mental equilibrium, in which unlike poles do not cancel each other out – the product of such a procedure would be immediate boredom – but keep each other in a balanced state of suspension.

In his best paintings Sigg achieves this equilibrium in many respects. To begin with the most general and most frequently observed: Sigg's art is neither mimetic, nor is it strictly related to itself, i.e. it is not, to use the customary language of art appreciation, non-representational; on the contrary, its translation has it contain the world, previously referred to as 'lyrical abstraction'. The colour contrasts are neither intellectualised into a vaporous or evaporated state, nor are they gummed together and dulled into coarse matter, but they are sonorous and vital in aspect. Moreover, the picture composition is neither rigid nor explosive, but well-balanced. The expression of the works is not clamorous or ambitious; it reaches the observer in the form of meaningful silence.

[7] 'H. A. Sigg, Recent Work', catalogue, Margaret Mathews-Berenson Fine Arts, New York, 1997 (no indication of the year)

Die Nacht über dem Fluss/Night over the River, 1977, Acryl/acrylic, 130×92 cm

The Ground Shade

Reviewing the whole, it seems to be a fundamental law that the artist Hermann Alfred Sigg constantly set out in search of himself. These departures did not always lead to what he hoped for. Sigg says himself: "Nothing comes to you, if you have no past, no paintings inside you". When the artist, sedentary and in his own words reluctant to travel, set out for India and East Asia, he found there the paintings that were, it is true, hidden deep down, but they were already prepared. On the other hand, his journeys to the Near East (1965) aroused but little in his soul. In the early nineties – the artist feels it himself – he arrives at a 'Reich der Mitte' (In the Middle Realm): the title of a large number of recent paintings. However, such a centre is never conquered indefinitely; it has to be restored in every new work.

Even the artist wrapped up in the depths of himself wants to express himself. Some want the truth and nothing but the truth; some seek to create beauty, only beauty; some want to cure themselves and/or the world; some aim to change the world; others set up for themselves and the observer opposite worlds, worlds to escape to. What does Sigg want to effect by means of his art? I have asked him this question time and again, directly and indirectly. The answer always went something like this:

"I believe that tranquillity and the meditative state harbour a vital force, the force of expression".[8]

Appendix: Remarks on Construction-Related Art

Hermann Alfred Sigg is a versatile artist. This book, however, focuses on his autonomous art; his commissioned works – illustrations, portraits and primarily 'Kunst am Bau' (art for building projects), including many stained-glass windows for both ecclesiastical and secular buildings – would merit a separate comprehensive presentation. Now follow just a few brief remarks on Sigg's recent significant commissioned works.

As the artist's reputation grew, so did the commissions he received, both in terms of the inner significance and the external scope. In 1978 he designed eight stained-glass windows for the Protestant Church in Fribourg; in 1985 the interior design of the nave decorated by a choir mural was completed.[9] In 1981 Sigg painted a mural for the University of Zurich-Irchel (3.5 by 6 metres) and another for Hotel Mariott, formerly Hotel Zurich, (2.2 by 12 metres) in Zurich. In 1995–1996 he designed the stained-glass window for the admissions hall of the emergency ward at Zurich University Hospital.

In 1993 the artist designed six stained-glass windows for the small 200-year-old church in Davos-Laret. He was responsible for the insertion of the round window, which did not exist before, in the choir using the ensuing central axis to provide the church interior with a clear alignment.

[8] From my notes taken during a discussion with Sigg on December 17, 1997

[9] Margrit Hahnloser-Ingold, 'H. A. Sigg, Farbfenster und Malerei. Reformierte Kirche Freiburg' (Stained-Glass Windows and Painting at the Reformed Church in Fribourg), Benteli Verlag, Bern 1994

The two previously mentioned murals for the University of Zurich-Irchel and Hotel Mariott are unreservedly the products of Sigg's whole oeuvre, which after 1968 assumed an increasingly versatile form. They correspond to what was described in this book as Sigg's Far Eastern landscape vision.

In the case of the stained-glass windows in Fribourg, Davos-Laret and Zurich University Hospital Sigg pushed the process of abstraction even beyond the non-commissioned Southeast Asian paintings. Admittedly, attempts were made by the church to impart to the windows in Fribourg certain motif-iconograph tendencies.[10] The artist himself primarily understood his task as creating through the medium of his form and colour rhythms the appropriate mood in the congregation for prayer. In the case of the stained-glass windows at the University Hospital Sigg said his main concern was "to allay the patients' stress and anxiety". He used a composition of flowing undulations, rising and falling. The latter are mainly set in blue and green tones against a bright background; the final descent glows strongly and gently in cyclamen red. Sigg compares these colour and form compositions to music: "In the orchestra individual parts grow stronger, brighter or darker to then re-immerge into the sound of the orchestra, and then other parts appear (…)".

[10] Ibid., p. 38 ff (contributed by Matthias Thurneysen)

Der Kimono III/The Kimono III, 1986, Acryl/acrylic, 175×81 cm

Frau im Kimono I/Woman in a Kimono I, 1985, Acryl/acrylic, 116×65 cm

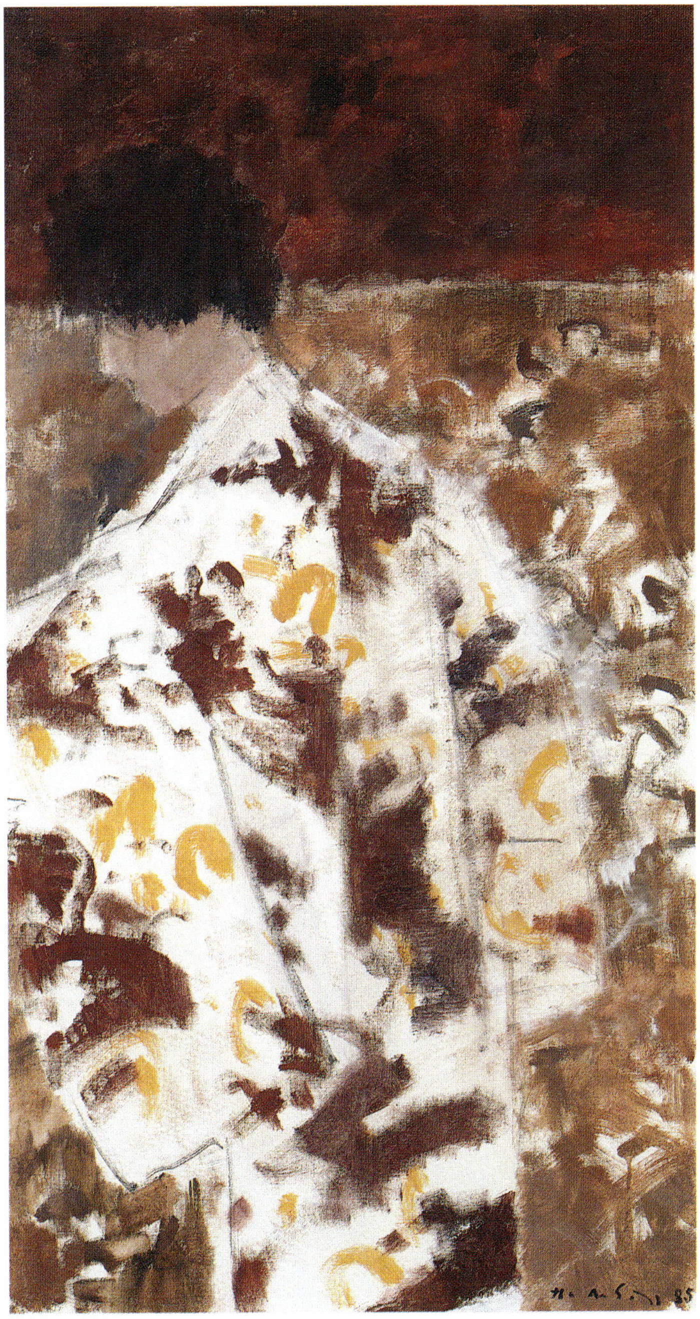

Der Traum/The Dream, 1986, Acryl/acrylic, 195×125 cm

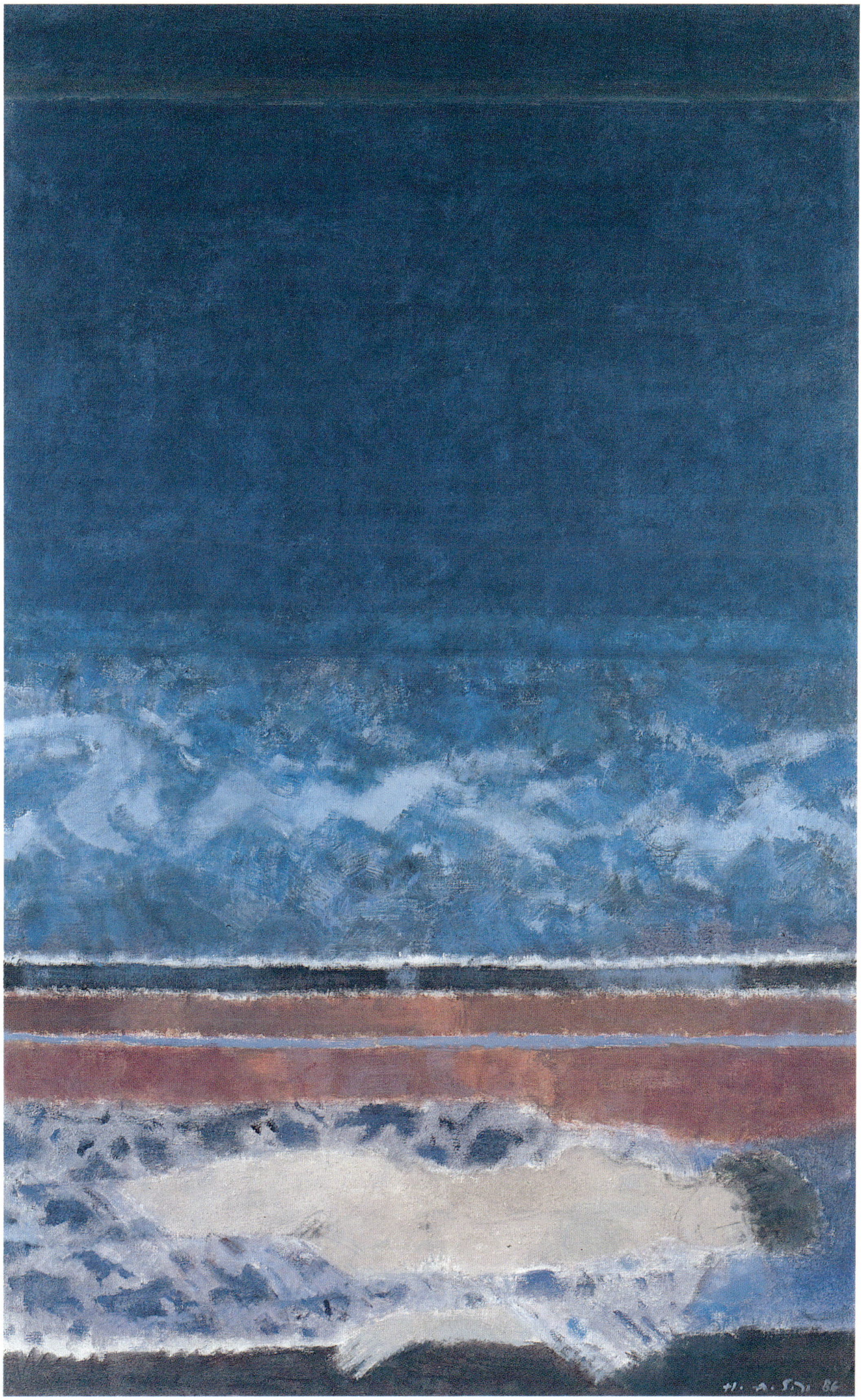

Im Lichte des Mondes/By the Light of the Moon, 1984, Acryl/acrylic, 175×81 cm

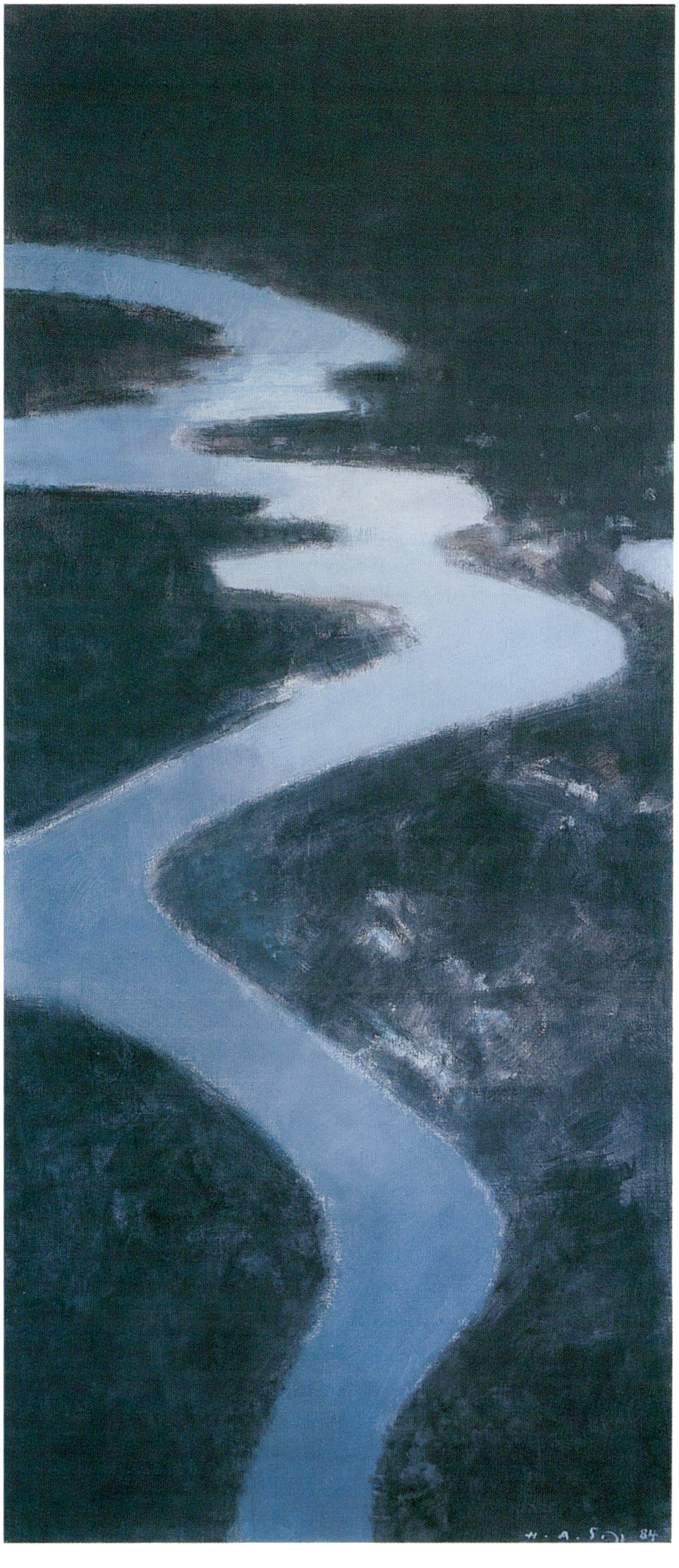

Die Insel des Poeten I/The Poet's Island I, 1989, Acryl/acrylic, 73×92 cm

Herbst/Autumn, 1984, Acryl/acrylic, 92×130 cm

Wintertag/Winter Day, 1976, Acryl/acrylic, 100×162 cm

Der Berg/The Mountain, 1994, Acryl/acrylic, 195×125 cm

Es hellt auf/Brightening Up, 1986, Acryl/acrylic, 162×116 cm

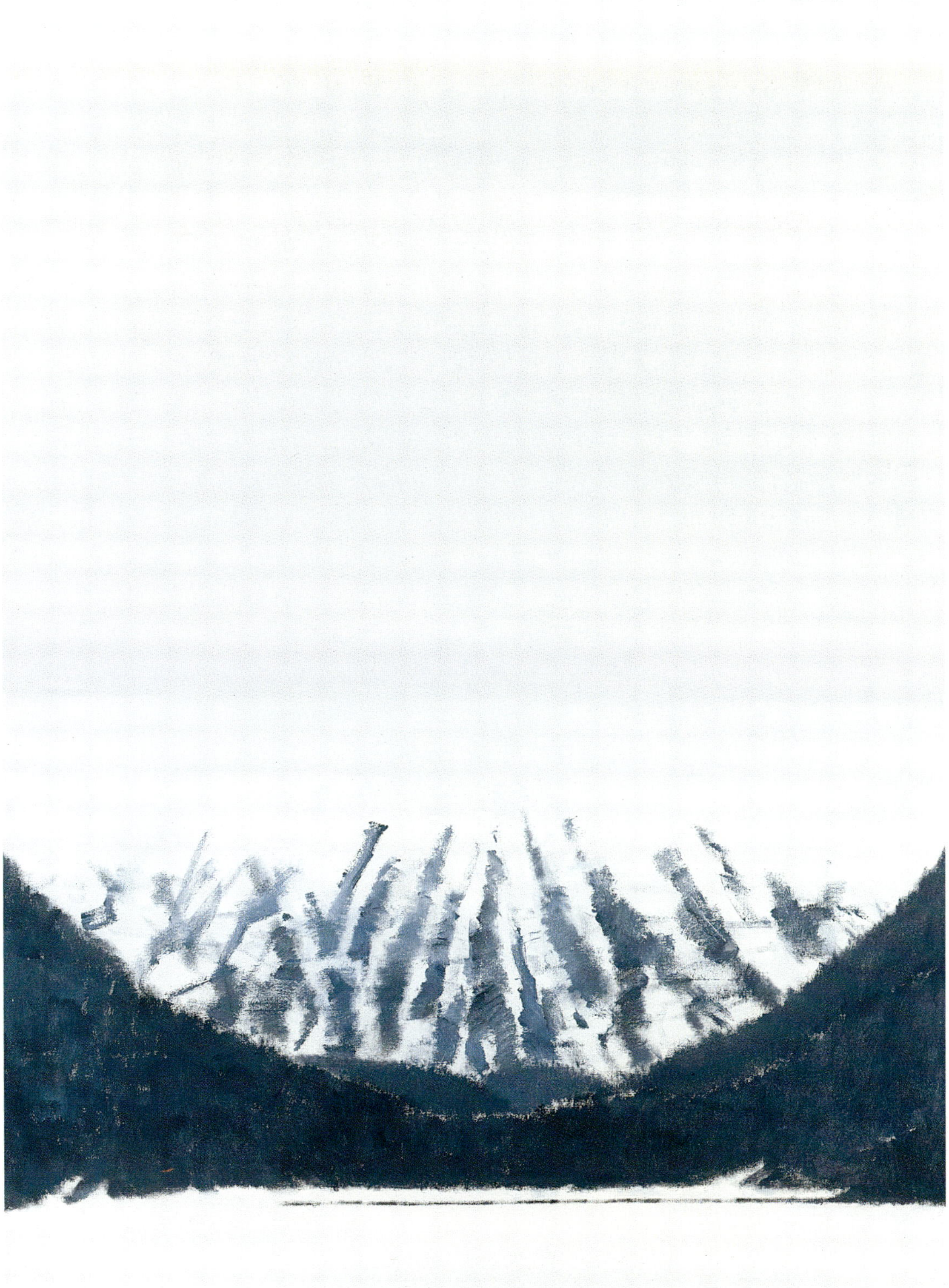

Vollmond, Wolken, Bergtal I/Full Moon, Clouds, Mountain Valley I, 1988, Acryl/acrylic, 175×81 cm

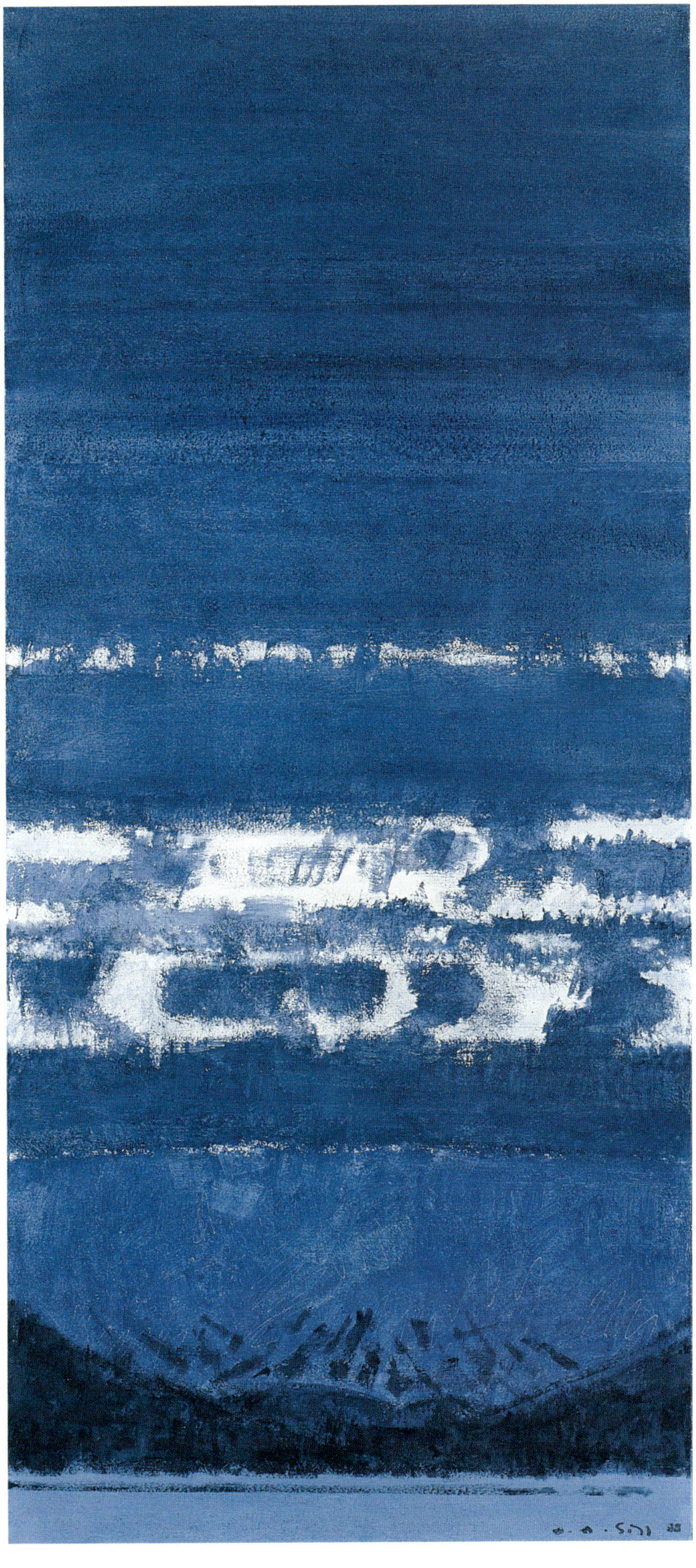

Das erste Licht II/The First Light II, 1988, Acryl/acrylic, 175×81 cm

Letztes helles Licht/The Last Bright Light, 1991, Acryl/acrylic, 195×125 cm

Fluss im Mondlicht/River by Moonlight, 1979/80, Acryl/acrylic, 195×125 cm

Nachklang II/Echo II, 1990/91, Acryl/acrylic, 92×130 cm

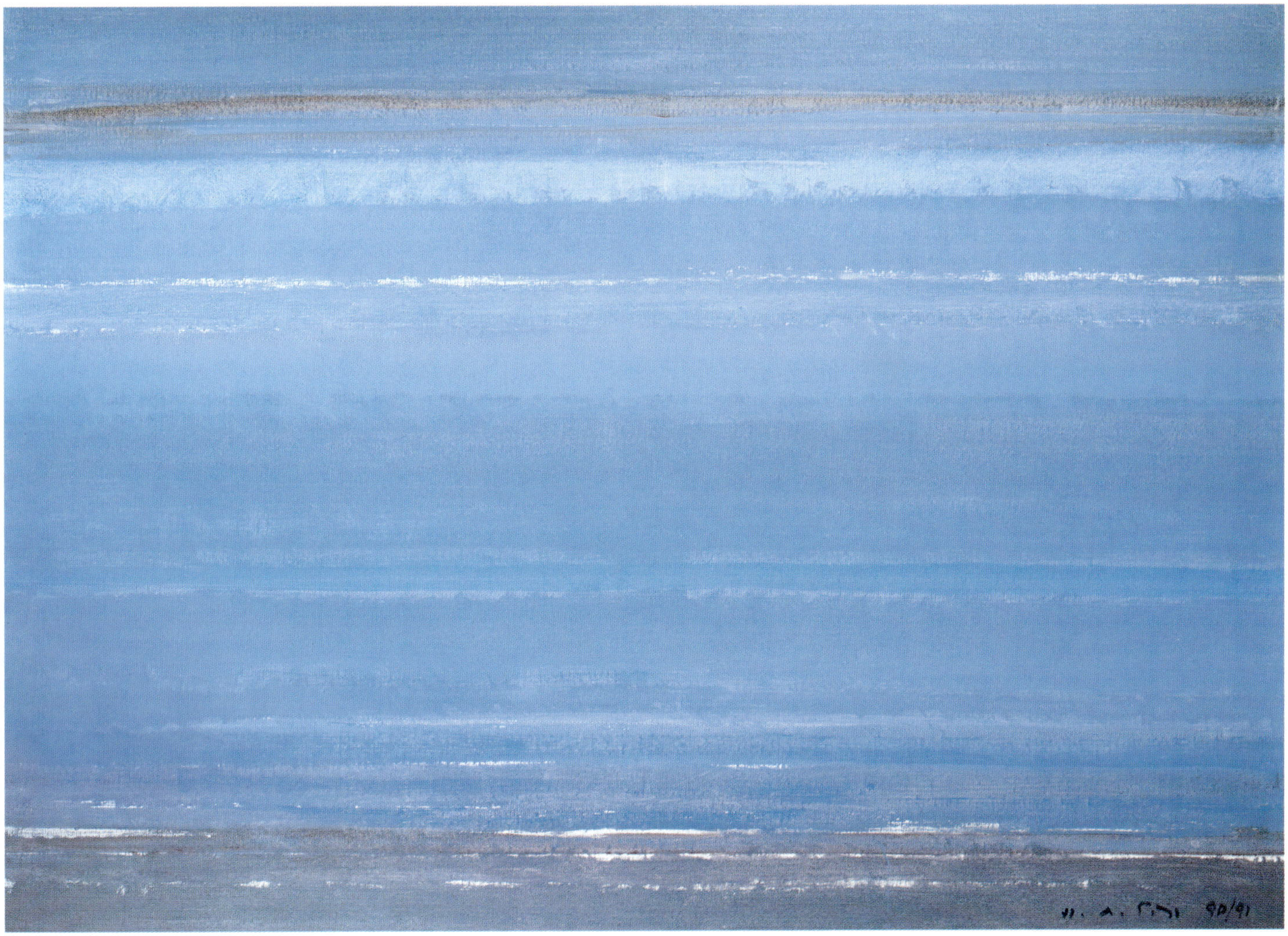

Licht des Himmels I/Light of the Sky I, 1988/92, Acryl/acrylic, 175×81 cm

Wolkenbänder III/Bands of Clouds III, 1988, Acryl/acrylic, 162×125 cm

Nachklang I/Echo I, 1990/91, Acryl/acrylic, 92×130 cm

Der Himmel/The Sky, 1982/83, Acryl/acrylic, 195×116 cm

Nacht über den Flussspuren I/Night over River Paths I, 1986, Acryl/acrylic, 210×125 cm

Abend am Meer III/Evening by the Sea III, 1988, Acryl/acrylic, 195×116 cm

Abend am Meer I/Evening by the Sea I, 1986, Acryl/acrylic, 195×125 cm

Erde – Himmel/Earth – Sky, 1989, Acryl/acrylic, 195×125 cm

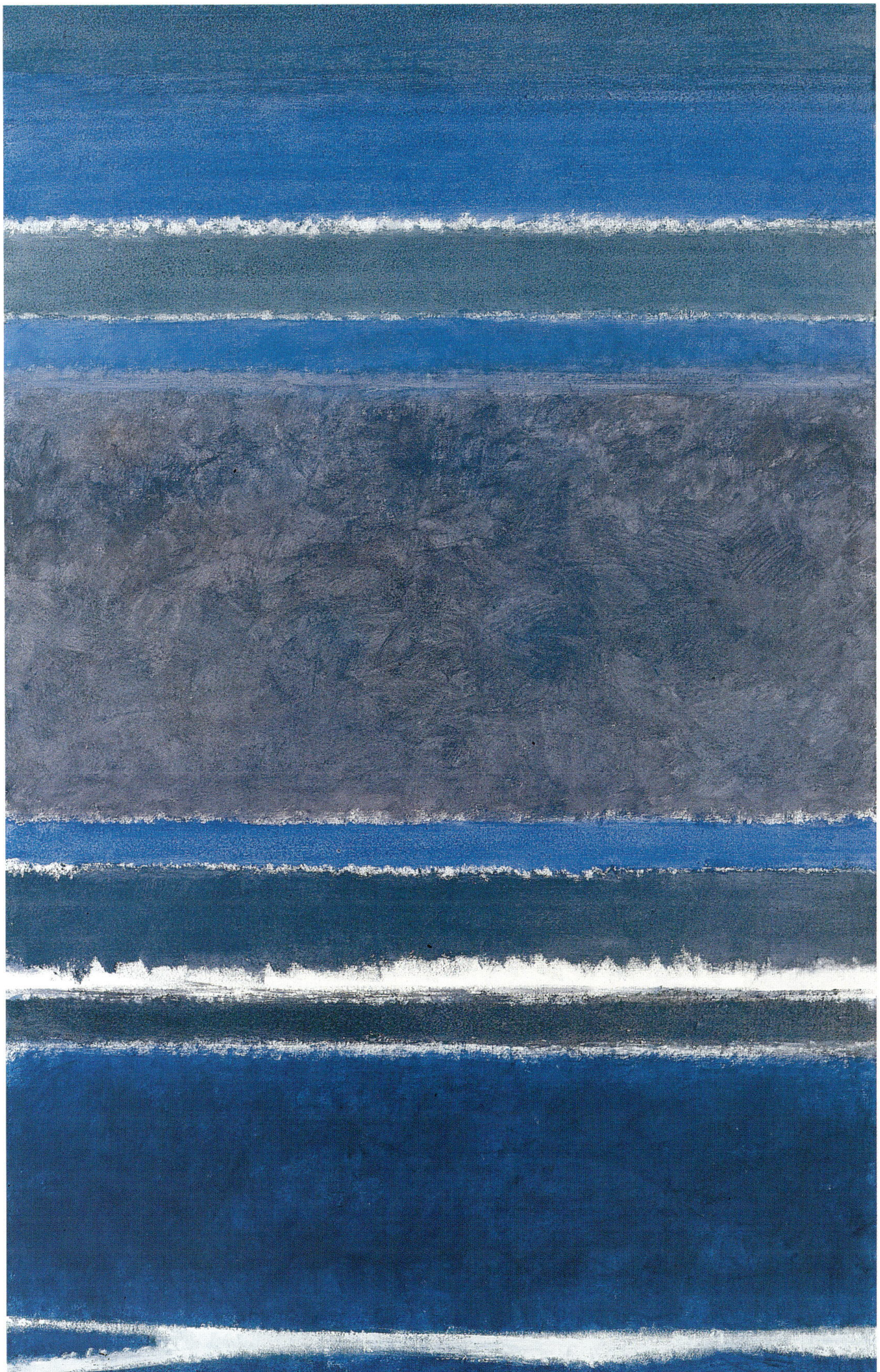

Nacht über den Flussspuren/Night over River Paths II, 1988, Acryl/acrylic, 195×125 cm

Träumende II/Dreamer II, 1986, Acryl/acrylic, 73×130 cm

Helle Flussspuren III/Bright River Paths III, 1986, Acryl/acrylic, 175×81 cm

Inseln im dunkelgrünen Wasser/Islands in Dark-Green Water, 1986, Acryl/acrylic, 195×116 cm

Meer und Himmel II/Sea and Sky II, 1979, Acryl/acrylic, 175×125 cm

Guido Magnaguagno **Ein Hohes Lied**

«Er spürte die Leichtigkeit eines Seidentuchs, das auf ihn herabsank. Und die Hände einer Frau – einer Frau –, die ihn abtrockneten und seine Haut liebkosten, überall: diese Hände und dieses aus nichts gesponnene Gewebe.» (Alessandro Baricco, Seide)

Ich habe mich in ein Bild verliebt. In ein kleines, 41,5 × 22,5 cm. Ein ziemlich hohes Format. Es wurde 1947 gemalt. Verliebt bin ich seit ein paar Jahren, seitdem ich es zum ersten Mal sah.

Das kleine Bild hängt im Atelier von Hermann Alfred Sigg. Aber nicht unten im grossen, geräumig hellen Arbeitsraum, ich entdeckte es oben auf der Galerie, dort, wo die Treppe anlangt. Es bildet das «Entrée» zum intimeren Atelier-Bereich des Ruhens, des Rückzugs, des Schlafens auch, von einer Art Ausguck blickt es auf die Besucher hinunter. Unscheinbar, aber trotzdem unübersehbar.

Das Bild ist nicht irgendeins im Werk von Hermann Alfred Sigg. Es wurde auch nicht «irgendwo» gemalt. Sondern in Paris, 1947.

Es zeigt ein Bett in einem hohen Zimmer, schräg im Raum, gegen die Wand, in eine Zimmerecke gestellt, auf einem blanken Holzbretterboden, darin ein schlafender Mensch. Eine Frau – eine Schlafende? Kein Gesicht, nicht einmal Haare, der Kopf ein brauner Farbfleck. Die räumliche Disposition vervollständigt ein leerer, oder beinahe leerer Holzstuhl, abgelegte Kleider fehlen fast ganz, von der Decke, die im Zimmerwinkel knapp sichtbar wird, baumelt eine Kordel, die Vertikale verstärkend. Nur wenige Accessoires kommen hinzu: ein paar Schuhe auf einer Art Bettvorlage, ein Landschaftsbild, zwei Bettdecken, ein Streifen weisses Leinen.

Was macht den grossen Reiz dieses kleinen Bildes aus? Seine Überhöhe, fast zweimal die Breite? Seine Leere, die vom Schlaf erfüllte Leere, das Schweigen, Innehalten, die Ruhe? Oder ist es das zweite Hauptmotiv des Bildes, die gelb-weiss-grau gewürfelte Tapete, ein einziges zartes Farbfeld, das mehr als die Hälfte der Bildfläche einnimmt? Das Bild verströmt Wohlbefinden, obwohl das Ambiente arm ist. Die Person, die hier schläft, das fühlt der Betrachter unwillkürlich, schläft tief und sicher, behaglich, vielleicht glückselig. Für sie ist gesorgt, gesorgt mit warmen Farben und der Wärme der Dinge, des Holzes, der Tücher, der Wandbespannung.

Das eigentliche Geheimnis des kleinen grossen Bildes ist aber vielleicht, dass die Schlafende (nennen wir sie doch so, so schläft kein Mann, behaupte ich) mit ihrem Schlafraum gleichsam verwoben ist. Die drei Tücher bergen, verbergen sie. Die grosse schwere Decke fällt sanft über die Kante, verbindet Bett mit Vorlage und Stuhl, die Muster des auf den unteren Teil des Bettes geschobenen Überzugs korrespondieren farblich mit der Zimmerdecke (zweimal «Bedeckung») sowie dem Kissen. Alle Muster und Ornamente, die Schrägen und Vertikalen bilden eine harmonische Einheit, und die reinen Farbflächen von Decke und Leintuch und Kissen hüten jenen Kopf, der genau in der Zimmerecke, am Ort des Zusammentreffens der Fluchtlinien liegt. Ein vollkommen komponiertes Bild, in Raum und Fläche, Farbe und Licht, Form und Stimmung. Ein Bild – natürlich – in der Art der frühen Nabis, à la Vuillard und Bonnard. Ein Bild gemalt nach der berühmten Devise von Maurice Denis, wonach ein Bild zuerst einmal eine farbige Fläche sei, bevor es Schlachtross etc. wäre. Ein Interieur gewoben wie ein Teppich, eine Bettdecke, eine Tapete. «Le Lit» – und darin ewiger, schöner Schlaf.

Hermann Alfred Sigg war 23 Jahre jung, als er 1947 nach Paris kam und dieses frühe Meisterstück malte. Hier begegnete er Hilda Jörger, die er zwei Jahre später heiratete. Und hier, bei André Lhote, lernte er, dass er seinen eigenen Weg zu gehen hatte. Er kam aus einer Bauernfamilie, wo ihm niemand den Weg zur Kunst wies, er besuchte von 1944–1947 die Kunstgewerbeschule Zürich, und löste sich mit diesem Pariser Bild von seinen Zürcher Lehrern, um sich an internationalen Grössen zu messen.

Achtunddreissig Jahre später fiel mir in seinem Atelier, unter seinen grossen, kaum gezeigten oder publizierten Produkten der letzten Jahre, ein verwandtes Bild auf. Grösser diesmal, «freier», wenn man so will. «Frau im Kimono» heisst es, 1985, 116×65 cm. Und diesmal dürfen wir sicher sein: Es ist eine Frau dargestellt. Sonst hat sich natürlich viel verändert, abgesehen vom Format. «Freier» sei das Bild, habe ich geschrieben, freier gemalt ist präziser. Die Schule der Nabis ist überwunden, die eigene Handschrift längst gefunden, eingeübt, virtuos beherrscht. Die matte Ölfarbe hat er mit dem geschmeidigeren Acryl vertauscht. Der Pinsel folgt nun der Handbewegung, auch dem Arm, sein Duktus ist unmittelbare Niederschrift, spontan und skizzenhaft. Ein beinahe homogenes Farbfeld belegt nur noch die oberste Bildzone, in welcher sich auch der Haarschopf der Frau befindet.

Wieviel anderes ist sich indessen gleich geblieben! Die warmen Brauntöne scheinen dem «Lit» so entnommen wie das orangene Muster auf dem Kimono an die Farbigkeit von Bettüberwurf, Kissen und Zimmerdecke erinnert. Und was damals die ästhetische Ordnung der Tapete ausmachte, formiert sich jetzt zum beschwingten Flächenornament des Kimonos. Und noch immer ist die Frau ohne Gesicht, auch wenn ihr Profil auftaucht, und nach wie vor scheint die Figur vollkommen in den Raum verwoben. Oder noch mehr: Figur und Raum bilden eine Fläche.

Das frühe Versprechen hat sich eingelöst, der Weg des Malers sich vollendet.

Nun steht das Bild «Frau im Kimono» im späten Schaffen des Künstlers nicht allein. Ein Jahr später entstanden eine zweite und dritte Fassung in Blau, wobei vom Bild «Der Kimono III» (175×81 cm) ein ähnlich grosser Zauber ausgeht. Obwohl sich Siggs malerische Errungenschaften auch auf allen gleichzeitig entstandenen Landschaften, wie allen Fluss- und Himmelbildern oder denen aus dem Engadin, mühelos einsehen lassen, schliesst sich mit «Der Traum» und «Die Träumende» aus demselben Jahr 1986 eine Werkgruppe zusammen, in der die Frauenfigur alles bündelt, was seit 1947 malerisch passiert ist. Aber mehr als nur dekorative Form und malerische Oberfläche, wie sie Malern wie Hermann Alfred Sigg manchmal auch zum Verhängnis werden können, indem die malerische Kultiviertheit ihren Gegenstand gleichsam erstickt oder «zumalt», ihre Botschaft zum Verschwinden bringt, lebt in diesen träumenden Frauen jenes Glück von Ruhe und Stille des Pariser Zimmers als geistig-meditative Kraft weiter. Form wird Stille, Stille Form. Eine Sehnsucht nach

Die hellen Inseln I/The Bright Islands I, 1993, Acryl/acrylic, 116×232 cm

Schönheit lebt in diesen Bildern, die nach mehr verlangt hat als bloss ausgewogenen Bildordnungen.

Ich weiss nicht, was etwas später der eigentliche Anlass zur China-Reise 1993 war. Aber ich könnte mir gut vorstellen, dass den Künstler nach 1986 eine neue Sehnsucht überfallen und beflügelt hat. Denn was er jetzt malt, der magistrale Werkzyklus «Im Reich der Mitte» (1994–1998), ist auf eine neue Art beseelt.

Wiewohl er jetzt die Figur wieder verliess und sich primär der Zeichensprache der chinesischen Tempel-Architektur zuwandte (über den «Umweg» von schwarzen Skulpturen, die ihm wohl die Tektonik neuer Bildräume öffneten), sind die Wände und Türen, die Spuren von Schriftzeichen und Flussmäandern, sind die freien Ornamente und Muster, die Allusionen an Lackfarben in einer Art poetischem Konzept eingebunden. Einer Annäherung an die Geheimnisse der fremden Schönheit des Fernen Ostens.

Wie Hervé Joncour in der bezaubernden Erzählung «Seide» von Alessandro Baricco, geht Sigg auf eine Reise ins Unbekannte, ausgestattet mit viel Wissen, viel Erfahrung auf seinem Gebiet, das die Malerei ist. Wie der Seidenraupen-Händler aus Lavilledien verliebt er sich – nicht in eine «japanische Prinzessin», aber vielleicht über sie, die «Frau im Kimono», in die Textur der chinesischen Kultur. Er spürt eine Verwandtschaft, die Ost-West-Osmose fliesst in gelöster Selbsttätigkeit, die Übersetzung des Fremden in die eigene Bildsprache vollzieht sich in unangestrengter Leichtigkeit. Das «alte» Gefühl des Wohlbefindens stellt sich wieder ein.

Sind wir damit einem Geheimnis im Kunstschaffen von Hermann Alfred Sigg auf der Spur? Einer so ganz eigenen Subtilität und Zartheit, wie er sie als Person auch zeigt, wenn er im Gespräch alles Direkte vermeidet, nichts festlegen, alles offen halten will? Sich ständig zurücknimmt hinter sein Werk. Durchlässig, könnte man ihn und seine Malerei vielmehr nennen, vom dünnen Farbauftrag bis zu den transparenten Nähten, die seine chinesischen Mauern teilen. Dass dabei die Erfahrungen mitwirkten, welche er mit den Glasfenstern für die Kirchen von Freiburg 1978 (als Buch im Benteli Verlag 1994 erschienen) und Davos Laret (1992–1993) machte, bedarf keiner weiterer Erläuterungen.

Transparenz – aber nicht als physikalische Erscheinung, sondern als spirituelle Qualität. Die Sehnsuchtsenergien strömen durch die Membran der Bildhaut.

Vom Hohelied Salomons, das Sigg 1967/68 als bibliophiles Buch gestaltete, zur indischen «Tempelwand» von 1973/74, einem 210 × 310 cm weiten Wandbild, wo sich Liebesgöttinnen ewig mit der Tempel-Architektur vermählen, ja vom Pariser «Lit» 1947 zur «Frau im Kimono» von 1985 und zum «Reich der Mitte, IX (1995/96), als Beispiel, wirkt das innere Kontinuum eines Künstlers, der nicht Bauer werden konnte, weil er einer anderen Ader zu folgen hatte. Ihr verdanken wir eine jener selten gewordenen Bildwelten, deren Ausstrahlung das Versprechen von erotisierter Schönheit verströmt.

Ein Hohes Lied der Malerei.

Guido Magnaguagno **Song of Songs**

"He felt the lightness of a silk foulard floating down towards him. And the hands of a woman – of a woman – drying him and caressing his skin, everywhere: those hands and the tissue woven from nothingness." (Alessandro Baricco, Silk, 1996)

I have fallen in love with a painting. In a small painting, 41.5 by 22.5 cm. A rather high format. Painted in 1947. I've been in love for a couple of years now, ever since I first saw it.

The little painting is hanging in Hermann Alfred Sigg's studio. But not down in the large, spacious, bright work-room; I discovered it up in the gallery, at the top of the stairs. It constitutes the 'entrée' to the more intimate part of the studio intended for resting, retiring to or sleeping; it gazes down at the visitor from a kind of look-out. Inconspicuous, but quite clear.

The painting is not just another of Hermann Alfred Sigg's works. Neither was it painted 'anywhere'. But in Paris, in 1947.

It portrays a bed in a tall room, slanting, pushed against the wall, in a corner of the room, on a bare wooden floor, containing someone asleep. A woman – a woman asleep? No face, not even any hair, the head is just a patch of brown. The spatial arrangement is completed by a vacant, an almost vacant wooden chair; there are hardly any shed clothes; a tassel dangling from the ceiling, just visible in a corner of the room, reinforces the vertical plane. Only a few extras complete the scene: some shoes on a kind of bedside rug, a landscape painting, two blankets, a strip of white linen.

What makes this little painting so attractive? Its extremely high format, almost twice the width? Its emptiness, its emptiness full of slumber, the silence, the repose, the tranquillity? Or the second main motif in the painting, the yellow-white-and-grey check wallpaper, a unique, gentle area of colour occupying over half of the picture? The painting emanates a feeling of well-being, despite the modesty of its ambience. The person sleeping here, the observer instinctively feels, lies in the sheltered depths of slumber, snugly tucked up, perhaps even in a state of bliss. He or she has been cared for, with warm colours and the warmth of the objects there, the wood, the drapes, the surface of the wall.

Perhaps the real secret of the small, but great painting lies in the fact that the woman (no man sleeps in this fashion, I would say) sleeping in the bed is interwoven, as it were, with the bedroom itself. The three drapes veil, conceal her. The large heavy blanket droops gently over the edge, joining the bed with the rug and the chair; the pattern of the bedcover pushed down to the lower end of the bed matches the colour of the ceiling, in both cases a 'cover', and the pillows. All the patterns and ornaments, the horizontal and vertical planes form a harmonious unity; the clear areas of colour represented by the ceiling, the linen drapery and the pillows protect the head, lying exactly in the corner of the room, the point where the lines intersect.

A perfectly composed painting, from the point of view of both space and surface, colour and light, form and atmosphere. A painting – of course – following in the tracks of the early Nabis, à la Vuillard and Bonnard. A picture painted along the lines of Maurice Denis' famous motto: a painting is first of all a coloured area before it becomes a war-horse or whatever. An interior woven like a carpet, a bed-cover, wallpaper. 'Le Lit' – affording eternal, beautiful slumber.

Hermann Alfred Sigg was merely 23 when he arrived in Paris in 1947 and painted this early masterpiece. It was here that he met Hilda Jörger, whom he was to marry two years later. Here, at the Académie André Lhote, he also learnt that he had to go his own way. He had grown up in a farmers' family, where no-one pointed out the way to art to him; he left to attend the Zurich College of Commercial Art from 1944 to 1947, and with this Paris painting he severed the ties with his Zurich teachers to make his mark on the international art scene.

Thirty-eight years later I was struck by an allied painting in his studio, amidst his large, hardly ever displayed or published works of recent years. Larger, 'more autonomous', as it were. Its name is 'Frau im Kimono' (Woman in a Kimono), dated 1985, 116 by 65 cm in size. This time there is no doubt that the subject portrayed is a woman. Of course, much had changed in the meantime, with the exception of the format. I said the painting was 'more autonomous'; 'more autonomously painted' would be more accurate. He has left the school of the Nabis behind him, he has discovered his own style and perfected it to the point of absolute virtuosity. The matt oil colour has been exchanged for smoother acrylic. The brush now follows the movement of the hand and the arm; the passage it follows brings it directly onto the canvas, spontaneously and sketchily. A virtually homogeneous field of colour occupies only the uppermost area of the painting, in which the woman's mane of hair is set.

So many other features have remained the same, however! Just as the warm brown tones seem to have been borrowed from 'Le Lit', the orange pattern on the kimono reminds us of the colourfulness of the bed-cover, the pillows and the ceiling. And the aesthetic composition of the wallpaper back then now forges the lively ornamental pattern on the kimono. Still the woman has no face despite the emergence of her profile; still the figure seems completely interwoven with the room. It goes even further: the figure and the room go to make up one area.

The early promise has come to fruition; the master's journey has been accomplished.

The painting 'Woman in a Kimono' does not stand alone in the artist's later oeuvre. One year later he painted a second and a third version in blue, the painting 'Der Kimono III' (The Kimono III), 175 by 81 cm, conjuring up an equally magic spell. Although Sigg's artistic achievements are easily discernible in all the landscapes produced during this period, for example all the river and sky paintings and those from the Engadin area of Switzerland, 'Der Traum' (The Dream) and 'Der Träumer' (The Dreamer) painted in 1986, the same year, comprise a group of works in which the woman's figure synthesises all the

Stiller Abend über hellem Fluss I/Quiet Evening over a Bright River I, 1986, Acryl/acrylic, 130×73 cm painter's developments since 1947. What is depicted here stretches way beyond decorative form and artistic shallowness, which may sometimes be fatal for artists such as Hermann Alfred Sigg when artistic sophistication stifles or 'paints over' the subject, despatching their message into oblivion. In these dreaming women the joy of the tranquillity and serenity of the room in Paris lives on as a spiritual-meditative force. Form becomes tranquillity, tranquillity form.

A yearning for beauty lives in these paintings, which has clearly asserted higher demands than merely well-balanced painting compositions.

I am not aware of what actually led to the journey to China in 1993. But I can well imagine that the artist was overwhelmed and uplifted by fresh aspirations after 1986. For what he paints now, the majestic cycle 'Im Reich der Mitte' (In the Middle Realm) (1994–98) features a new form of inspiration.

Although he has now left the figure in order to devote himself primarily to the symbolic language of the Chinese temple architecture – via the 'detour' of black sculptures, which paved the way to the tectonics of new painting dimensions –, the walls and doors, the traces of writing characters and river meanders, the autonomous ornaments and patterns, the allusions to varnish paints are integrated into a kind of poetic concept. A signpost pointing towards the secrets of the exotic beauty of the Far East.

Like Hervé Joncour in the charming racconto 'Silk' by Alessandro Baricco, Sigg embarks on a journey to the unknown, equipped with a wealth of knowledge and experience in his field of painting. Like the silk-worm merchant from Lavilledia he falls in love – not with a 'Japanese Princess', but perhaps 'about' her, the 'Woman in a Kimono', namely the quality of Chinese culture. He senses an affinity; the East-West osmosis flows spontaneously; the foreign culture is translated into his own pictorial language with considerable ease. That 'old' feeling of well-being is restored.

Have we unearthed the clue to the secret of Hermann Alfred Sigg's artistic creativity? His very special subtlety and tenderness, which he himself shows when avoiding all directness in discussion, all precision, keeping everything open, when he constantly withdraws to behind his oeuvre? He and his painting could be described as transparent, referring to his thin application of colour and the limpid seams dividing his Chinese walls. That this was enriched by the experience he gathered in his creating the stained-glass windows project for the churches in Fribourg in 1978 (reproduced as a book by Benteli Verlag in 1994) and Davos-Laret (1992–1993) goes without saying.

Transparency – but not as a physical phenomenon but as a spiritual quality. The energies triggered by his yearning stream through the membrane of the painting surface.

The inner continuity of an artist who could not become a farmer because he was destined to follow another path is apparent throughout his oeuvre, ranging from The Song of Solomon, which Sigg designed as a bibliophilic edition, to the Indian 'Tempelwand' (Temple Wall), 1973–74, a 210 by 310 cm wide mural featuring love-goddesses who unite

Im Land der Flüsse II/In the Land of the Rivers II, 1992, Acryl/acrylic, 73×162 cm with the temple architecture for all eternity, and the Paris painting 'Le Lit' (1947), the 'Woman in a Kimono' (1985) and the 'Im Reich der Mitte XI' (Middle Realm) (1995–96). We owe to it one of those now rare pictorial worlds whose aura issues the promise of erotic beauty.

Painting's Song of Songs.

Flusslauf – Erde – Himmel/River Course – Earth – Sky, 1988/89, Acryl/acrylic, 210×125 cm

Aufleuchtende Flussspuren/Gleaming River Paths, 1988, Acryl/acrylic, 175×125 cm

Helle Wasserläufe/Bright Watercourses, 1986, Acryl/acrylic, 175×81 cm

Die weissen Flussformen/White River Forms, 1989, Acryl/acrylic, 146×81 cm

Beschwingter Flusslauf II/Lively River Course II, 1989/90, Acryl/acrylic, 200×400 cm

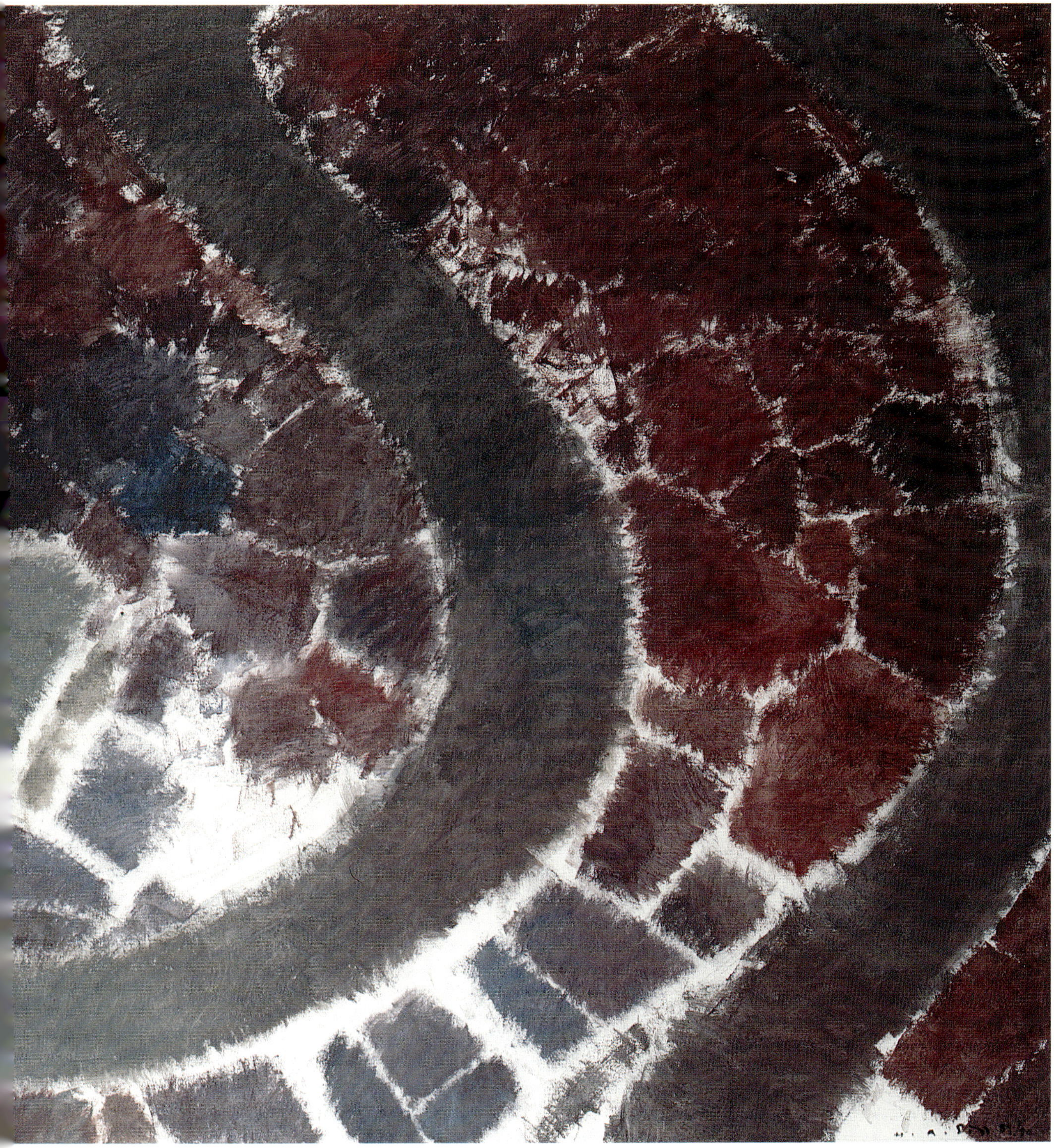

Im Land der Flüsse IV/In the Land of the Rivers IV, 1993, Acryl/acrylic, 81×175 cm

Skulptur II/Sculpture II, 1989, Bronze/bronze, 85,5×24×12 cm

Skulptur III/Sculpture III, 1989, Bronze/bronze, 124×30×17,5 cm

Nacht-Traum/Night-Dream, 1994, Acryl/acrylic, 116×232 cm

Zwischen Tag und Traum III/Between Day and Dream III, 1991, Acryl/acrylic, 116×310 cm

Nacht-Blau/Night-Blue, 1995, Acryl/acrylic, 195×116 cm

Karl Ruhrberg Malerische Meditationen

Zu den Arbeiten von Hermann Alfred Sigg

«Wie ich sehe» – diese Formulierung des Wiener Literaten Peter Altenberg könnte das Leitmotiv für die Arbeiten des Schweizer Malers Hermann Alfred Sigg sein. Was seine Bilder und Skulpturen zum optischen Erlebnis macht, ist die Verwandlung konkreter Realität. Auf sein Werk liesse sich Werner Haftmanns Terminus «Weltinnenbilder» anwenden. Ganz gleich, ob Landschaften, Akte, Portraits oder Tierherden Thema der Darstellung sind: Stets spielt der biographische Hintergrund des weltläufigen Bauernsohn als Quelle der Inspiration eine mitbestimmende Rolle. Dem entspricht die Schwebelage zwischen Gegenständlichkeit und Abstraktion, Meditation und Anschauung. Grundstimmung der Bilder ist eine klangvolle, malerisch instrumentierte Ruhe, künstlerisches Merkmal die hohe Qualität der «peinture», auch im grossen Format bis hin zu den Wandbildern in öffentlichen Räumen.

Sigg malt nicht, wie Cézanne es tat, «vor dem Motiv»; seine Bilder sind vielmehr Antworten auf Gesehenes und Erlebtes; die Farbfelder und Mäander sind bildnerische Zeichen für Flüsse, Felder und – seltener – für Ansiedlungen unter weiten Horizonten und für die Struktur einer teils unberührten, teils bereits vom Menschen kultivierten, aber noch nicht domestizierten, vom Zivilisationsmüll verschütteten, verkrebsten südostasiatischen Natur. Eduard Hüttinger hat in diesem Zusammenhang gesagt, die Bilder von Sigg seien das Medium zur «Erhellung des Standorts des Menschen in einer masslos erweiterten Welt.»

Natürlich sind Siggs malerische Mittel ganz andere als die des bewunderten grossen Franzosen Edouard Monet: nicht Farbpunkt und Farbkomma, sondern Farbfleck und Farbfeld. Doch es erscheint kaum verwunderlich, wenn man erfährt, dass auch Pierre Bonnard, der Meister der Farbe und des in sie eingeschlossenen und zugleich aus ihr herausleuchtenden Lichts, der Maler, der den Impressionismus über sich selbst hinausführte, zu den inspirierenden Anregern des Schweizers gehört.

Weite der Empfindung und der Anschauung kennzeichnet bereits die frei variierten Landschaften, die unter dem Eindruck Apuliens und des Engadin entstanden. Aber noch wichtiger waren Siggs Flugerlebnisse vom Cockpit aus, in dem er neben den Piloten sitzen durfte, als er sich Flugtickets statt fälliger Honorare für künstlerische Arbeiten erbeten hatte. Diese «Blickpunkte» haben seinen Horizont erweitert.

Auslösender Impuls für die lange Reihe der malerisch sensiblen meditativen Bilder, die seit dem Ende der sechziger Jahre entstanden sind, war die Begegnung mit Südostasien, fern von Europa. Sigg hat diese Weltgegend immer wieder vom Flugzeug aus gesehen. Nicht nur in seinem Fall hat diese Optik in den ersten Nachkriegsjahren, als das Fliegen noch nicht selbstverständlich war und das Bordkino noch nicht den Blick ins Freie ersetzte, der Malerei durch die «Vogelschau» neue Blickpunkte erschlossen. Die jahrhundertealte Tradition der «Reisebilder» gewann dadurch eine vorher nicht gekannte Dimension hinzu.

Siggs meditativ-philosophische Lebenshaltung hält sich fern von der Hektik des Alltags in Amerika und Europa. Doch so tief ihn Ostasien, – seine Landschaften, seine Kunst und die Menschen – beeindruckt haben, so unverkennbar ist er auch im fernen und mittleren Osten Europäer geblieben. Seine Bilder zeigen in ihrer klangvoll instrumentierten Ruhe, in der gelassenen Harmonie statischer Figurationen, in ihrer unverkrampften Schwebelage zwischen Abstraktion und Gegenständlichkeit, in der Sensibilität der kalligraphischen Elemente eine starke Affinität zu asiatischem Denken und Empfinden. Doch Sigg gerät nicht in die Versuchung zur totalen Anverwandlung fremden Wesens durch Identifikation, eine Versuchung, der manche andere Künstler erlegen sind. Ihr Scheitern war die unvermeidliche Folge. Siggs Bilder hingegen sind Widerhall des tiefen und formenden Eindrucks, den Asien auf einen Europäer macht. Es sind Bilder der Verwandlung erlebter Realität, nicht der Nachempfindung, keine Abbilder, sondern Zeugnisse innerer Wahlverwandtschaft.

Die bildnerischen Zeichen des Künstlers sind mäandrisch und ornamental, gefächert für das beherrschende Leitmotiv Fluss, mosaikartig geordnet für die Struktur der Erde, horizontal geschichtet für Himmel und Meer. Sie vermitteln zwischen den teils konzentrierten und dichten, teils locker miteinander verbundenen Form- und Farbfeldern, zwischen teils weiten, ortlosen Flächen. Auf diese Weise geben sie dem frei gestalteten Bild seinen kompositorischen Halt. Die parallelen Reihungen, die differenzierte Monochromie der farbigen Flächen über tiefliegenden Horizonten weisen über den Bildrand hinaus. Sie sind «unbegrenzt, aber endlich». Wenn man den Vergleich nicht überanstrengt, könnte man sich mitunter an Bildordnungen von Paul Klee oder Mark Rothko erinnert fühlen, ohne dass jedoch die suggestive Räumlichkeit des Amerikaners russisch-jüdischer Herkunft angestrebt würde. Siggs Arbeiten sind demgegenüber flächig, nicht räumlich konzipiert und realisiert.

Im Laufe der Jahre setzt der Maler seine malerischen Mittel bei fortschreitender Sensibilisierung immer sparsamer ein. Die Zwischentöne, die leisen Klänge, die Nuancen bestimmen das Bild. Die Farbe aber bleibt immer lebendig, «couleur vivante». Sigg bewältigt mit diesen zurückhaltenden, quasi lyrischen Mitteln ohne vordergründig dramatische Gesten auch das grosse Format. Dabei kommt er ohne Anleihen aus. Er bewegt sich ausserhalb der gängigen Trends, und verzichtet auf jegliche Anpassung an den Zeitgeist, den der grosse Kunsthistoriker Ernst H. Gombrich einmal als den «Geschäftsführer des Weltgeists» bezeichnet hat. Insofern ist sein Werk durchaus «unzeitgemäss».

Nachdenklichkeit und eine – mitunter melancholisch durchsetzte – Heiterkeit charakterisieren die Grundstimmung, die Atmosphäre des Werks. In den besten Fällen ist eine insistierende Dichte das Kennzeichen. Siggs Arbeiten sind aber auch auf eine unverkrampfte, entspannende Weise dekorativ im positiven Sinne.

In einer Komödie, die diesen Namen verdient, kann man lächeln, ohne sich anschliessend genieren zu müssen. Vor Hermann Alfred Siggs Bildern darf man sich an der Schönheit der Farben und am Melos der lebendigen, oft dem Antropomorphen sich nähernden

Formen erfreuen, ohne das Gefühl zu haben, vor der problembeladenen Wirklichkeit der eigenen Zeit in ein ästhetisches Nirwana zu fliehen. Die ruhige Freude, die man bei ihrem Anblick empfindet, ist künstlerisch legitimiert durch die sinnlich-geistige Substanz, die ihnen zugrundeliegt.

Das gilt auch für die Skulpturen des Künstlers, die sein Schweizer Landsmann René Wehrli ebenfalls als «Bilder» verstanden hat: vertikale, abstrakte Figurationen, die in ihren symmetrischen Ordnungen um eine imaginäre Mitte herum mit den gemalten Arbeiten korrespondieren, ohne ihre Selbständigkeit einzubüssen.

Ohne Titel I/No title I, 1989, Acryl/acrylic, 116×210 cm

Karl Ruhrberg   **Artistic Meditations**

Hermann Alfred Sigg's Works

"How I see " – this expression coined by the Viennese writer Peter Altenberg could be the leitmotiv for the works by the Swiss painter Hermann Alfred Sigg. What makes his paintings and sculptures an optical experience is the transformation of concrete reality. Werner Haftmann's term 'world interior paintings' provides an apt description for his oeuvre. Regardless whether landscapes, nudes, portraits or herds of animals are the theme, the biographical background of the worldly-wise farmer's son always plays a decisive role as his source of inspiration. This is reflected in the suspended state between objective realism and abstraction, meditation and intuition. The fundamental mood of his paintings is sonorous, picturesquely composed serenity, their artistic hallmark being the high quality of the 'peinture', in both large-format works and murals in public halls.

Sigg does not paint like Cézanne before him, 'in front of the motif'; his paintings are the responses to what he has seen and experienced; the fields of colour and meanders are the sculptural symbols for rivers, fields and – more rarely – for settlements lying beneath wide horizons, for the structure of Southeast Asian nature partly unspoilt, partly cultivated by man but not yet fully subjugated to his domestic needs, not diseased and buried under the waste of modern civilisation. In this connection, the well known Swiss art historian Eduard Hüttinger said that Sigg's paintings were the medium for "elucidating man's location in an immeasurably extended world".

Of course, Sigg's painting means and approaches differ radically from those of the great, much admired Frenchman Edouard Monet: not dots and strokes of colour, but patches and fields of colour. But this is hardly surprising when one hears that Pierre Bonnard, the master of colour and of the light that colour includes and emanates, the painter that stretched Impressionism beyond its own borders, is one of the Swiss painter's inspirators.

The vastness of sensation and perception characterises the unrestrictedly varied landscapes arising from the artist's impressions of Apulia and Engadin. But even more important were Sigg's experiences from a plane cockpit, where he was permitted to sit next to the pilot, having requested air tickets instead of the normal commission for his works of art. These 'perspectives' broadened his horizons.

The impulse that triggered the long series of artistically sensitive, meditative paintings after the late sixties was Sigg's encounter with Southeast Asia, far away from Europe. He saw this part of the world time and again from a plane. In the immediate post-war period when travelling by plane was not an everyday occurrence and the on-board cinema had not yet taken over from the view across vast expanses of sky, his was not the only case of where the optical effect resulting from this 'bird's-eye view' opened up new perspectives for painting. The century-old tradition of 'travel scenes' thus took on a completely new dimension.

Sigg's meditative-philosophical life remains aloof from the hustle-and-bustle of everyday life in America and Europe. Notwithstanding the deep impressions East Asia – its landscapes, art and people – had on him, he remained unmistakably a European in the Far and Middle East. His paintings, in their sonorous tranquillity, in their serene harmony of static figurations, in the relaxed suspension between abstraction and realism, in the sensitivity of the calligraphic elements, display a strong affinity to Asiatic thinking and feeling.

But Sigg does not succumb to the total assimilation of a foreign entity by way of identificaition, a temptation many an artist has yielded to. Failure in their case was inevitable. Sigg's paintings, on the other hand, reflect the deep and formative impression Asia has on a European. They are paintings of the transformation of experienced reality, not the re-creation, not the reproduction but testimonies of an inner affinity.

The artist's sculptural symbols are ornamental, assuming various forms: meanders fanning out for the predominant leitmotiv, the river; mosaics for the structure of the earth; horizontal layers for the sky and the sea. They mediate between the partly concentrated and dense, partly loosely connected form and colour fields, between partly wide, uninhabited expanses; they impart to the freely structured painting its composition stability. The parallel rows, the variegated monochrome of the coloured areas above low-lying horizons point to beyond the edge of the painting. They are "boundless, but finite". Without stretching the analogy too far, one could feel they are reminiscent of the painting structures of Paul Klee or Mark Rothko, not that the suggestive spatiality of the Russian-Jewish American was at all aspired to. By comparison, Sigg's works are flat, not spatially conceived and executed.

In the course of time the painter applied the artistic means at his disposal increasingly economically the more his sensitivity grew. The intermediate tones, the gentle sounds, the nuances determine the painting. The colour, however, always remains vivid, a 'couleur vivante'. Sigg also applies these reserved, virtually lyrical means, without any superficial dramatic gestures, to conquer the large format. He accomplishes this without borrowing from other sources. He moves outside current trends, eschewing any inclination to adapt the the *zeitgeist*, once described by the great art historian Ernst H. Gombrich as the "general manager of the *weltgeist*". In this respect, his oeuvre is quite 'out-of-date'. Contemplation and mirth, occasionally imbued with melancholy, characterise the basic mood, the atmosphere of his oeuvre. In the most favourable cases the main feature is their compelling intensity. On the other hand, in an informal, relaxing way Sigg's works are also decorative in the positive sense of the term. Only occasionally does the "enchanting sweetness" prevail that Hüttinger once referred to en passant.

In a comedy worthy of the name one can laugh without any subsequent embarrassment. Looking at Hermann Alfred Sigg's paintings, one can rejoice in the beauty of their colours and the melos of their lively, often anthropomorphic forms, without sensing that one is fleeing from the many problems of contemporary reality to some aesthetic

Nirvana. The serene pleasure one experiences when contemplating these paintings is artistically legitimated by the sensuous-spiritual substance they are founded on.

The same applies to the artist's sculptures, which his Swiss fellow countryman René Wehrli also understood to be 'paintings': vertical, abstract figurations corresponding to the painted works in their symmetrical structures around an imaginary centre, without forfeiting their autonomy.

Triptychon (links)/Triptych (left), 1994,
Acryl/acrylic, 33×116 cm, 232×116 cm

Triptychon (Mitte)/Triptych (middle), 1994,
Acryl/acrylic, 33×116 cm, 232×116 cm

Triptychon (rechts)/Triptych (right), 1994,
Acryl/acrylic, 33×116 cm, 232×116 cm

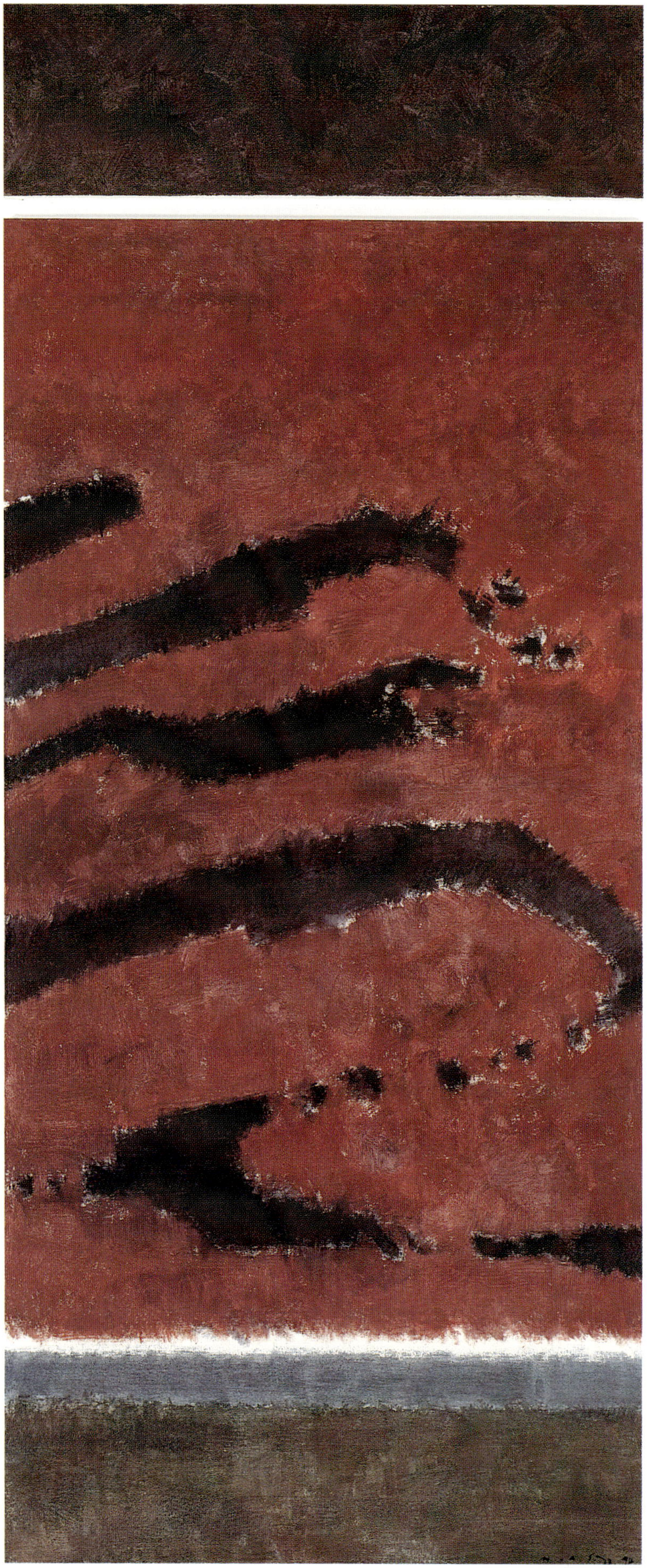

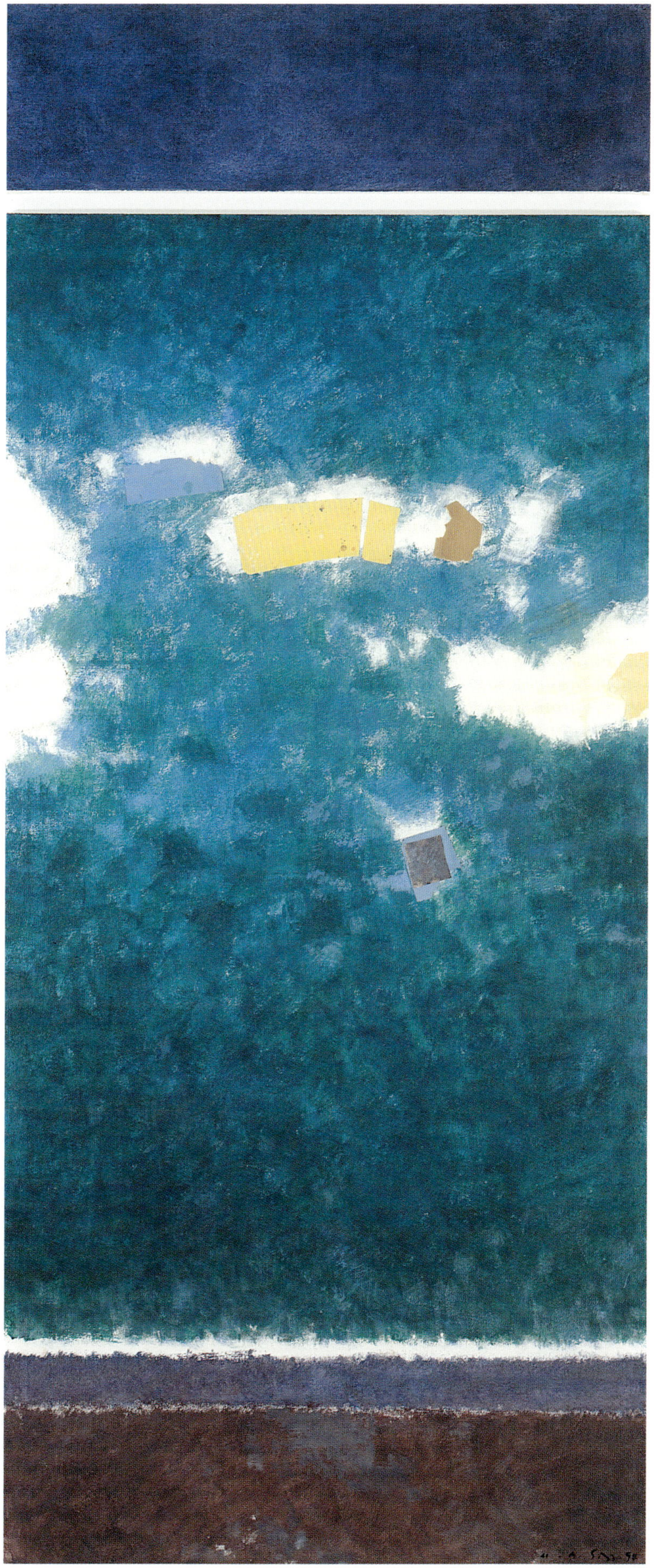

Im Reich der Mitte III/In the Middle Realm III, 1994, Acryl/acrylic, 125×175 cm

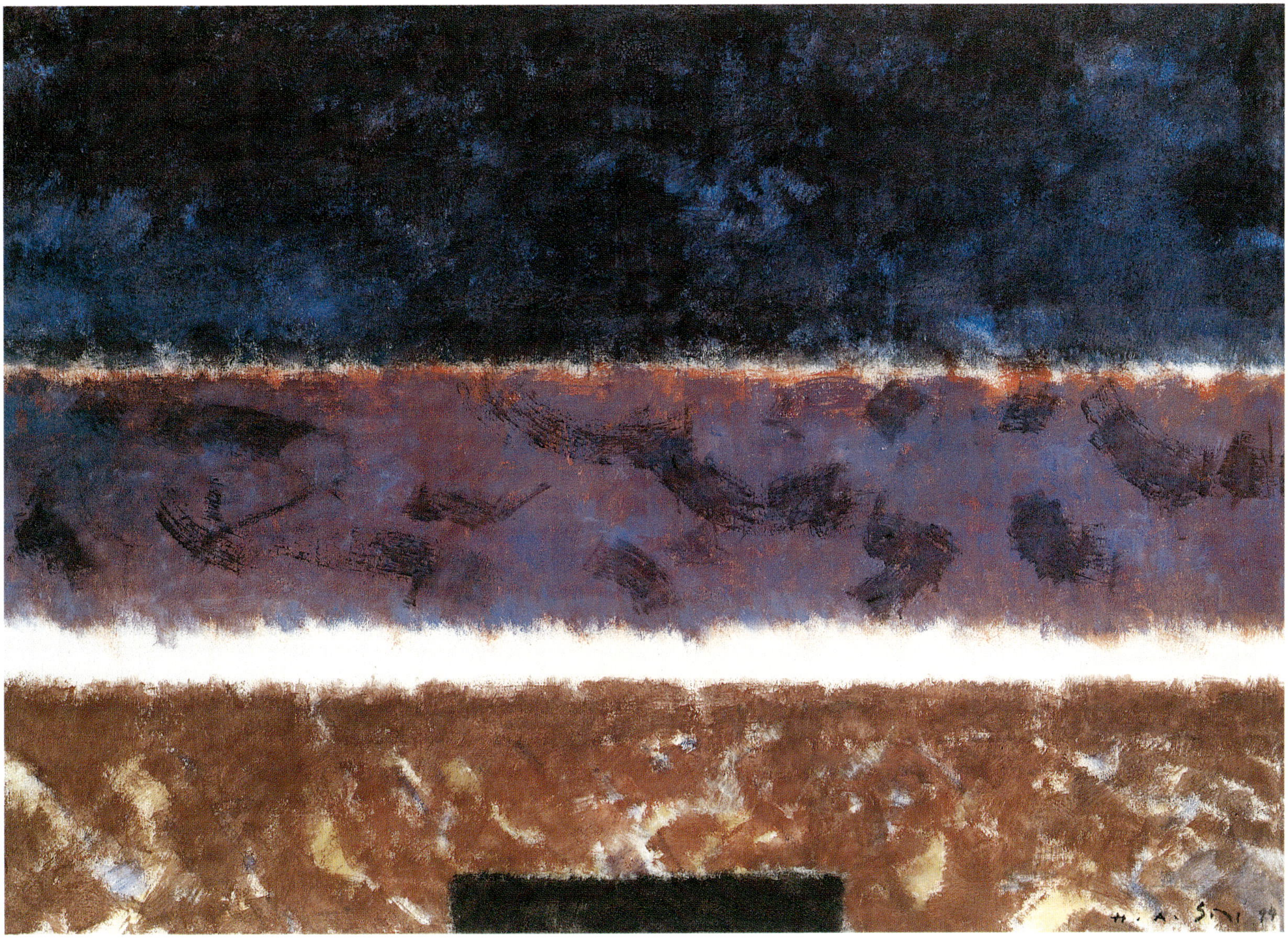

Mündung III/Estuary III, 1995, Acryl/acrylic, 81×232 cm

Ohne Titel 1/No title 1, 1994, Stahl und Kupfer, bemalt/steel and copper, painted, 64×23×17 cm

Im Zeichen des Flusses III/Under the Sign of the River III, 1990/91, Acryl/acrylic, 162×116 cm

Ohne Titel 3/No title 3, 1994, Holz, Kunststoff, Metall, bemalt/wood, plastic, metal, painted, 61,5×25×17 cm

Ohne Titel II/No title II, 1993, Acryl/acrylic, 195×116 cm

Im Reich der Mitte IV/In the Middle Realm IV, 1994, Acryl/acrylic, 210×116 cm

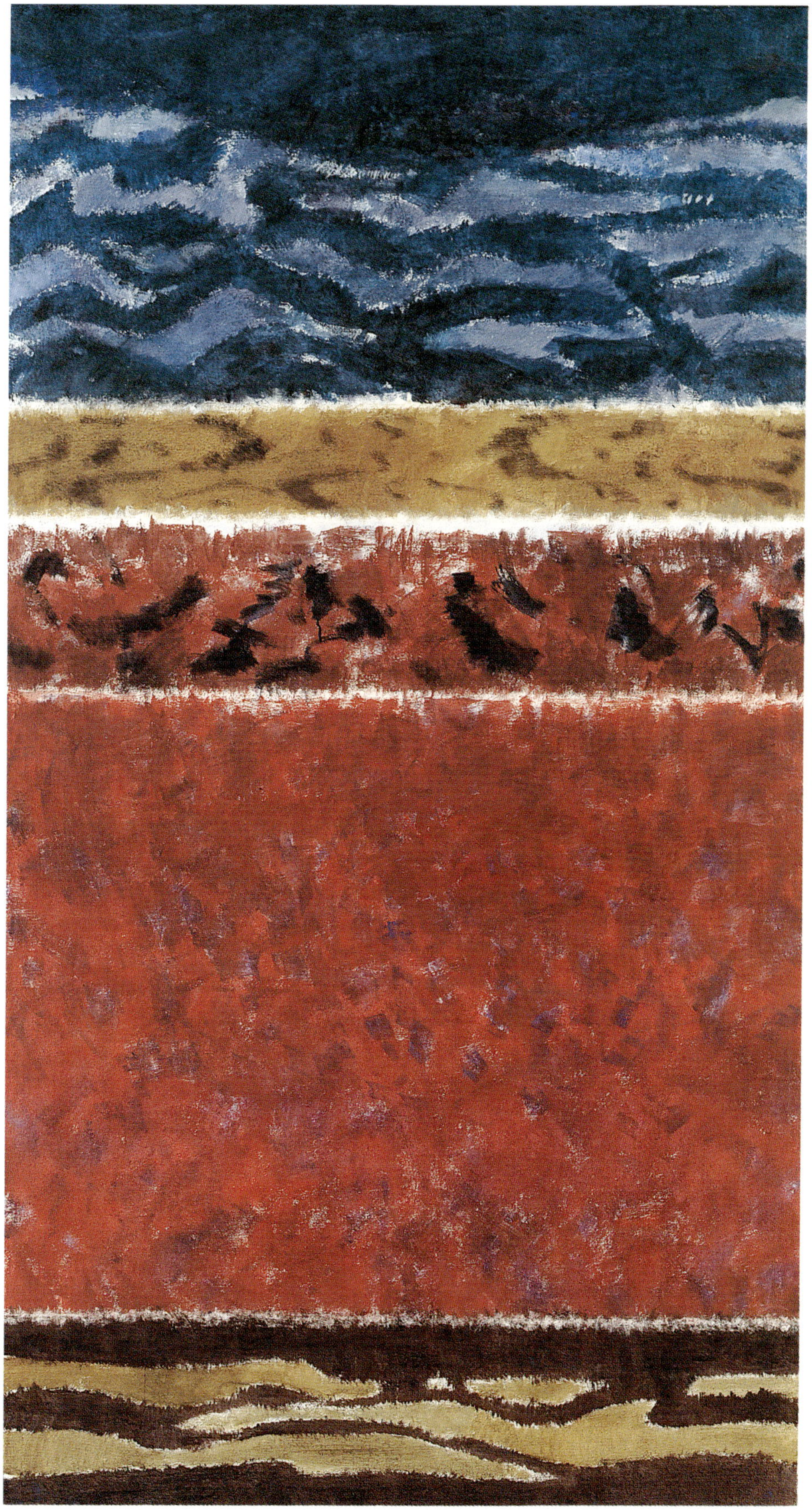

Ohne Titel 5/No title 5, 1994, Holz, Kunststoff, bemalt/wood, plastic, painted, 64,5×27×27 cm

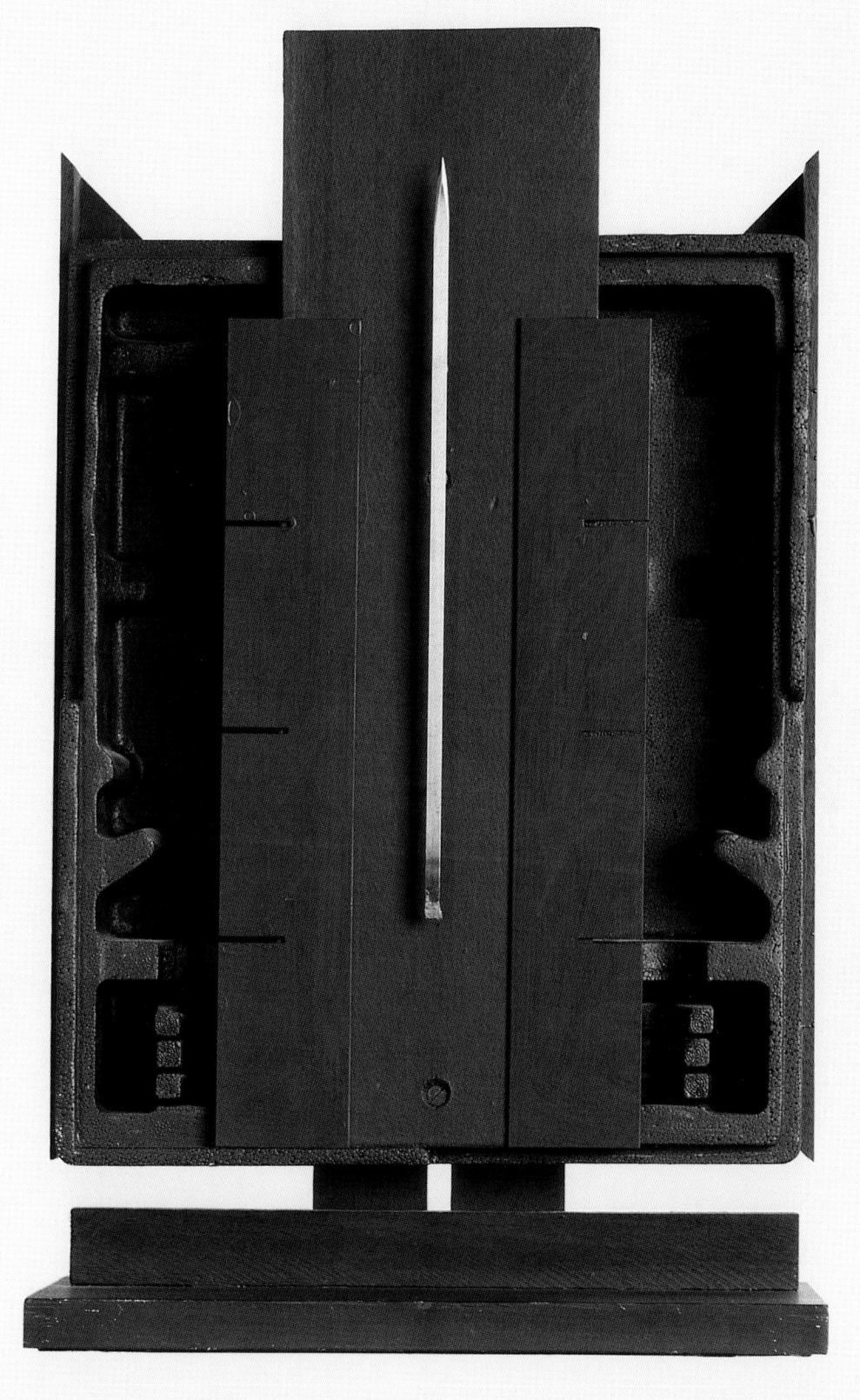

Ohne Titel 4/No title 4, 1994, Holz, Kunststoff, Metall, bemalt/wood, plastic, metal, painted, 52,5×32×17 cm

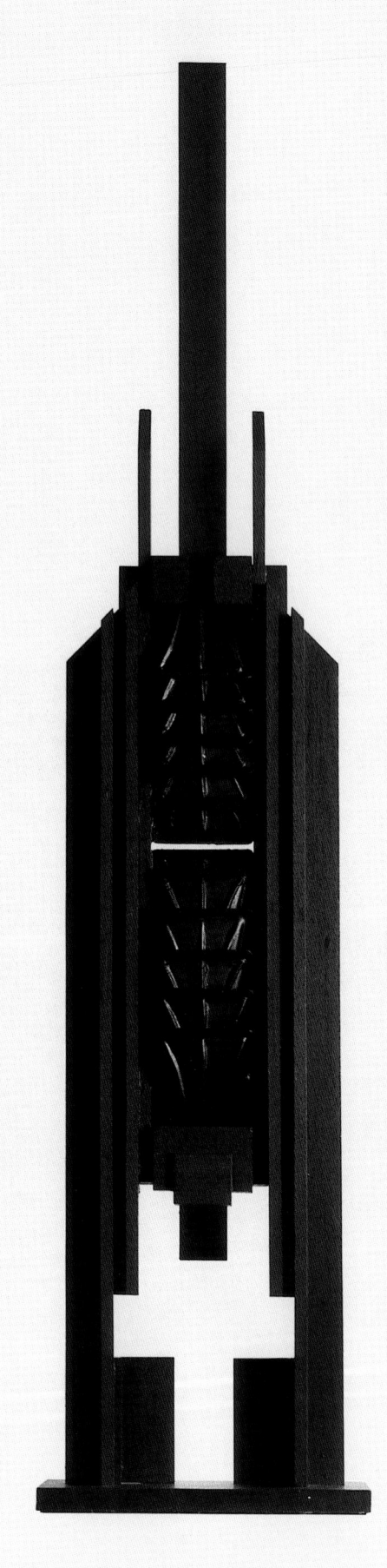

Ohne Titel 10/No title 10, 1995, Holz, Kunststoff, bemalt/wood, plastic, painted, 101,5×25,5×18 cm

Ohne Titel 11/No title 11, 1994, Holz, Kunststoff, bemalt/wood, plastic, painted, 64,5×23×17 cm

Ohne Titel 2/No title 2, 1994, Holz, Kunststoff, bemalt/wood, plastic, painted, 62×25×17 cm

Im Reich der Mitte I/In the Middle Realm I, 1994, Acryl/acrylic, 175×116 cm

Im Reich der Mitte VII/In the Middle Realm VII, 1995, Acryl/acrylic, 232×138 cm

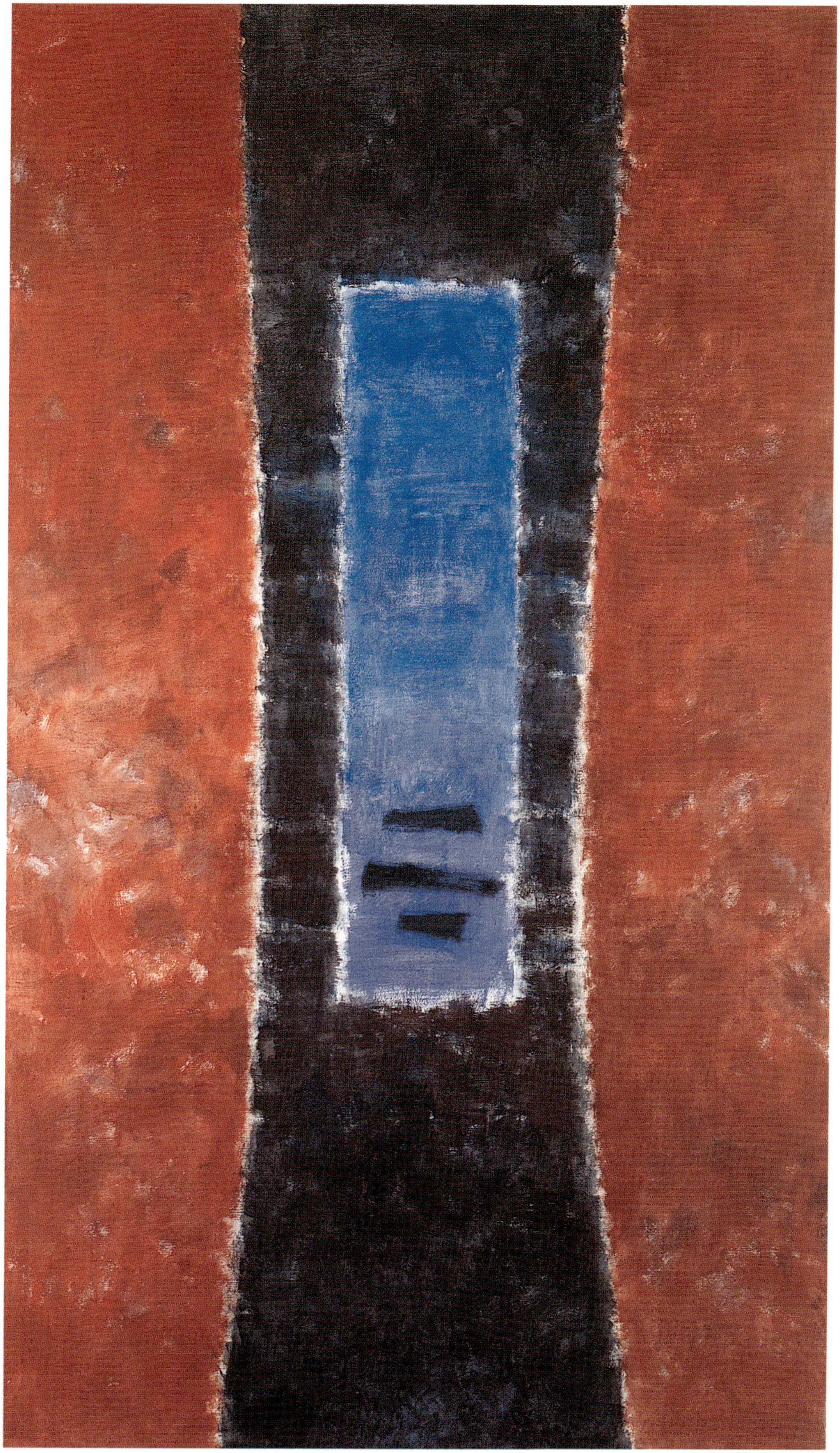

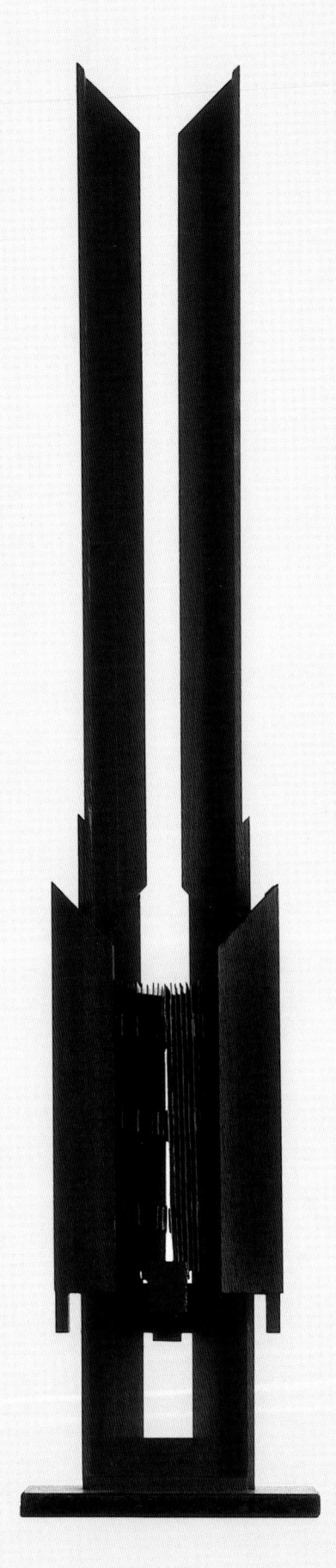

Ohne Titel 7/No title 7, 1995, Holz, Kunststoff, bemalt/wood, plastic, painted, 101×23×17 cm

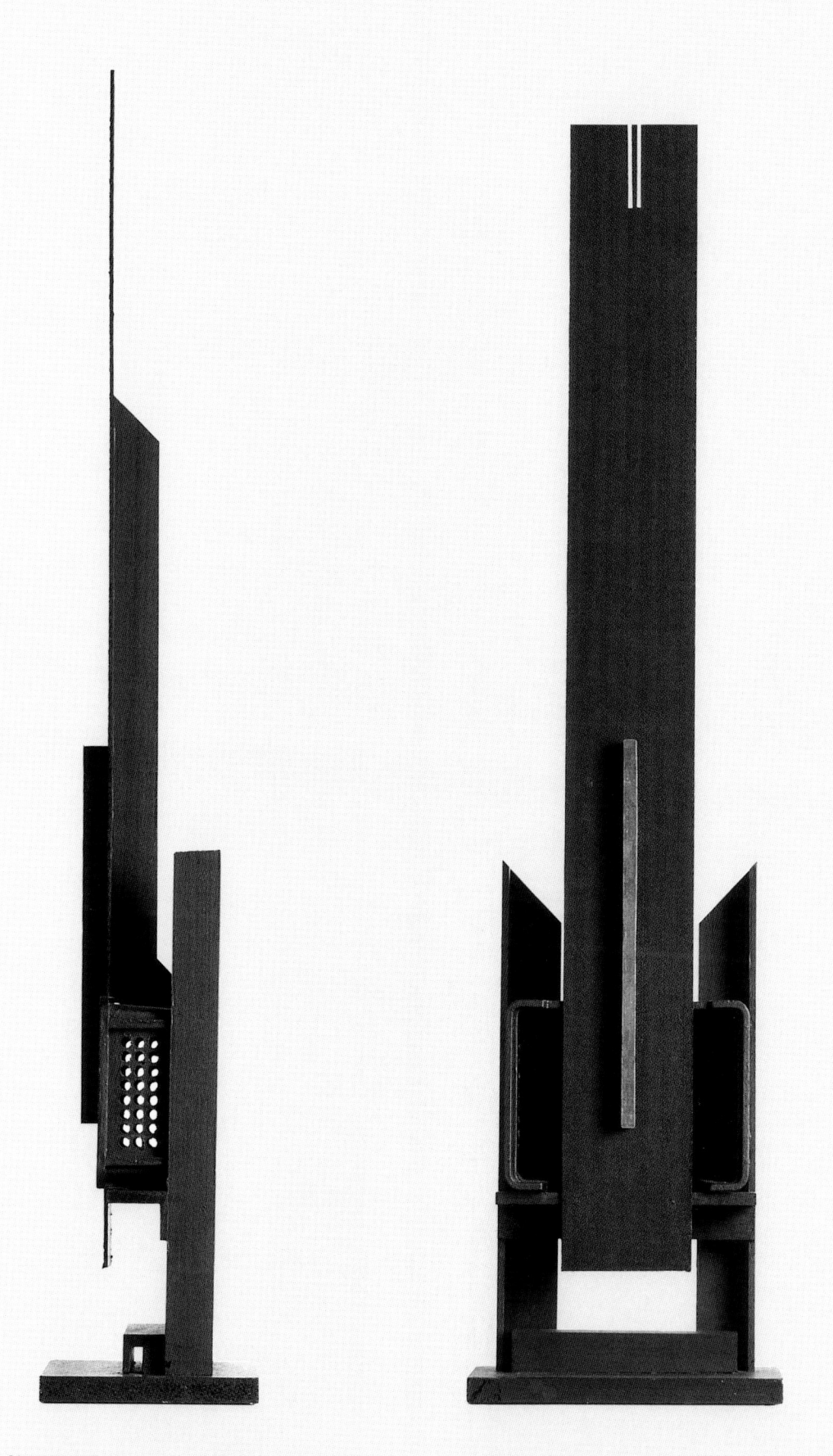

Ohne Titel 8/No title 8, 1995, Holz, Kunststoff, Kupfer, bemalt/wood, plastic, copper, painted, 105×25×17 cm

Ohne Titel 9/No title 9, 1994, Holz, Kunststoff, bemalt/wood, plastic, painted, 70,5×24×17 cm

Ohne Titel 12/No title 12, 1994, Holz, Kunststoff, Metall, bemalt/wood, plastic, metal, painted, 64,5×23,5×17 cm

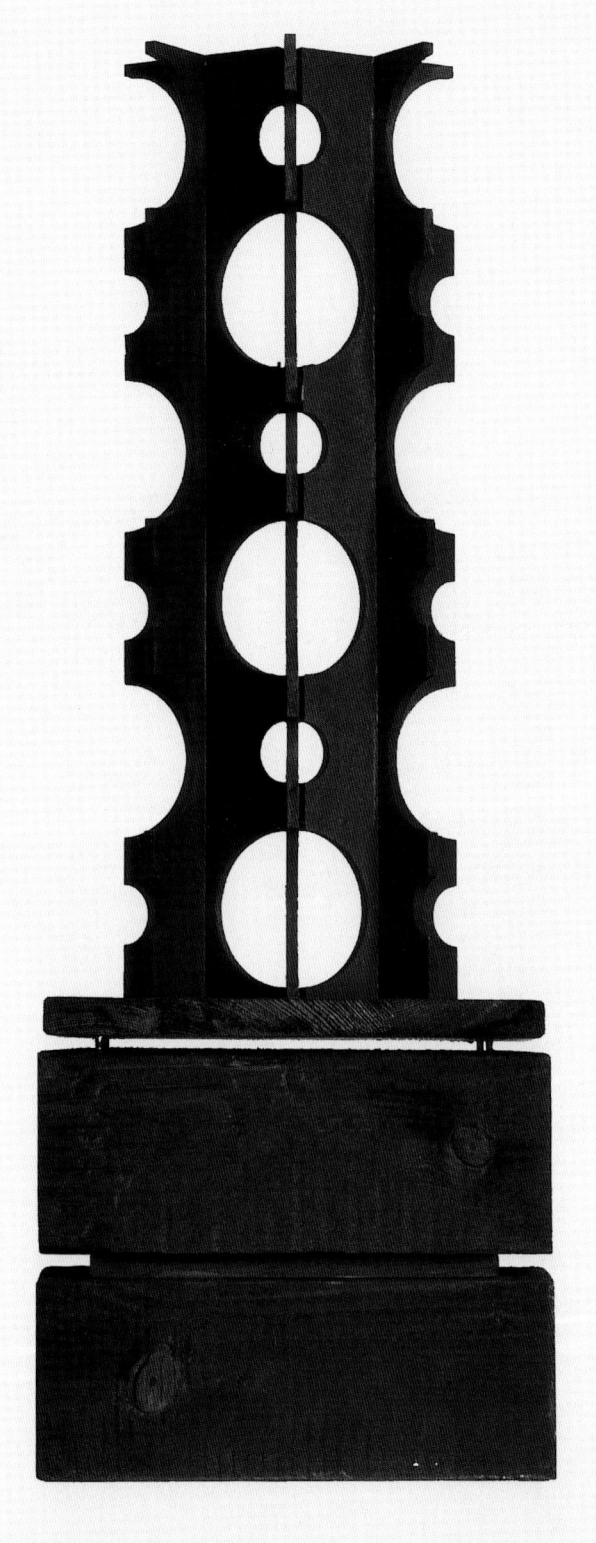

Ohne Titel 15/No title 15, 1996, Holz, bemalt/wood, painted, 70,5×26×17,5 cm

Ohne Titel 16/No title 16, 1996, Holz, bemalt/wood, painted, 89×25×13,5 cm

Ohne Titel 17/No title 17, 1996, Holz, bemalt/wood, painted, 84,5×26×14 cm

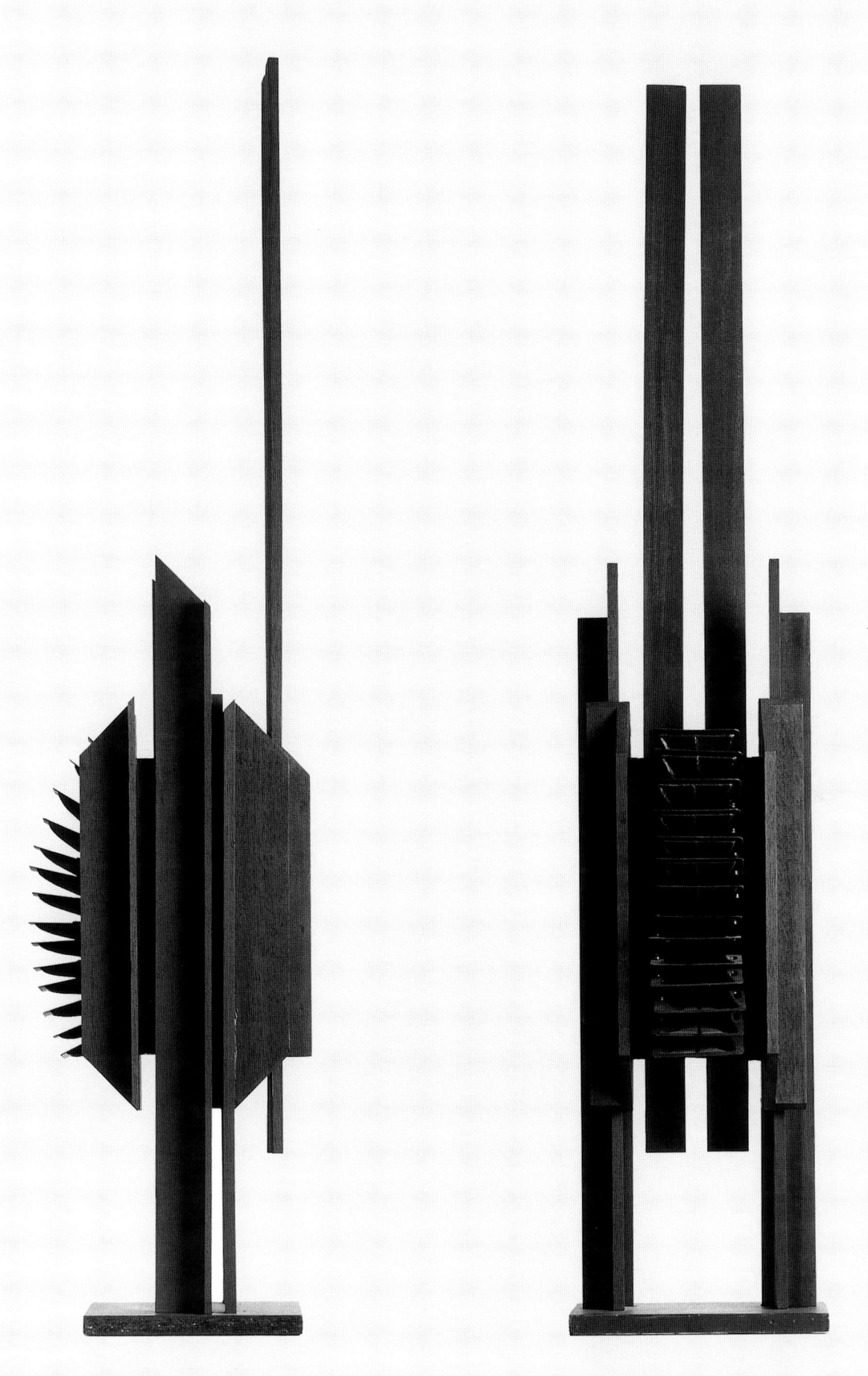

Ohne Titel 14/No title 14, 1995, Holz, Kunststoff, bemalt/wood, plastic, painted, 110×23×19 cm

Ohne Titel 13/No title 13, 1995, Holz, Kunststoff, bemalt/wood, plastic, painted, 110×27,5×19 cm

Im Reich des Herbstes/In the Realm of Autumn, 1994/95, Acryl/acrylic, 195×116 cm

Im Zeichen des Flusses I/Under the Sign of the River I, 1990/91, Acryl/acrylic, 175×81 cm

Im Reich der Mitte XI/In the Middle Realm XI, 1995/96, Acryl/acrylic, 81×210 cm

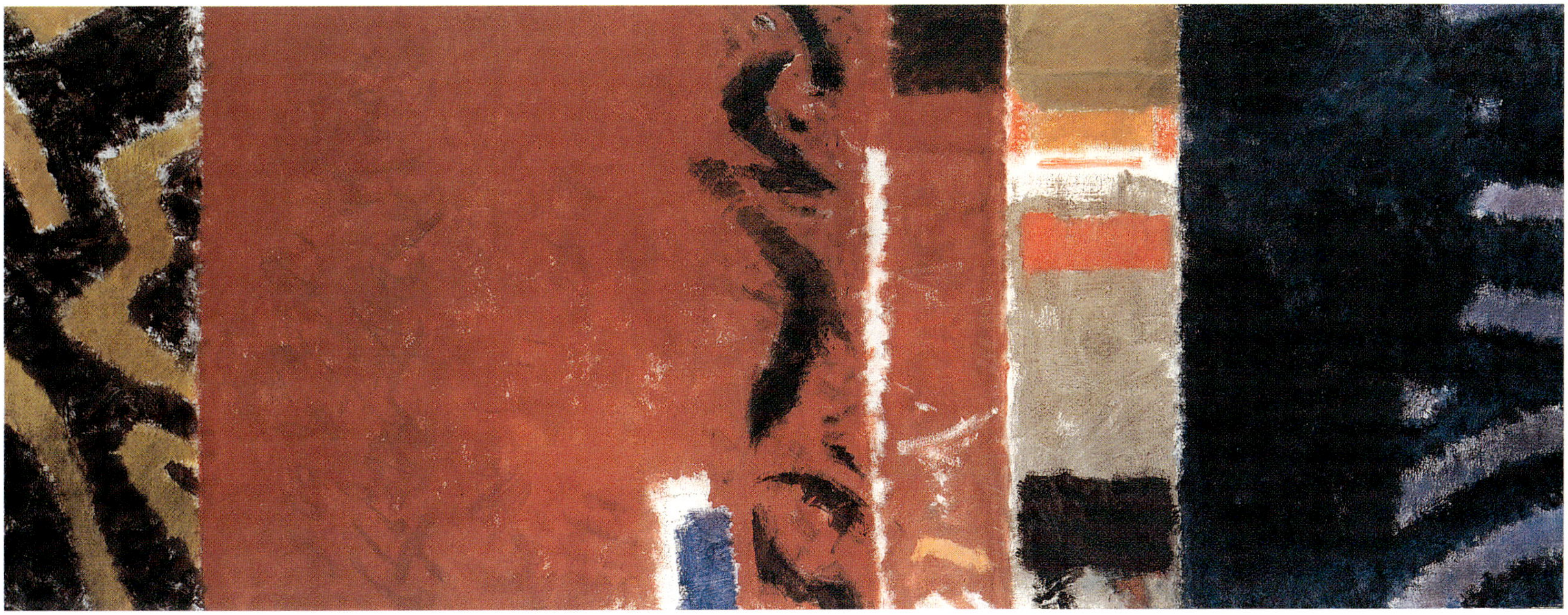

Im Reich der Mitte IX/In the Middle Realm IX, 1994/95, Acryl/acrylic, 195×125 cm

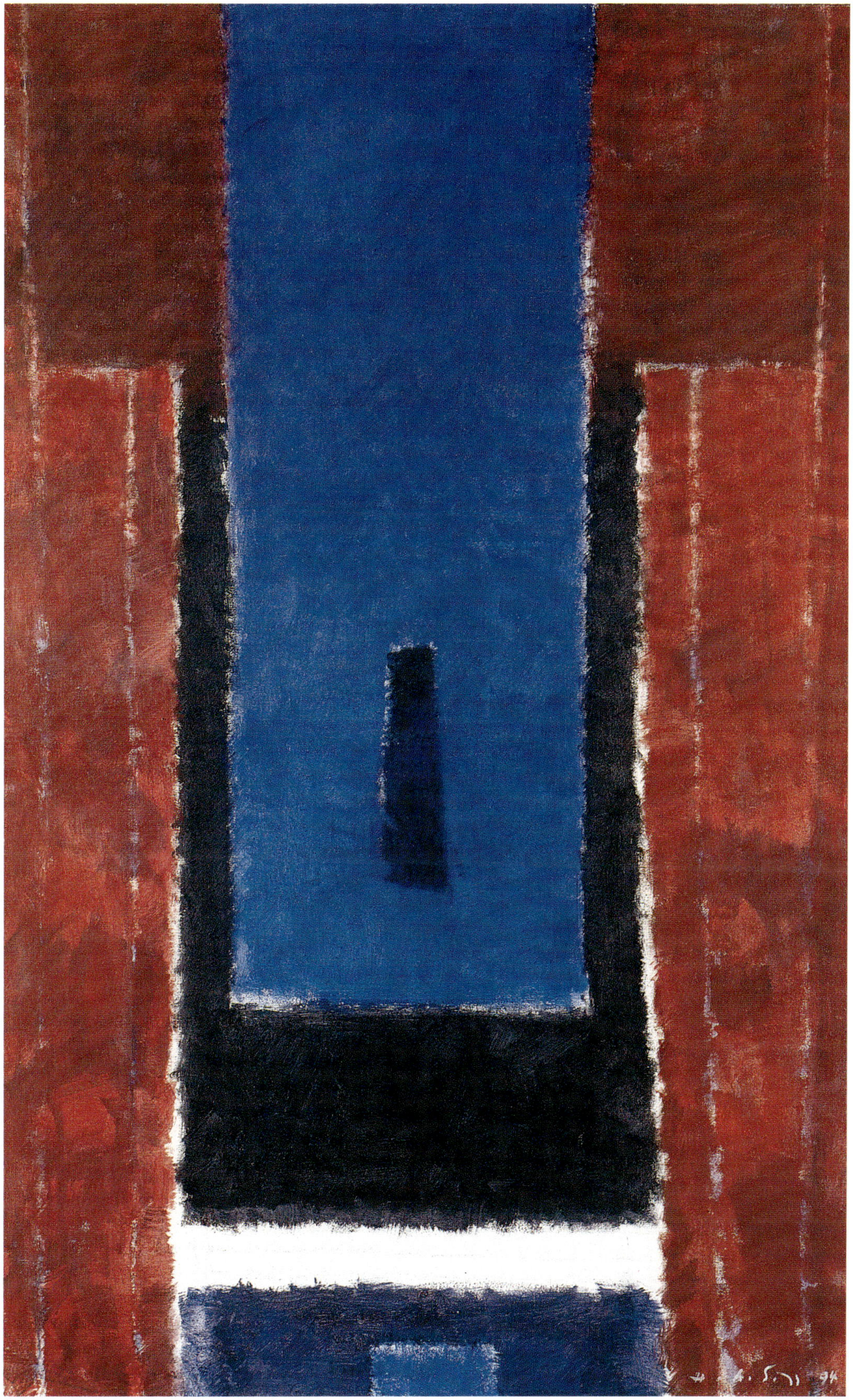

Im Reich der Mitte X/In the Middle Realm X, 1995/96, Acryl/acrylic, 175×125 cm

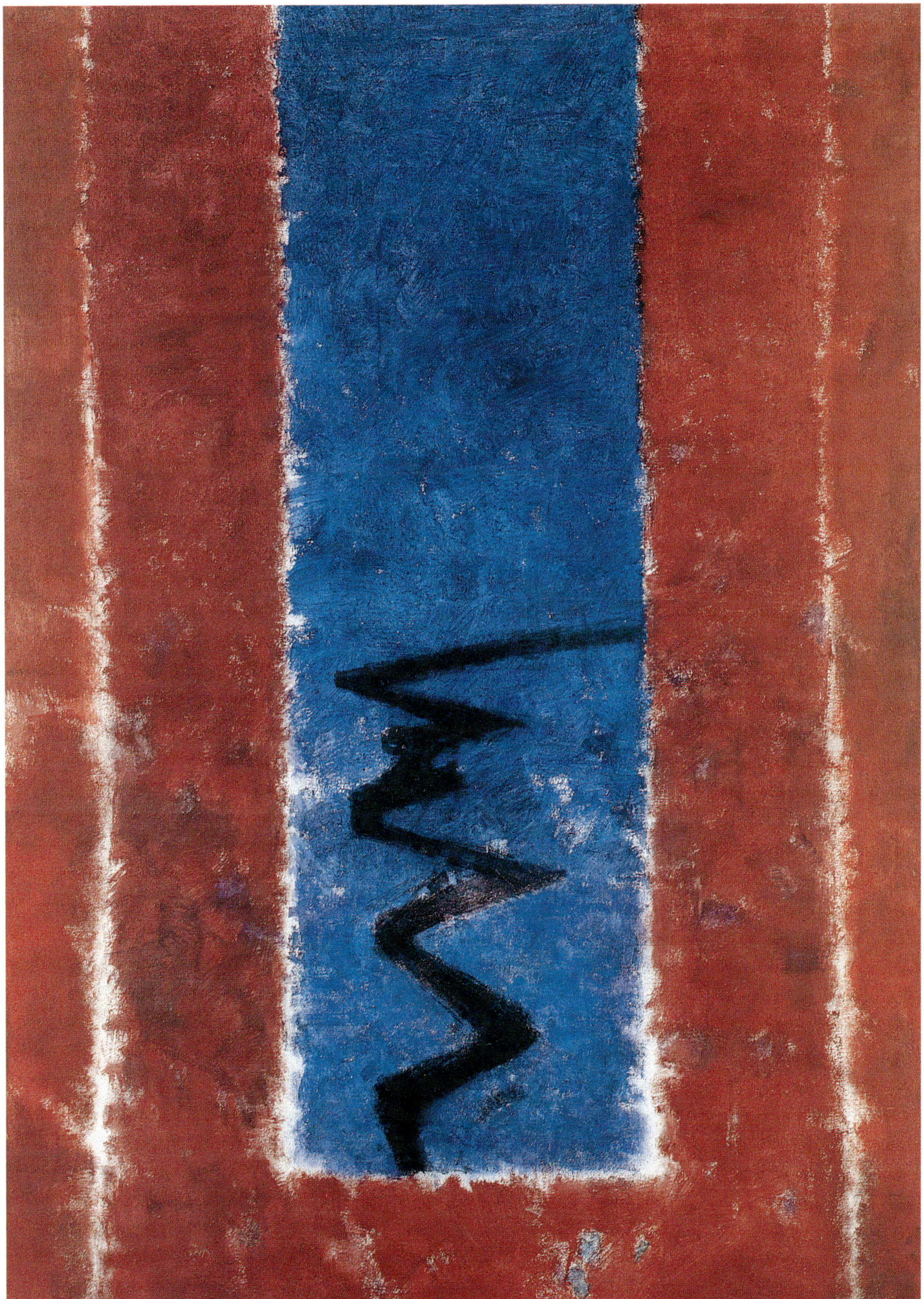

Im Reich der Mitte VIII/In the Middle Realm VIII, 1995, Acryl/acrylic, 232×130 cm

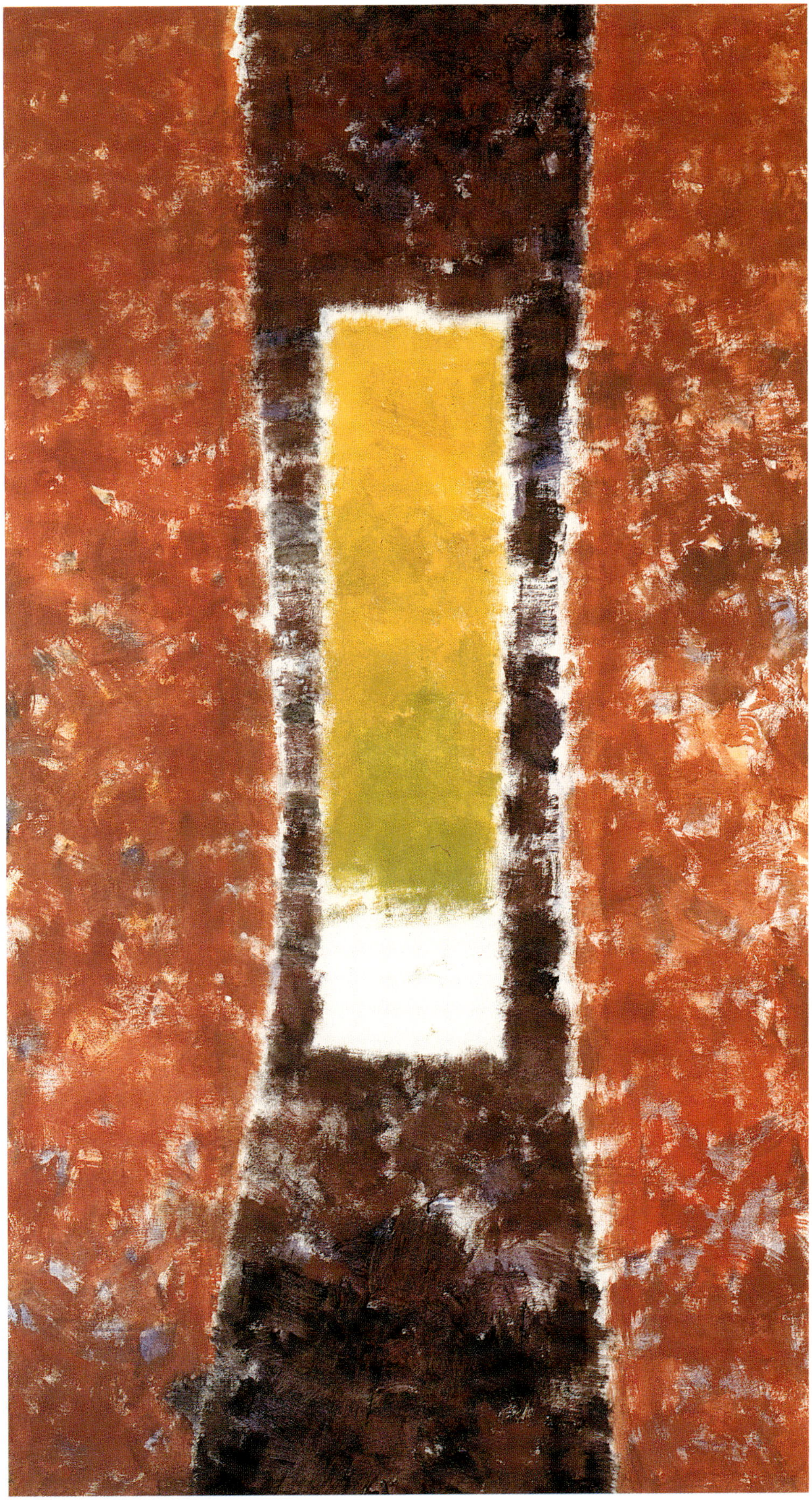

Im Reich der Mitte II/In the Middle Realm II, 1994, Acryl/acrylic, 175×116 cm

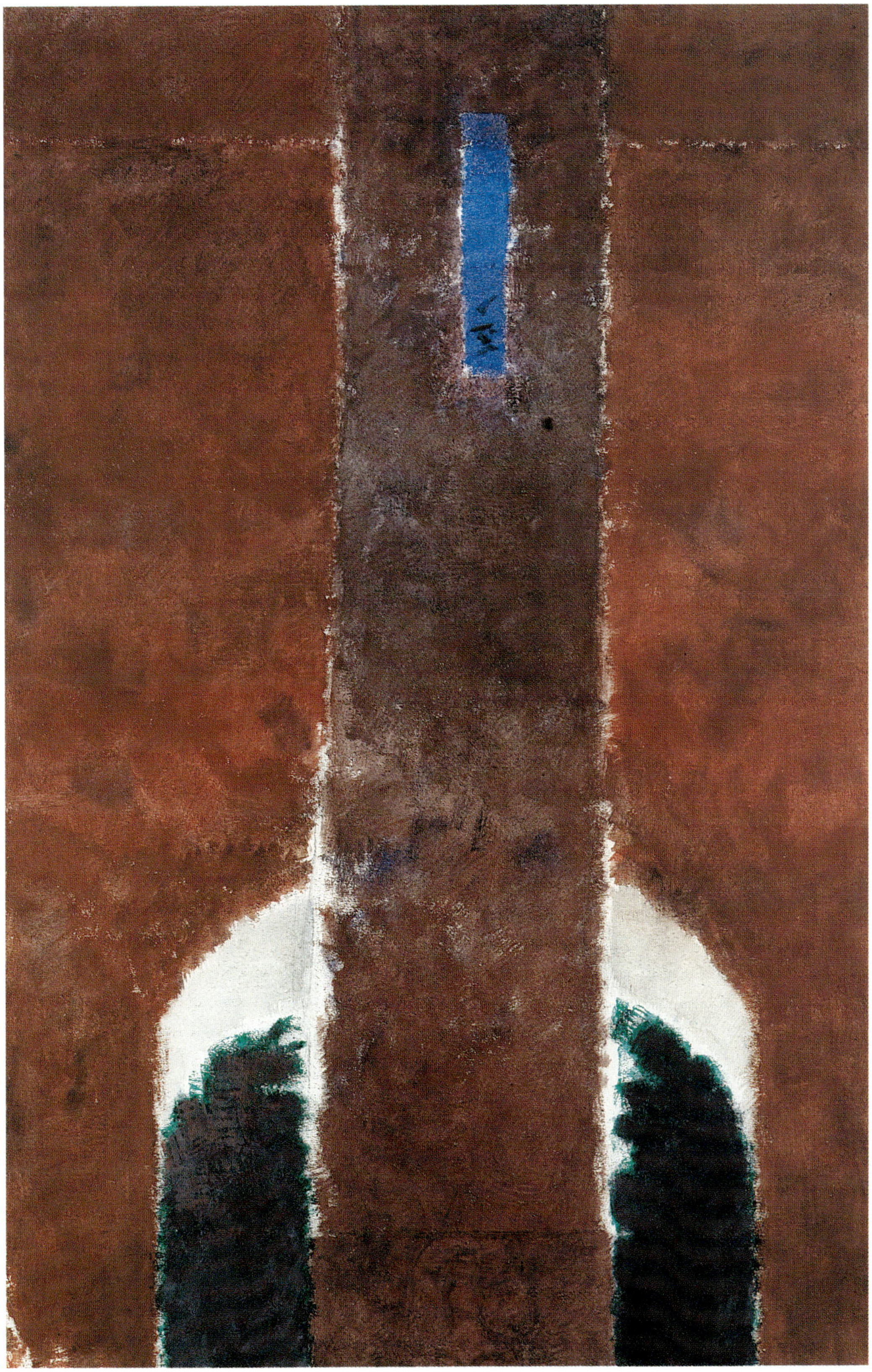

Nachdenkend verweilen/Lingering in Contemplation, 1994, Acryl/acrylic, 175×116 cm

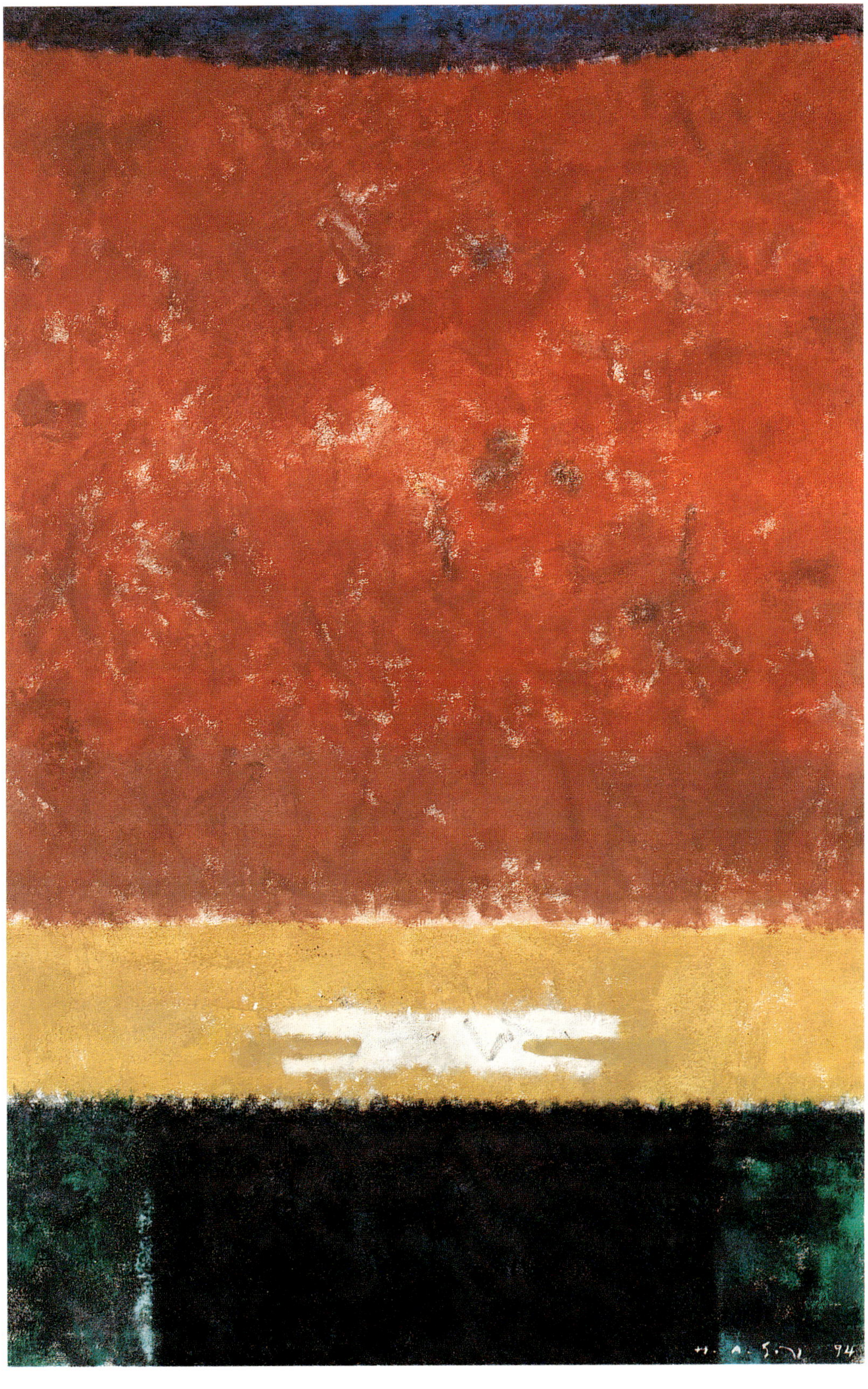

Im Reich der Mitte XIV/In the Middle Realm XIV, 1996, Acryl/acrylic, 195×125 cm

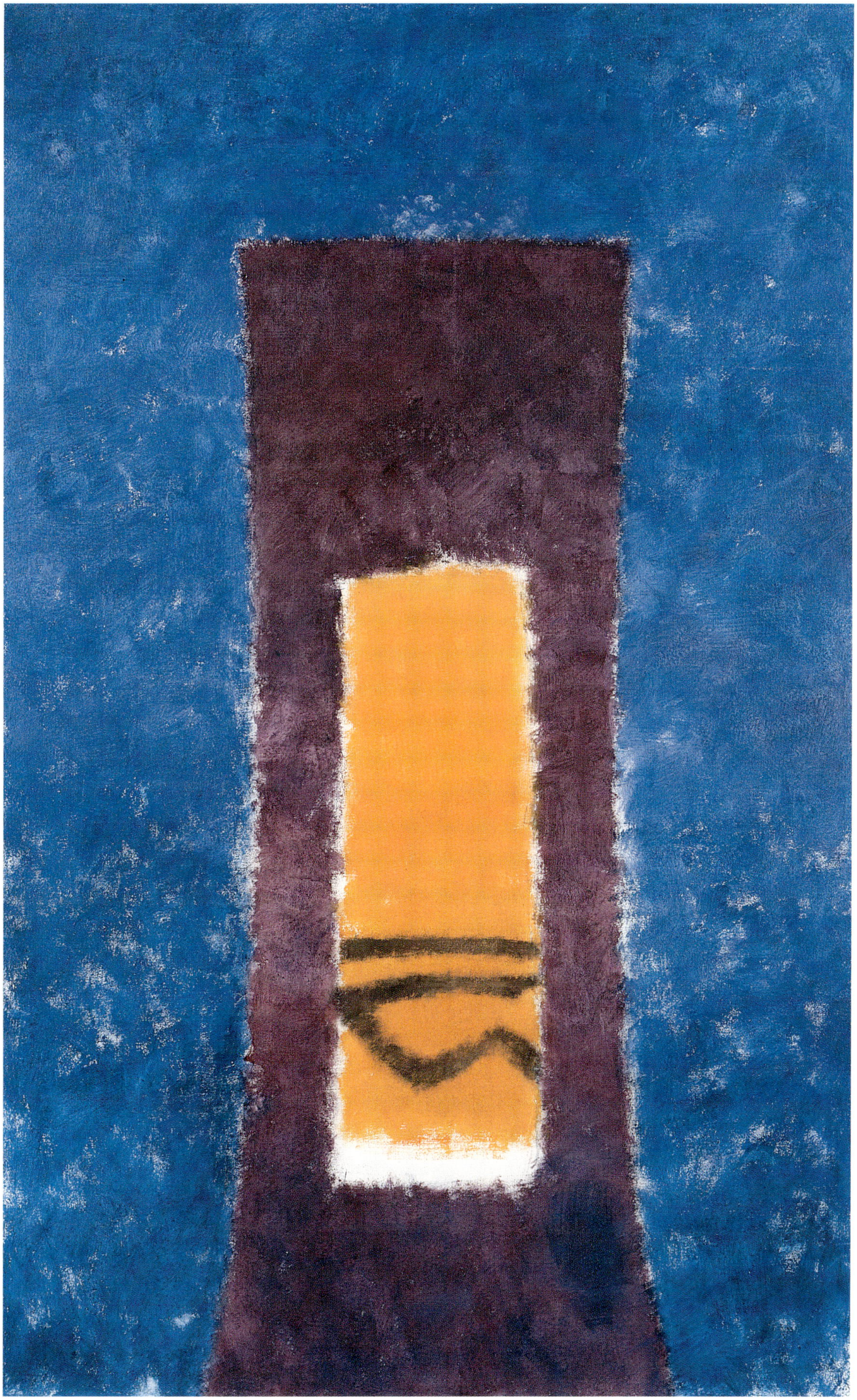

Im Reich der Mitte XII/In the Middle Realm XII, 1996, Acryl/acrylic, 175×125 cm

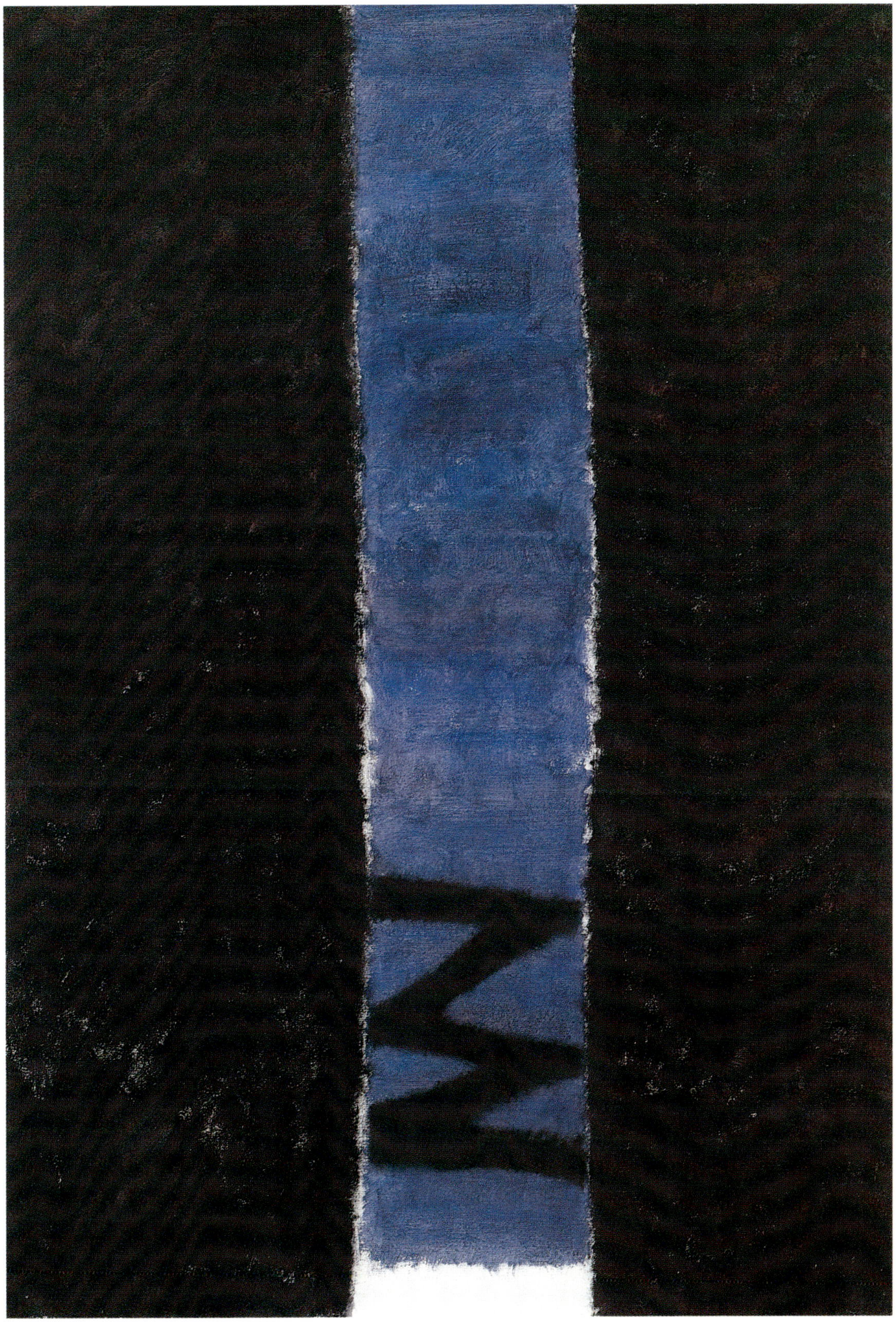

Im Reich der Mitte XV/In The Middle Realm XV, Acryl/acrylic, 1998, 195×116 cm

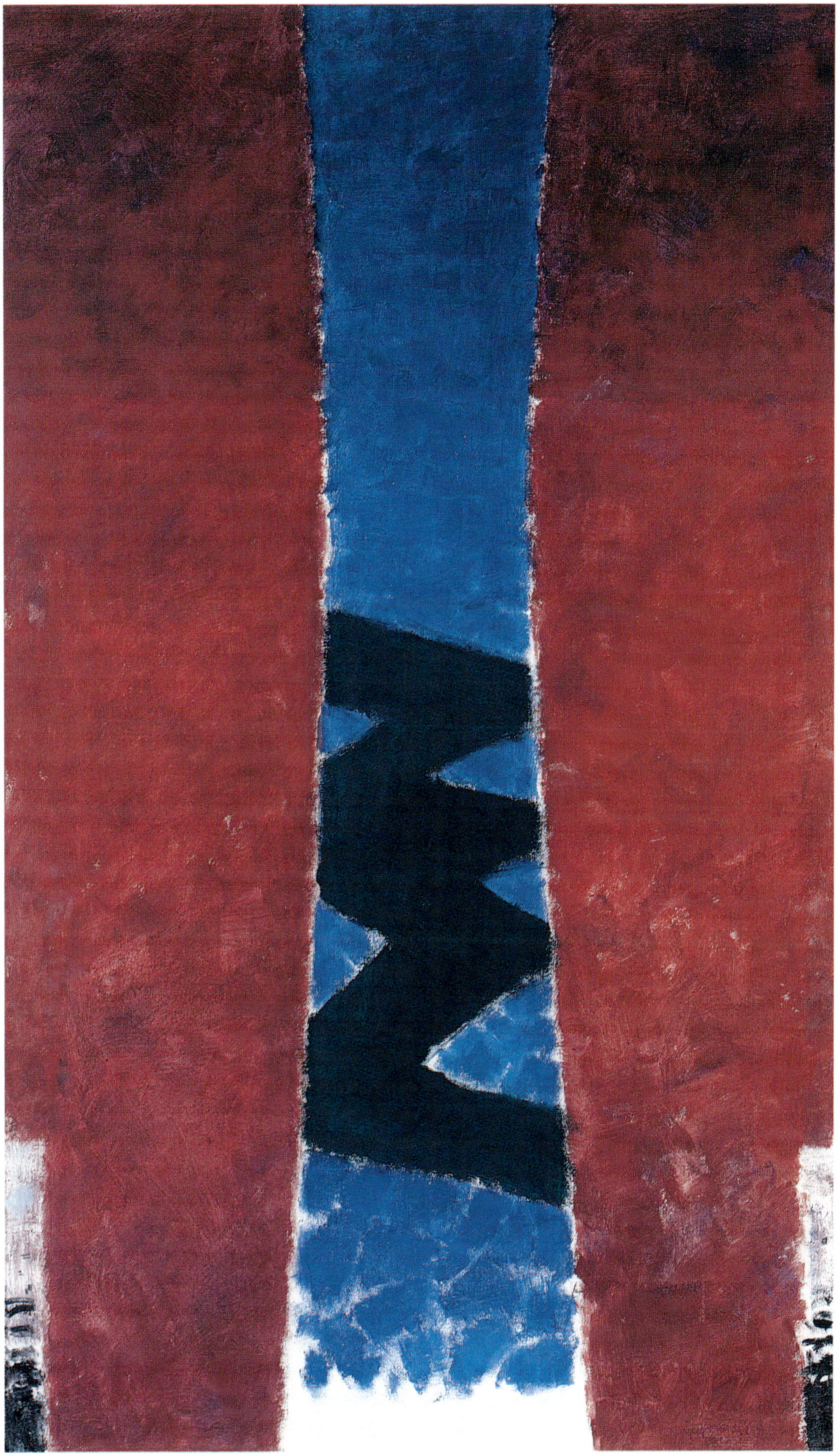

Im Reich der Mitte XVI/In the Middle Realm XVI, Acryl/acrylic, 1997/98, 232×138 cm

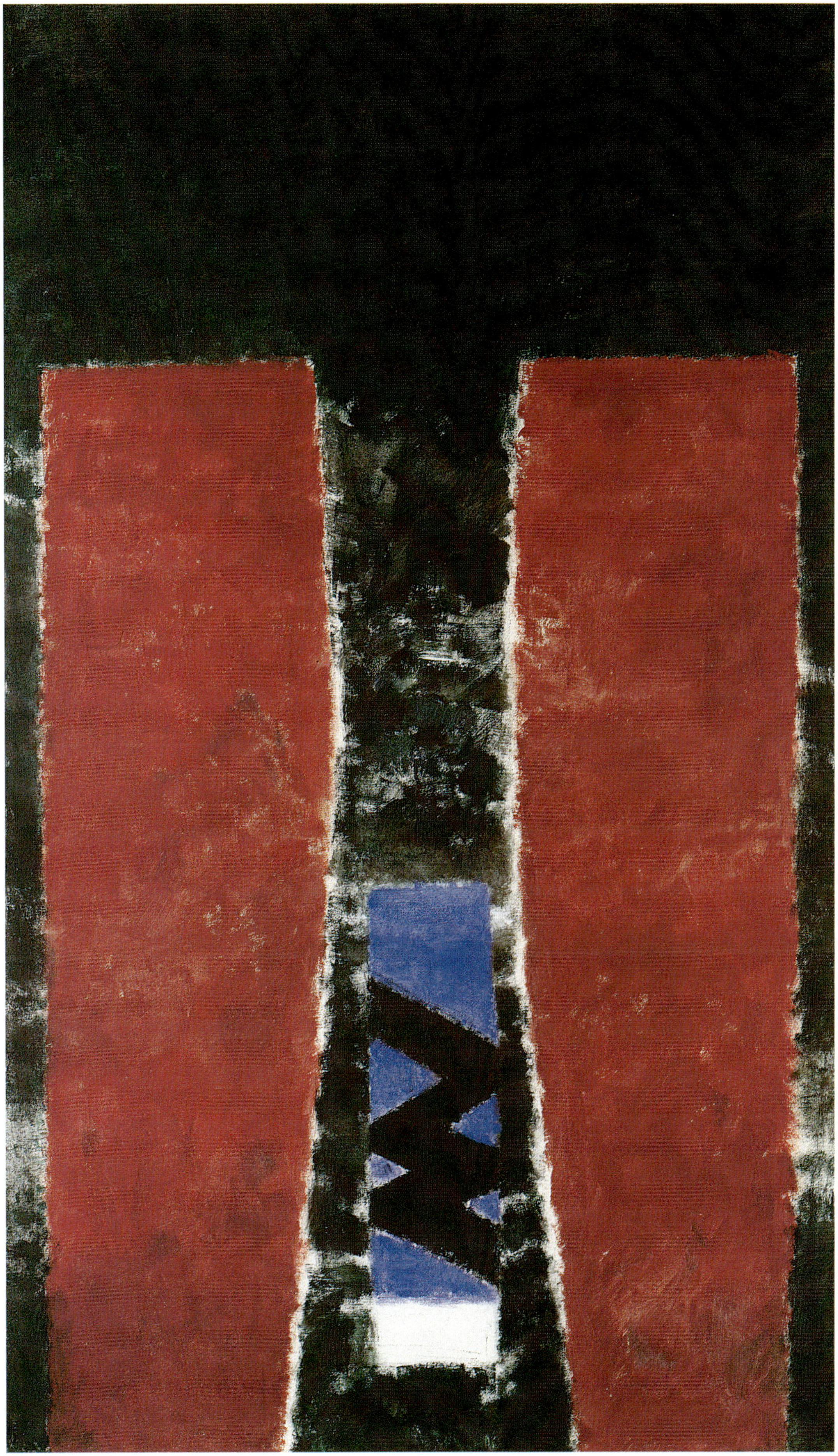

Kunst am Bau

Construction-Related Art

8 Farbfenster Reformierte Kirche Freiburg
8 Stained-Glass Windows, Reformed Church Fribourg, 1978
und Chorwandbild/and Choir Mural, 1985

Rundfenster Reformierte Kirche Freiburg/
Round Window, Reformed Church Fribourg, 1985, Ø 264 cm

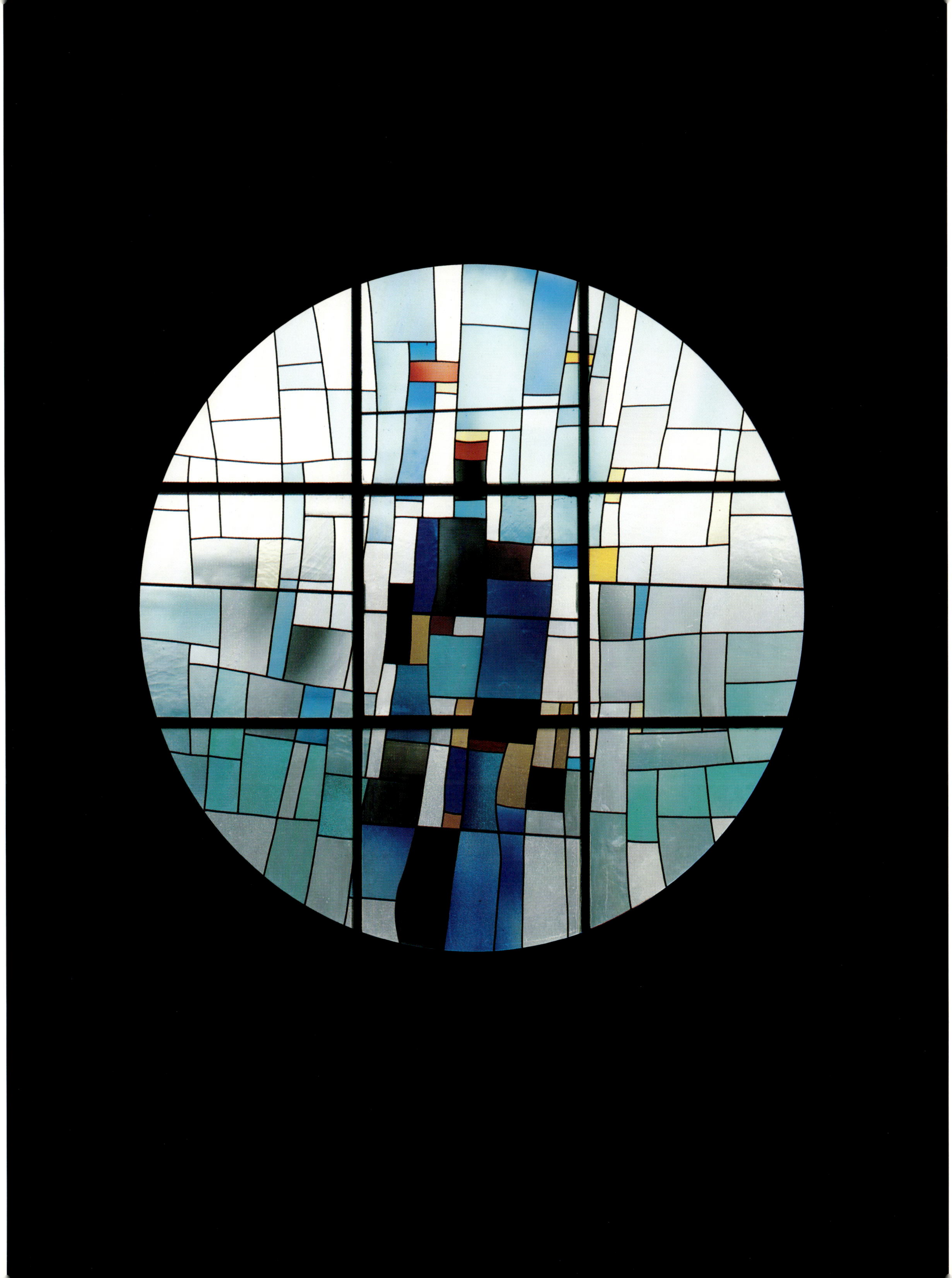

Wandbild Universität Zürich-Irchel/Mural University of Zurich-Irchel, 1981, 350×600 cm

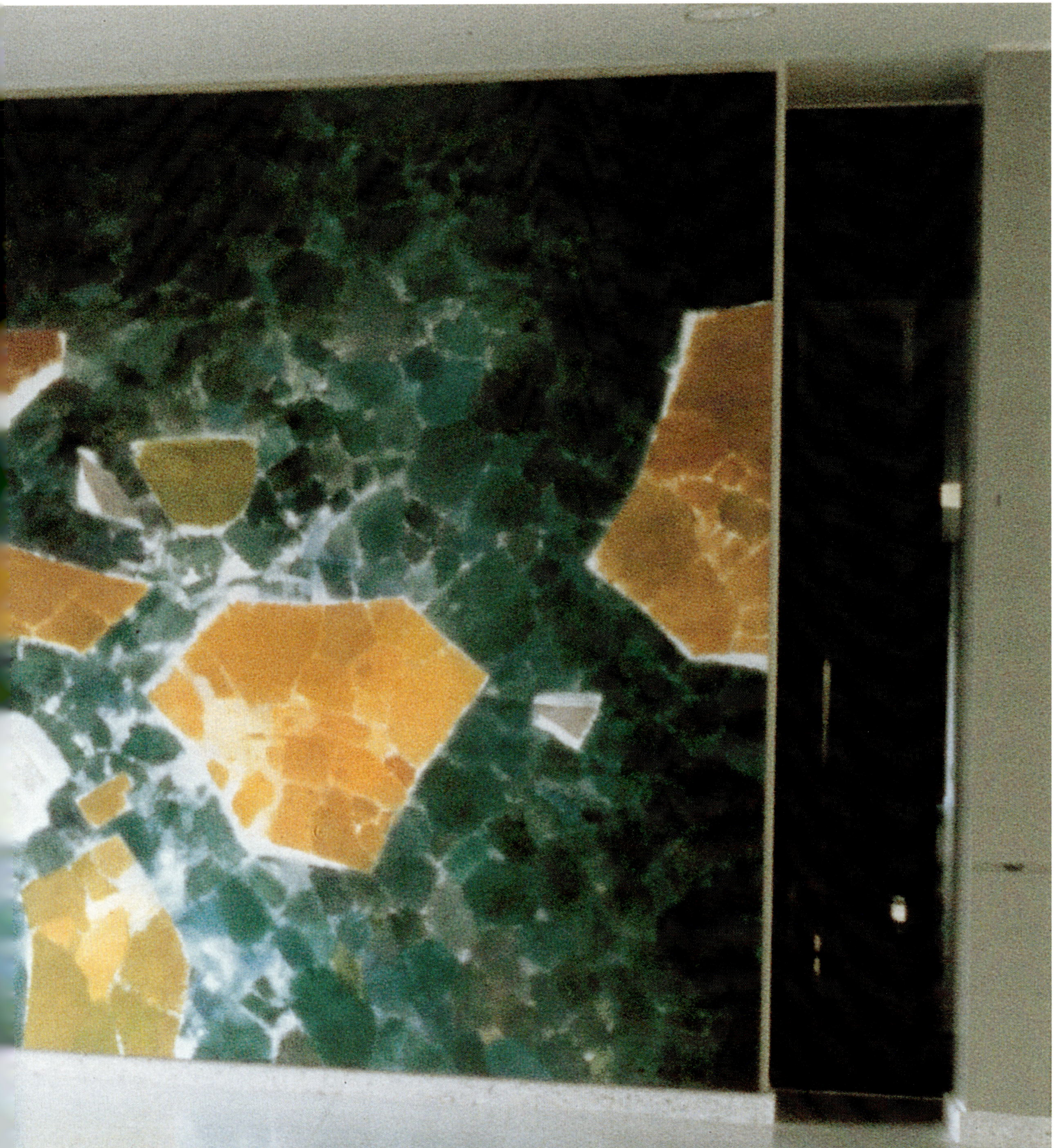

Im Atelier/At the Studio, 1990

Wandbild/Mural 1990, 220×1200 cm, ehemals Hotel Zürich, heute Hotel Mariott Zürich/Former Hotel Zurich, today Hotel Mariott Zürich

101 1 4 5
102 1 4

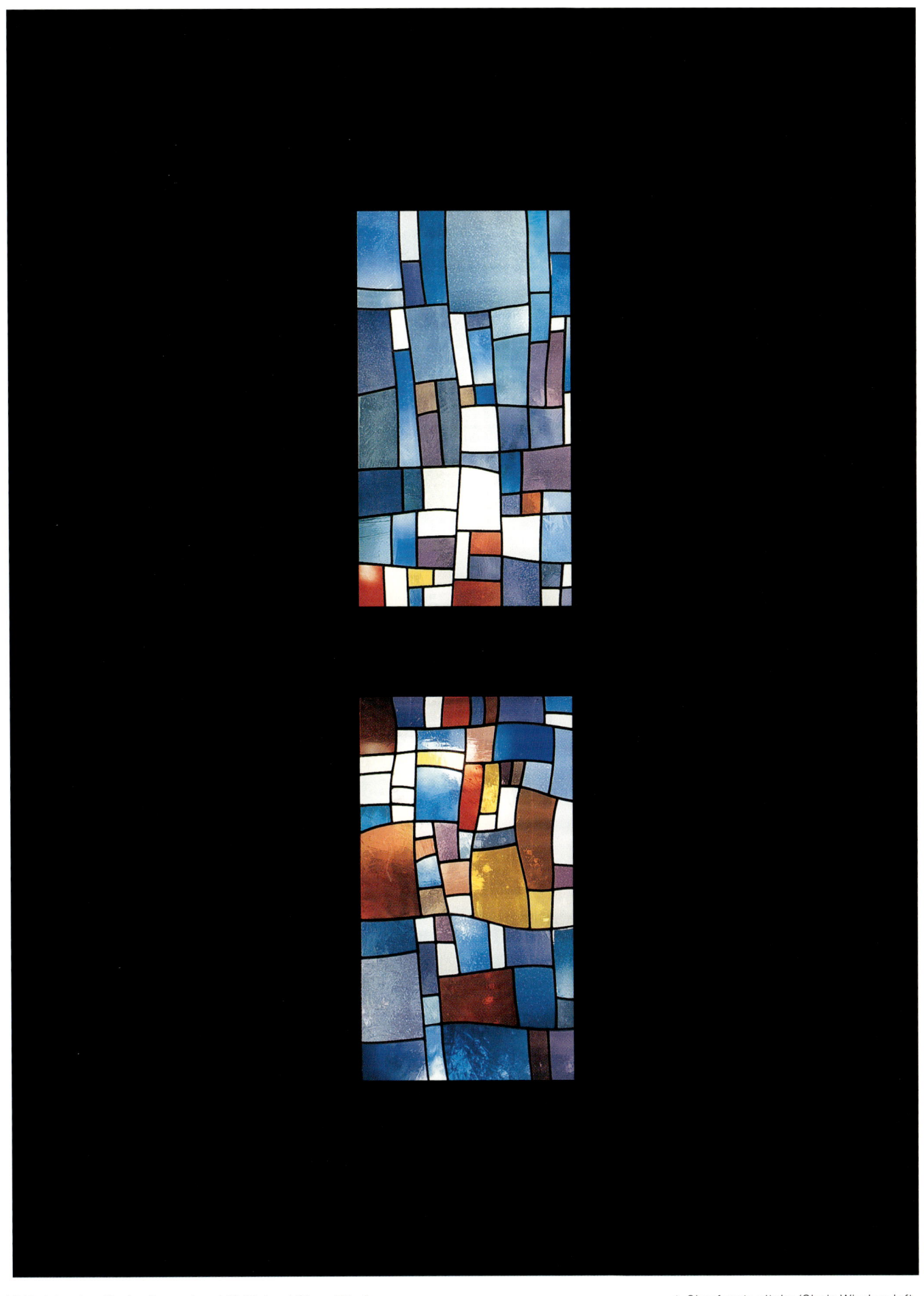

◄ 6 Farbfenster Kirche Davos-Laret/6 Stained-Glass Windows, Davos-Laret Church, 1992/93

▲ Chorfenster links/Choir Window left, 1992/93, 170×43,5 cm

Farbfenster, Universitätsspital Zürich, Aufnahmetrakt/Stained-Glass Window, University Hospital Zurich, Admissions Hall, 1995/96, 260×750 cm

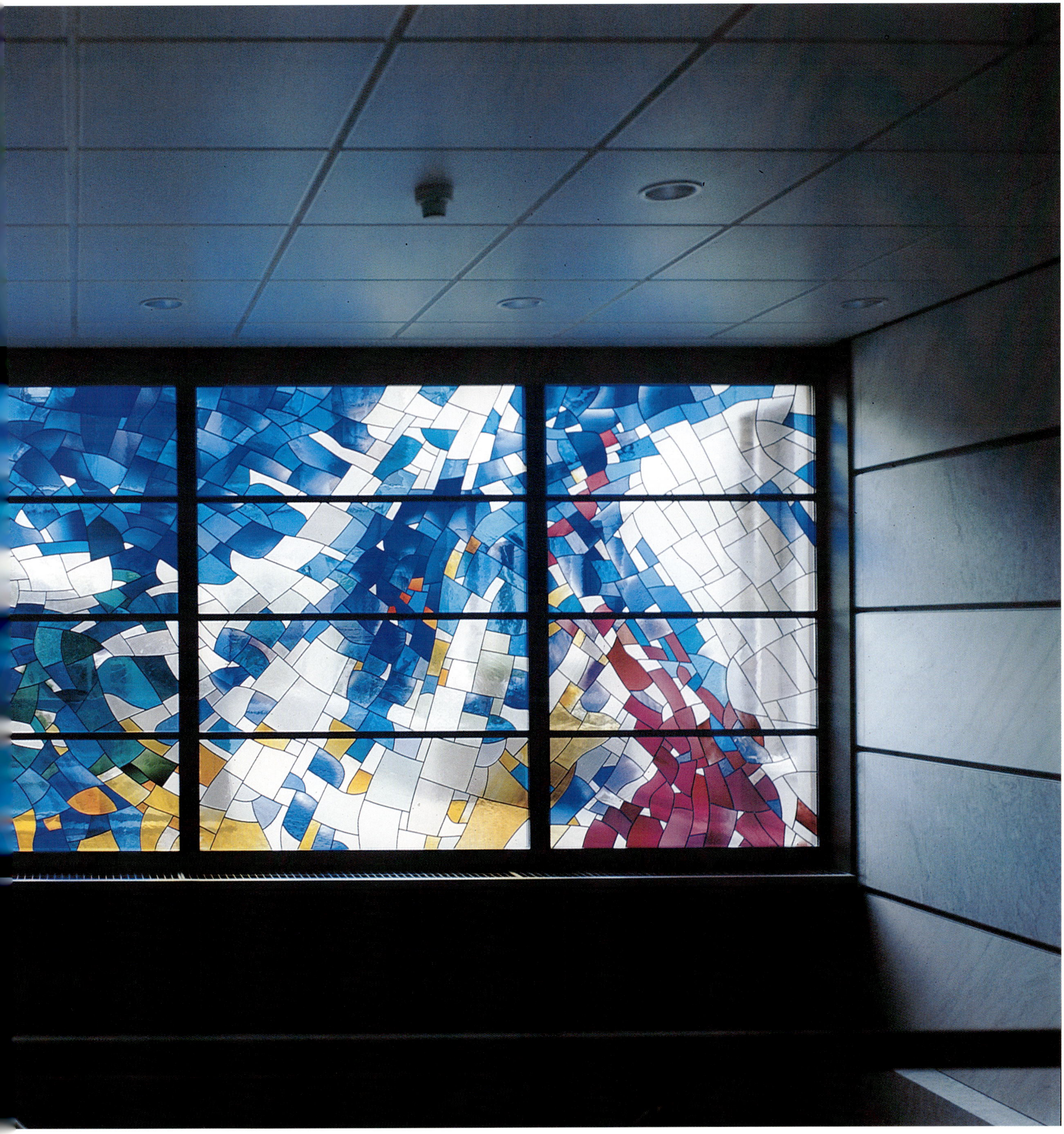

Biographische Notizen

Biographical Notes

1924
Geboren in Zürich am 29. Juni.
Verbringt seine Jugendzeit auf dem elterlichen Bauernhof in Oberhasli ZH.

1944–1947
Studien an der Kunstgewerbeschule Zürich.
Lehrer: Johannes Itten, Heinrich Müller, Ernst Georg Rüegg, Carl Fischer, Otto Morach, Ernst Gubler und andere.

1947
Studien an der Akademie André Lhote, Paris.
An der Akademie lernt er Hilda Jörger kennen, die er 1949 heiratet.
Rückkehr in die Schweiz. Verdient seinen Lebensunterhalt als Graphiker auf dem Gebiet der Illustration, der Ausstellungsgestaltung und der Schaufensterkonzeptionen. Arbeitet auch als Zeichenlehrer. Bühnenbildner für das zeitkritische Theater «Zeitbühne». Beginn der Freundschaft mit Oskar Reck, der kurze Zeit als Textautor bei der «Zeitbühne» mitwirkt.

1924
Born in Zurich on June 29.
Spent his childhood on his parents farm at Oberhasli, Canton of Zurich.

1944–1947
Studied at the College of Commercial Art, Zurich.
His teachers: Johannes Itten, Heinrich Müller, Ernst Georg Rüegg, Carl Fischer, Otto Morach, Ernst Gubler and others.

1947
Studied at the Académie André Lhote, Paris.
Here he met Hilda Jörger, whom he married in 1949.
Returned to Switzerland, where he earned his living as a graphic designer working in illustration, exhibition design and window display. Also worked as an art teacher and a stage designer for the sociocritical theatre "Zeitbühne".
Beginning of a friendship with Oskar Reck, who for a time was a writer for the same theatre.

Kunsthaus Aarau «Zehn junge Schweizer Künstler» (1950).

Kunsthaus Aarau "Ten young Swiss artists" (1950).

Erste Farbfenster, Kantonsspital Schaffhausen. 1957 wurde das Farbfenster «Barmherzigkeit» (rechts) die offizielle Bundesfeierkarte der Schweiz (1950).

First stained-glass windows, Schaffhausen Canton Hospital. In 1957 the stained-glass "Charity" (right) was adopted as the official "Bundesfeier" card (in commemoration of the first Swiss league on 1st August). (1950)

1949
Verleihung des Conrad-Ferdinand-Meyer-Preises.
In den folgenden Jahren zweimaliger Beitrag der Kiefer-Hablitzel-Stiftung.

1950
Studienreisen durch Italien, Sizilien und die Liparischen Inseln. Italien wird in der Folge fast jährlich aufgesucht.

1951
Beginn der ersten Serie von Lithographien bei E. Matthieu AG.

1952
Ausstellung im Palais Zappeion Athen. Reise durch Griechenland.
Erste Ankäufe durch das Sammlerehepaar Nelly und Werner Bär. Beginn der Freundschaft mit den Familien Bär.

1953
Erster grosser Wettbewerbserfolg: 1. Preis für die Wandmalerei, die Sgraffitis und die Farbfenster im Kantonsspital Schaffhausen. Sie ermöglichen ihm, sich ganz der Malerei zu widmen. In den folgenden Jahren intensive Beschäftigung mit dem künstlerischen Schmuck an Bauwerken.

1954
Studienreise nach Deutschland.

1949
Awarded the Conrad Ferdinand Meyer Prize.
In the next few years twice received a bursary from the Kiefer-Hablitzel Foundation.

1950
Study trips through Italy, Sicily and the Aeolian Islands. Visited Italy almost every year from now on.

1951
Started the first series of lithographs at the studios of E. Matthieu AG.

1952
Exhibition in the Zappeion Palace, Athens. Trip through Greece.
First pictures bought by the collectors Nelly and Werner Bär. Beginning of a friendship with the Bär families.

1953
First major competition success: 1st. Prize for the mural, sgraffiti and stained-glass windows at Schaffhausen Canton Hospital. This enables him to devote all his efforts to painting. In the years to follow he develops an intense interest in the artistic ornamentation of buildings.

1954
Study trip to Germany.

Mosaik Kantonsschule Wetzikon (1957).
Mosaic for Wetzikon Canton School (1957).

1955
Ausstellung «Drei Zürcher Künstler» im Kunsthaus Chur.

1956
Wandmalereien Theater Schaffhausen, Fischer-Werke Schaffhausen, Schulhaus Regensdorf.
Geburt des Sohnes Daniel.

1957
Erste Ausstellung Galerie Verena Müller, Bern, dank Anregung des Sammlers Josef Müller.

1958
Zweite Studienreise nach Griechenland (Insel Paros).
Wandbild Schule Adliswil ZH.

1959
Ausmalung des Esszimmers der Sammler Nelly und Werner Bär, Zürich.
Vertiefung der Freundschaft auch mit den anderen Familien Bär.
In diesem Kreis entstehen Bekanntschaften und Freundschaften mit Wissenschaftlern, bildenden Künstlern, Musikern und Dirigenten aus aller Welt.
Wandmalerei Schulhaus Schwanden GL.

1955
Exhibition of three Zurich artists ("Drei Zürcher Künstler") at Kunsthaus Chur.

1956
Murals for Schaffhausen Theatre, the Fischer works in Schaffhausen and a school in Regensdorf near Zurich.
Birth of his son Daniel.

1957
First exhibition at the Galerie Verena Müller in Bern, inspired by the collector, Josef Müller.

1958
Second study trip to Greece (island of Paros).
Mural for a school in Adliswil near Zurich.

1959
Painting of the dining-room of the collectors Nelly and Werner Bär, Zurich.
Closer friendship with the other branches of the Bär family. In this circle friendships and acquaintances with scientists, visual artists, musicians and conductors from all over the world.
Mural for a school at Schwanden, Glarus.

Portrait-Reihe des Sammlers Josef Müller (1964).

Series of portraits of the collector Josef Müller (1964).

1960
Farbfenster Kirche Oberhasli ZH.
Studienreise nach Marokko.

1961
Vier Lithographien für das Buch «Die Episode Randa» von C. J. Burckhardt zu dessen 70. Geburtstag.

1962
Fünf Farbfenster Kirche Männedorf ZH.

1963
Sieben Farbfenster, Türe und Kanzelgestaltung Kirche Sternenberg ZH.
Erneute Studienreise nach Spanien und Tunesien.

1964
Portraitreihe des Sammlers Josef Müller, Solothurn.
Wandbild Direktion des Militärflugplatzes Dübendorf.
Wandbild Schule der Stadt Zürich in Bülach.

1960
Stained-glass windows for Oberhasli Church, Canton of Zurich.
Study trip to Morocco.

1961
Four lithographs for the book "Die Episode Randa" on the occasion of the 70th. birthday of its author, C. J. Burckhardt.

1962
Five stained-glass windows for Männedorf Church.

1963
Seven stained-glass windows, doors and pulpit design for Sternenberg Church, Canton of Zurich.
Further study trips to Spain and Tunisia.

1964
Series of portraits of the collector Josef Müller, Solothurn.

Eröffnung Werner Bär-Saal Kunsthaus Zürich. Direktor Dr. René Wehrli im Gespräch mit Dr. Franz Meyer, Kunstmuseum Basel. Wehrli ist einer der Autoren des 1976 im Orell-Füssli-Verlag erschienenen Buches über den Künstler. Rechts der Künstler mit dem Bildhauer O. Ch. Bänninger (1966).

Opening of the Werner Bär Hall at Kunsthaus Zürich. Director Dr. René Wehrli talking to Dr. Franz Meyer of the Kunstmuseum Basel. Wehrli is one of the authors of the book published on the artist by Orell-Füssli-Verlag in 1976. On the right, the artist with the sculptor, O. Ch. Bänninger (1966).

1965
Ausstellung im Museum zu Allerheiligen Schaffhausen, Ansprache: Prof. Dr. Eduard Hüttinger.
Überreichung der Goldmedaille durch die Schweizer Sportjournalisten für seine Bilderserie über die Pferderennen.
Reise durch den Näheren Orient: Libanon, Syrien, Jordanien, Israel.
Portrait der Familie der Sammler Dr. Walter und Minnie Bechtler, Zollikon.
Zwei Farbfenster Kirche Ellikon an der Thur ZH.
Erneute Reise nach Tunesien (Djerba) gemeinsam mit dem Bildhauer Otto Ch. Bänninger, Zürich.

1966
Zweite Reise nach Marokko.
Wahl in die Ausstellungskommission Kunsthaus Zürich.

Mural for the Directorate of Military Airfields, Dübendorf near Zurich.
Mural for a City of Zurich school in Bülach.

1965
Exhibitions at the Museum zu Allerheiligen, Schaffhausen, address by Prof. Eduard Hüttinger.
Presentation of a gold medal by Swiss sports journalists for his painting series on horse races.
Trip to the Near East: Lebanon, Syria, Jordan, Israel.
Portrait of the whole family of the collectors Dr. Walter and Minnie Bechtler, Zollikon.
Two stained-glass windows for the church of Ellikon an der Thur, Canton of Zurich.
Further trip to Tunisia (Jerba) with Otto Ch. Bänninger, a sculptor from Zurich.

1966
Second trip to Morocco.
Election to the exhibition committee of Kunsthaus Zürich.

Der Künstler mit seiner Frau Hilda und der befreundeten Ellen Weyl auf der grossen Studienreise (1968).

The artist with his wife Hilda and friend Ellen Weyl on a long study trip (1968).

1967
Fünf Farbfenster Kirche Lichtensteig SG.
Ausstellung Schloss Arbon, Ansprache: Dr. Felix Baumann, Kunsthaus Zürich.
Studienreise nach Sardinien.

1968
Das bibliophile Buch «Das Hohe Lied von Salomo» mit 34 Lithographien erscheint bei Arta, Zürich.
Grosse Studienreise durch Indien, Thailand, Kambodscha und Hongkong.
Beginn der Periode mit den Flussbildern und Tempelfiguren.

1969
Ausstellung im Musée d'art et d'histoire Fribourg, Ansprache: Directeur Michel Terrapon.

1970
Wandbild Krankenpflegeheim Schaffhausen.
Drei Farbfenster Limmattalspital, Urdorf ZH.
Farbfenster Rikon ZH.
Reise nach Griechenland (Kreta).

1967
Five stained-glass windows for Lichtensteig Church, Canton of St. Gall.
Exhibition at Arbon Castle, address by Dr. Felix Baumann of Kunsthaus Zürich.
Study trip to Sardinia.

1968
A collector's edition of the Song of Solomon illustrated by 34 lithographs, published by Arta, Zurich.
Extensive study trip to India, Thailand, Cambodia and Hong Kong.
Beginning of the period of paintings of rivers and temple figures.

1969
Exhibition at the Musée d'art et d'histoire, Fribourg, address by the director, Michel Terrapon.

1970
Mural for Schaffhausen Nursing Home. Three stained-glass windows for Limmat Hospital in Urdorf near Zurich.
Stained-glass window for Rikon, Canton of Zurich.
Trip to Greece (Crete).

1971

Ausstellung Kunsthaus Zürich im Helmhaus, 15 Künstler «Die Farbe als sinnliche Erfahrung».

1972

Studienreise nach Ceylon, Java und Bali.

1973

Tropea-Aufenthalt (Kalabrien) mit dem Theologen Walter Bernet und den Kunsthistorikern Christel Sauer und Eduard Hüttinger. Serie der Himmel-Wasser-Bilder.

1974

Biennale Internazionale Campione mit Bill, Moser, Coghuf. Wandbild Schulhaus Niederhasli ZH.
Studienreise nach Südindien und Ceylon, im Herbst erste Reise nach New York.

1971

Exhibition staged by Kunsthaus Zurich at the Helmhaus in Zurich: "Die Farbe als sinnliche Erfahrung" (Colour as a Sensuous Experience), 15 artists.

1972

Study trip to Ceylon, Java and Bali.

1973

Stay in Tropea, Calabria, accompanied by the theologians Walter Bernet and the art historians Christel Sauer and Eduard Hüttinger. Series of sky-water paintings.

1974

Exhibition with Bill, Moser and Coghuf at the Biennale Internazionale Campione.
Mural for school in Niederhasli near Zurich.

Ausstellung Helmhaus Zürich (1976).	Exhibition Helmhaus Zurich (1976).

In der New York Times (1976).
From the New York Times (1976).

1975
Studienreise nach Nepal, Nord- und Zentralindien.

1976
Serie der Radierungen «Die Freuden indischer Liebestempel».
Ausstellung, Kunstgesellschaft Zürich, Helmhaus.
Bilder 1988–1976 und Skulpturen aus Indien und Südostasien aus dem Besitz des Künstlers und des Museum Rietberg Zürich. Ansprache: Dr. Felix Baumann, Kunsthaus Zürich.
Reise zur eigenen Ausstellung in New York.

1978
Acht Farbfenster Reformierte Kirche Freiburg i.Üe.

Study trip to Southern India and Ceylon, in autumn first visit to New York.

1975
Study trip to Nepal, North and Central India.

1976
Series of etchings: "Die Freuden indischer Liebestempel" (The Joys of Indian Temples of Love).
Exhibition Helmhaus Zurich.
Paintings Sigg 1988–1976 and sculptures from India and Southeast Asia (from the artist's personal property and the Rietberg Museum collection in Zurich). Address given by Dr. Felix Baumann, Kunsthaus Zürich.
Trip to his own exhibition in New York.

1978
Eight stained-glass windows for the "Temple de Fribourg".

Erwin Leiser 1977 im Atelier. Arbeit am Film über den Künstler.
Erwin Leiser at the artist's studio, 1977. Working on the film about the artist.

Portraitsitzung mit dem befreundeten Verleger, Photographen und Publizisten Dr. Martin Hürlimann (1978).

Portrait session with his friend, the publisher, photographer and publicist, Dr. Martin Hürlimann (1978).

1979
Studienreise nach Ägypten.
Kurzer Aufenthalt in Venedig.

1980
Drei Farbfenster Kirche St. Peter und Paul, Zürich, auf Anregung des Sammlers Gustav Zumsteg.
Farbfenster Kirche Niederglatt ZH.

1981
Studienreise nach Sizilien.
Wandbild Universität Irchel Zürich.
Bau des zweiten Ateliers in Oberhasli, um Platz für grössere Arbeiten zu haben. So konnte auf die teilweise Benützung der Roten Fabrik in Zürich verzichtet werden.

1979
Study trip to Egypt.
Short stay in Venice.

1980
Three stained-glass windows for the church of St. Peter and Paul, Zurich, on the initiative of the collector Gustav Zumsteg.
Stained-glass windows for Niederglatt Church, Zurich

1981
Study trip to Sicily.
Mural for University of Zurich.
Construction of the second studio in Oberhasli to create space for large works. This allowed the artist to give up partly using the "Rote Fabrik" studio in Zurich.

In der Roten Fabrik Zürich. Arbeit an einem Wandbild für Harro M. Bodmer (1980).

"Rote Fabrik" studio in Zurich. Working on a mural for Henry M. Bodmer (1980).

Am Portrait des Bildhauers Silvio Mattioli (1986).

Working on the sculptor Silvio Mattioli's portrait (1986).

1982
Studienreise nach Thailand, Burma und Malaysia.

1983
Studienreise nach Südmarokko.

1984
Farbfenster Kirche Sulgen TG.
Reise nach Hamburg.
Studienreise nach New York.
Wandbild Depositen- und Kreditbank Zürich.
Farbfenster Abdankungshalle Niederhasli ZH.

1982
Study trip to Thailand, Burma and Malaysia.

1983
Study trip to the Southern Morocco.

1984
Stained-glass window, Sulgen Church, Canton of Thurgau.
Trip to Hamburg.
Study trip to New York.
Mural for "Depositen- und Kreditbank Zürich".
Stained-glass window in the Funeral Chapel, Niederhasli, Zurich.

Ausstellung in der Galerie Kornfeld, Zurich (1984).

Exhibition at the Galerie Kornfeld in Zurich (1984).

Im Atelier. V. l. nach r.:Schriftsteller P. K. Wehrli, Theologe Prof. Walter Bernet, Journalistin Hildegard Schwaninger, Redaktor Jürg Ramspeck, Meieli Bernet, Schauspielerin Julia Vonderlinn, Kunstkritiker Dr. Fritz Billeter (1984).

In the artist's studio. Left to right: the writer P. K.Wehrli, the theologian Prof. Walter Bernet, the journalist Hildegard Schwaninger, the editor Jürg Ramspeck, Meieli Bernet, the actress Julia Vonderlinn, the art critic Dr. Fritz Billeter (1984).

1985

Chorwandbild Reformierte Kirche Freiburg i.Üe.
Mit diesem Bild ist nach langem Ringen zusammen mit den acht Farbfenstern der Kreis geschlossen und ein theologisch und künstlerisch Ganzes entstanden. Seit diesem Zeitpunkt jährlich mehrmalige Arbeitsaufenthalte in Südfrankreich.
Neue Serie der Himmel-Wasser-Bilder.

1985

Choir mural at the "Temple de Fribourg".
This mural completes the work comprising eight stained-glass windows, marking the end of a long battle over the creation of a theological and artistic integral complex. Subsequently, several studies in the South of France every year.
New series of sky-water paintings.

Arbeit mit farbigem Papier am
Familienbild Dr. Bucher-Bechtler (1986).

Working with coloured paper on the
Dr. Bucher-Bechtler family painting
(1986).

1986
Studienreise nach New York,
in den Westen Amerikas und nach Hawaii.

1988
Studienreise nach New York, Guatemala und Mexiko.

1989
Studienreise nach Chicago und New York.

1986
Study trip to New York, West America and Hawaii.

1988
Study trip to New York, Guate-mala and Mexico.

1989
Study trip to Chicago and New York.

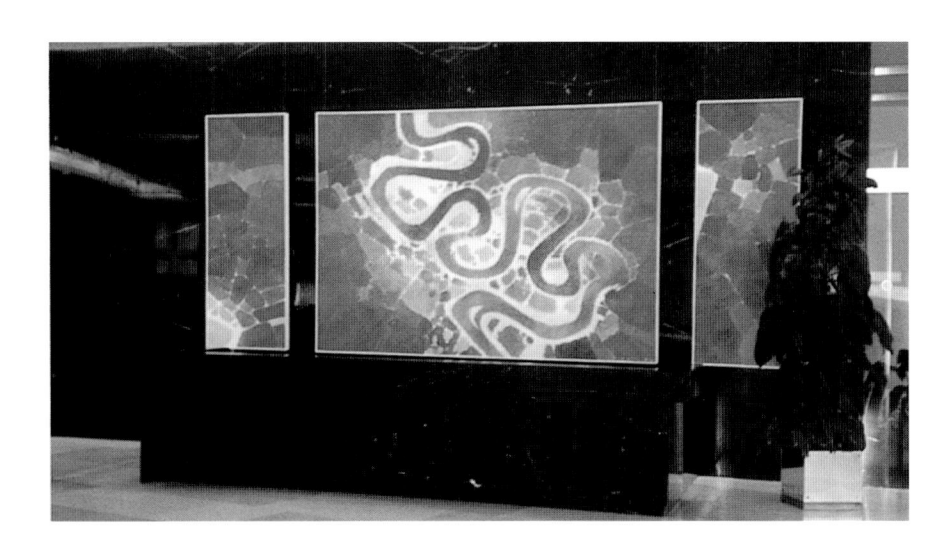

Ausstellung in der Galerie Baukunst, Köln (1988).

Exhibition at the Galerie Baukunst in Cologne (1988).

Der Künstler mit seinem Sohn Daniel in der Galerie Baukunst, Köln.

The artist with his son Daniel at the Galerie Baukunst in Cologne.

1990
Wandbild Hotel Zürich, heute Hotel Mariott Zürich.
Leihgabe Familie Bührle an das Hotel Zürich.

1990
Mural at Hotel Zürich, today Hotel Mariott Zürich.
On loan from the Bührle family to Hotel Zürich.

Beginn der Portrait-Reihe von Dr. Hans Gerling, Köln (1989).

Beginning of the portrait series of Dr. Hans Gerling, Cologne (1989).

Exhibition 50 Years of Zürich-Land, Kunstmuseum Winterthur (1990).

Ausstellung 50 Jahre Zürich-Land. Kunstmuseum Winterthur (1990).

1991
Studienreise nach New York.

1992–1993
Sechs Farbfenster Kirche Davos-Laret, gestiftet von Ingeborg und Otto Haab sowie ihren Freunden.
Zusätzlich zu den bestehenden Fenstern fügt der Künstler

1991
Study trip to New York.

1992–1993
Six stained-glass windows for Davos-Laret Church, donated by Ingeborg and Otto Haab and friends.
Besides the existing windows the artist inserts in the middle

Der Künstler mit dem Kunstglaser Heini Mäder (1993).

The artist with the glass artist Heini Mäder (1993).

Mit seiner Frau Hilda, dem Sohn Daniel und dessen Frau Ellen auf der Chinesischen Mauer (1993).
The artist with his wife Hilda, his son Daniel and wife Ellen on the Chinese Wall (1993).

Karton für Farbfenster Universitätsspital Zürich (1995/96).
Cartoon for stained-glass window at Zurich University Hospital (1995/96).

in der Chormitte ein Rundfenster in die 200jährige Kirche ein und erreicht damit eine klare Ausrichtung des Raumes. Dank einem Freund des Künstlers konnte durch ein Legat auch die Kirche renoviert werden.

1993
Studienreise nach Taiwan, Hongkong und China. Anschliessend Beginn einer Serie von Skulpturen.

1994
Das Buch «H. A. Sigg, Farbfenster und Malerei. Reformierte Kirche Freiburg» erscheint im Benteli Verlag. Autoren: Margrit Hahnloser, Stefan Trümpler und Matthias Thurneysen.

1996
Farbfenster Universitätsspital Zürich.
Studienreise nach New York.

1997
Portrait-Reihe Dr. Nicolas Bär.

of the choir a round window in the 200-year-old church, providing the interior with a clear alignment.
The bequest of one of the artist's frien≠ds also made it possible to renovate the church.

1993
Study trip to Taiwan, Hong Kong and China. Subsequently, the initiation of a series of sculp-tures.

1994
Book published by Benteli Verlag: "H. A. Sigg, Farbfenster und Malerei. Reformierte Kirche Freiburg" (H. A. Sigg, Stained-glass Windows and Painting in the Reformed Church of Fribourg). Authors: Margrit Hahnloser, Stefan Trümpler and Matthias Thurneysen.

1996
Stained-glass window for Zurich University Hospital.
Study trip to New York.

1997
Series of portraits of Dr Nicolas Bär.

Mit wachen Augen: der Künstler und seine Frau Hilda.

Eyes alert: the artist and his wife Hilda.

Werkverzeichnis
Catalogue of Works

Seite/page

7	**Selbstbildnis**/Self-Portrait, 1946/47
8	**Mutter**/Mother, 1945
10	**Am Tisch**/At the Table, 1946
11	**Die Entscheidung**/The Decision, 1946
17	**Le lit,** Paris 1947
21	**Das Fenster**/The Window, 1948 Kanton Zürich
22	**Auf dem Balkon I**/On the Balcony I, Paris, 1947
23	**Nacht-Café III**/Night-Café III, Paris 1947
24	**Hilda mit Hund**/Hilda with Dog, 1954
25	**Café Select**/Café Select, 1946/47
27	**Stadt im Süden**/Town in the South, 1965 Hans und Annemarie Hubacher, Zürich
28	**Die Sonnenstreifen**/Sun Streaks, 1964 Ursula Nyffenegger, Neuhausen
30	**Schafe**/Sheep, 1962 Collection Hans und Bessie Bechtler, Zürich
31	**Schafe im Schnee**/Sheep in the Snow, 1962 Ellen Weyl, Zürich
32	**Herde unterwegs**/Roving Herds, 1965 Collection Bank Julius Bär, Zürich
33	**Das schwarze Feld**/The Black Field, 1961
34	**Das Rennen**/The Race, 1961/68 Hanspeter Zweidler, Küsnacht
35	**Pferderennen**/The Horse Race, 1961 Private collection, Bassersdorf
37	**Familie des Sammlers Dr. W. A. Bechtler** The Family of the Collector Dr. W.A. Bechtler, 1964/65 Foundation Dr. Walter Bechtler, Zollikon
38	**Der Sammler Josef Müller I** The Collector Josef Müller I, 1964/65 Collection Barbier-Müller, Genf
41a	**Harlekin vor dunklem Bild** Harlequin by a Dark Picture, 1965 Private collection, Zumikon
41b	**Harlekin**/Harlequin, 1957 Andreas und Marguerite Fanconi, Zürich
43a	**Rückenakt**/Rear-View Nude, 1964 Private collection
43b	**Nach dem Bade**/After the Bath, 1966
45	**Apulischer Frühling**/Apulian Spring, 1967 Ray und Peter Bär, Küsnacht
47	**In den Gärten Salomos**/In Solomon's Gardens, 1971
48	**Im Lichte des Winters**/In the Light of Winter, 1971/72 Collection Gerling-Konzern, Köln
55	**Weit verzweigter Strom**/Ramified River, 1971
56	**Fleuve,** 1969 Collection Schweiz. Bankverein, Zürich
61	**Reisfelder**/Rice Fields, 1969 Collection Schweiz. Nationalbank, Zürich
65	**Nachklänge, Zyklus indische Figurationen** Echoes, Cycle of Indian Figurations, 1974/82
66	**Die grosse Tempelfigur** The Large Temple Figure, 1973
67	**Der Eingang zum Tempel** The Entrance to the Temple, 1971/72
68	**Indische Tempelfigur I** Indian Temple Figure I, 1973
69	**Die Tempelwand**/The Temple Wall, 1973/74 Private collection Bioley-Magnoux
70	**Geburtstagsblatt**/Birthday, 1975
71	**Indische Tempelfigur II** Indian Temple Figure II, 1975
74	**Die grosse Biegung**/The Large Bend, 1975 Collection Zürcher Kantonalbank
76	**Die Flusswindungen III**/River Meanders III, 1976/84
79	**Inselformen II**/Island Forms II, 1975 Collection Credit Suisse Group, New York
80	**Zwischen Tag und Traum II** Between Day and Dream II, 1990 Christine und Diether Kuhn
81	**Licht über dunklem Wasser** Light above Dark Water, 1986 Private collection, New York
82	**Inselformen I**/Island Forms I, 1975 Collection Credit Suisse Group, New York

83	**Die Inseln im Strom**/Islands in the River, 1980 Private collection, New York	127	**Nachklang II**/Echo II, 1990/91 Collection A.+M. Giedion, Zürich
84	**Inselreich**/Island Kingdom, 1991 Nelly und Hans Ruegger, Aarau	128	**Licht des Himmels I**/Light of the Sky I, 1988/92 Collection Credit Suisse Group, Zürich
89	**Rote Erde, dunkler Fluss** Red Earth, Dark River, 1977/78 Collection R.+L. Blum, Zumikon	129	**Wolkenbänder III**/Bands of Clouds III, 1988
		130	**Nachklang I**/Echo I, 1990/91 N.H. Meyerhofer, Zürich
91	**Heller Fluss im Dunkel der Nacht** Bright River in the Dark of the Night, 1981 Private collection, Zürich	131	**Der Himmel**/The Sky, 1982/83 Collection Bank Julius Bär, Zürich
95	**Der geheimnisvolle Fluss**/Secret River, 1990	133	**Nacht über den Flussspuren I** Night over River Paths I, 1986 Private collection, New York
97	**Die Spur des Flusses**/The Course of the River V, 1985		
99	**Nacht über der Küste**/Night over the Coast, 1975 Hans-Ulrich und Barbara Doerig, Zumikon	134	**Abend am Meer III**/Evening by the Sea III, 1988
		135	**Abend am Meer I**/Evening by the Sea I, 1986
101	**Die Wasserstellen**/The Watering Places, 1973 Monika und Thomas Bär, Erlenbach	137	**Erde – Himmel**/Earth – Sky, 1989
		138	**Nacht über den Flussspuren** Night over River Paths II, 1988
104	**Die Nacht über dem Fluss** Night over the River, 1977 Collection Credit Suisse Group, New York	139	**Träumende II**/Dreamers II, 1986
		140	**Helle Flussspuren III**/Bright River Paths III, 1986
107	**Der Kimono III**/The Kimono III, 1986	141	**Inseln im dunkelgrünen Wasser** Islands in Dark-Green Water, 1986
109	**Frau im Kimono I**/Woman in a Kimono I, 1985		
111	**Der Traum**/The Dream, 1986	142	**Meer und Himmel II**/Sea and Sky II, 1979 Collection Zürcher Kantonalbank
113	**Im Lichte des Mondes** By the Light of the Moon, 1984 Private collection, Köln	145	**Die hellen Inseln I**/The Bright Islands I, 1993
		149	**Stiller Abend über hellem Fluss I** Quiet Evening over a Bright River I, 1986 Private collection, New York
114	**Die Insel des Poeten I**/The Poet's Island I, 1989 Collection Karin und Peter Schindler, Zürich		
115	**Herbst**/Autumn, 1984 Marianne und Jörg Kern, Forch	150	**Im Land der Flüsse II** In the Land of the Rivers II, 1992 Collection Paul und Margrit Hahnloser, Fribourg
116	**Wintertag**/Winter Day, 1976 Robert A. Jecker, Basel	153	**Flusslauf – Erde – Himmel** River Course – Earth – Sky, 1988/89
117	**Der Berg**/The Mountain, 1994		
119	**Es hellt auf**/Brightening Up, 1986	155	**Aufleuchtende Flussspuren** Gleaming River Paths, 1988
121	Vollmond, Wolken, Bergtal I/Full Moon, Clouds, Mountain Valley I, 1988	156	**Helle Wasserläufe**/Bright Watercourses, 1986 Private collection, Winterthur
122	**Das erste Licht II**/The First Light II, 1988		
123	**Letztes helles Licht**/The Last Bright Light, 1991	157	**Die weissen Flussformen**/White River Forms, 1989 Collection Zürcher Kantonalbank
125	**Fluss im Mondlicht**/River by Moonlight, 1979/80 Sonja Koblet, Uitikon	158	**Beschwingter Flusslauf II** Lively River Course II, 1989/90

160	**Im Land der Flüsse IV**/In the Land of the Rivers IV, 1993 Rudolf W. Hug	207	**Im Zeichen des Flusses I** Under the Sign of the River I, 1990/91
161	**Skulptur II**/Sculpture II, 1989 Private collection, New York	209	**Im Reich der Mitte XI** In the Middle Realm XI, 1995/96
162	**Skulptur III**/Sculpture III, 1989	211	**Im Reich der Mitte IX** In the Middle Realm IX, 1994/95 Private collection, Germany
163	**Nacht-Traum**/Night-Dream, 1994		
164	**Zwischen Tag und Traum III** Between Day and Dream III, 1991	213	**Im Reich der Mitte X** In the Middle Realm X, 1995/96
166	**Nacht-Blau**/Night-Blue, 1995	215	**Im Reich der Mitte VIII** In the Middle Realm VIII, 1995
170	**Ohne Titel I**/No title I, 1989		
176– 178	**Triptychon (links, Mitte, rechts)** Triptych (left, middle, right), 1994	217	**Im Reich der Mitte II** In the Middle Realm II, 1994
179	**Im Reich der Mitte III**/In the Middle Realm III, 1994	219	**Nachdenkend verweilen**/Lingering in Contemplation, 1994 Kanton Zürich
180	**Mündung III**/Estuary III, 1995		
182	**Ohne Titel 1**/No title 1, 1994, Minnie Bechtler, Zollikon	221	**Im Reich der Mitte XIV**/In the Middle Realm XIV, 1996
183	**Im Zeichen des Flusses III** Under the Sign of the River III, 1990/91	223	**Im Reich der Mitte XII**/In the Middle Realm XII, 1996 Private collection, New York
184	**Ohne Titel 3**/No title 3, 1994	225	**Im Reich der Mitte XV**/In The Middle Realm XV, 1998
185	**Ohne Titel II**/No title II, 1993	227	**Im Reich der Mitte XVI** In the Middle Realm XVI, 1997/98
187	**Im Reich der Mitte IV**/In the Middle Realm IV, 1994		
188	**Ohne Titel 5**/No title 5, 1994	230	**8 Farbfenster,** 1978, und **Chorwandbild,** 1985, Reformierte Kirche Freiburg 8 Stained-Glass Windows, 1978, and Choir Mural, 1985, Reformed Church Fribourg
189	**Ohne Titel 4**/No title 4, 1994		
190	**Ohne Titel 10**/No title 10, 1995		
191	**Ohne Titel 11**/No title 11, 1994		
192	**Ohne Titel 2**/No title 2, 1994	231	**Rundfenster,** Reformierte Kirche Freiburg Round Window, Reformed Church Fribourg, 1985
193	**Im Reich der Mitte I**/In the Middle Realm I, 1994		
195	**Im Reich der Mitte VII**/In the Middle Realm VII, 1995	232	**Wandbild Universität Zürich-Irchel** Mural University of Zurich-Irchel, 1981
196	**Ohne Titel 7**/No title 7, 1995		
197	**Ohne Titel 8**/No title 8, 1995	235	**Wandbild**/Mural, 1990, ehemals Hotel Zürich, heute Hotel Mariott Zürich/Former Hotel Zurich, today Hotel Mariott Zürich Leihgabe Familie Bührle/on loan by the Bührle family
198	**Ohne Titel 9**/No title 9, 1994		
199	**Ohne Titel 12**/No title 12, 1994		
200	**Ohne Titel 15**/No title 15, 1996		
201	**Ohne Titel 16**/No title 16, 1996	236	**6 Farbfenster,** Kirche Davos-Laret 6 Stained-Glass Windows, Davos-Laret Church, 1992/93
202	**Ohne Titel 17**/No title 17, 1996		
203	**Ohne Titel 14**/No title 14, 1995	237	**Chorfenster links,** Kirche Davos-Laret Choir Window left, Davos-Laret Church, 1992/93
204	**Ohne Titel 13**/No title 13, 1995		
205	**Im Reich des Herbstes**/In the Realm of Autumn, 1994/95 Collection Credit Suisse Group, Zürich	238	**Farbfenster,** Universitätsspital Zürich, Aufnahmetrakt Stained-Glass Window, University Hospital Zurich, Admissions Hall, 1995/96

Anhang

Appendix

Einzelausstellungen
One-man Exhibitions

1951	Zürich, Galerie Wolfsberg
1952	Athen, Palais Zappeion
1953	Zürich, Galerie Orell Füssli
1955	Zürich, Galerie Orell Füssli
1956	Winterthur, Galerie ABC
1957	Bern, Galerie Verena Müller
	Zürich, Galerie Läubli
1958	Zürich, Galerie Orell Füssli
1959	Bern, Galerie Verena Müller
1960	Langenthal, Galerie Leuenbrüggli
	Luzern, Galerie Im Ronca-Haus
1962	Bern, Galerie Verena Müller
	Zürich, Galerie Läubli
	Zürich, Galerie Orell Füssli
1963	Lenzburg, Galerie Rathausgasse
1964	Zug, Galerie Altstadt
	Uster, Stadthaus
	Zürich, Galerie Orell Füssli
	Zürich, Galerie Läubli
1965	Schaffhausen, Museum zu Allerheiligen
	Bern, Galerie Verena Müller
1967	Arbon, Schloss von Arbon
1968	Zürich, Galerie Orell Füssli
	Zofingen, Galerie Zur alten Kanzlei
1969	Fribourg, Musée d'art et d'histoire
1970	Bern, Galerie Verena Müller
	Zürich, Galerie Orell Füssli
1971	Chur, Galerie Zur Kupfergasse
	Zofingen, Galerie Zur alten Kanzlei
1973	Bern, Galerie Verena Müller
1974	Zürich, Galerie Orell Füssli
1975	Zürich, Galerie Roswitha Haftmann, Modern Art
1976	Zürich, Kunstgesellschaft, Helmhaus
	New York, Galerie William Wolff
1978	Schaffhausen, Galerie des Kunstvereins
	Zofingen, Galerie Zur alten Kanzlei
	Zürich, Galerie Orell Füssli
1979	Klosters, Galerie 63
1980	Ascona, Galerie AAA
	Savognin, Vereinigung Pro Segantini
1982	Zofingen, Galerie Zur alten Kanzlei
1983	Bern, Galerie Kornfeld «Bilder der Jahre 1973–1982»
	Langenthal, Galerie Leuenbrüggli
1984	Zürich, Galerie Kornfeld «Bilder der Jahre 1975–1984»
1985	Romont, Musée Suisse du Vitrail
	Oetwil, Kunstcollegium Limmattal
1986	Zofingen, Kunsthaus zum alten Schützenhaus
1987	Herrliberg, Galerie Vogtei
	Wangen a. Aare, Galerie Steinke
1988	Köln, Galerie Baukunst und Folgeausstellungen Mannheim und Brüssel
1989	Frauenfeld, Kunstverein
	Zofingen, Kunsthaus zum alten Schützenhaus
1990	Zug, Galerie Bommer
	Chur, Galerie Giacometti
1991	Zürich, Galerie Kornfeld «Bilder der Jahre 1985–1991»
1992	Wangen a. Aare, Galerie Steinke
1993	Langenthal, Galerie Leuenbrüggli
1995	Flughafen Kloten, Galerie Wolfsberg
1996	Lenzburg, Galerie Rathausgasse

Auswahl Gruppenausstellungen
Selected Group Exhibitions

1946 Winterthur, Kunstmuseum, «Zürcher Künstler»
1947 Zürich, WbK
1948 Zürich, WbK
1949 Zürich, Kunsthaus, «Junge Zürcher Künstler»
1950 Aarau, Kunsthaus, «Zehn junge Schweizer Künstler»
 Zürich, Kunsthaus, GSMBA, Sektion Zürich
 Winterthur, Kunstmuseum, «Zürcher Künstler»
1951 Zürich, Kunsthaus, «Nationale Ausstellung der GSMBA»
 Uster, «Zürcher Künstler»
1952 St. Gallen, Kunstmuseum
 Aarau, Galerie Strebel
 Winterthur, Kunstmuseum, «Zürcher Künstler»
1953 Bern, Kunstmuseum, «Nationale Ausstellung der GSMBA»
 Schaffhausen, Museum zu Allerheiligen, «Schaffhauser Künstler»
1954 Zürich, Kunsthaus, «Christliche Kunst der Gegenwart»
 Zürich, Kunsthaus, GSMBA, Sektion Zürich
 Schaffhausen, Museum zu Allerheiligen, «Schaffhauser Künstler»
 Konstanz, Kunstverein
 Küsnacht, «Zürcher Künstler»
1955 Chur, Kunsthaus, «Drei Zürcher Maler» H. Müller, W. Sautter, H.A. Sigg
 Olten, Atelhaus
 Schaffhausen, Museum zu Allerheiligen, «Schaffhauser Künstler»
 Luzern, Kunstmuseum, «Zürcher Maler und Bildhauer»
 St. Gallen, Olmahalle, «Nationale Ausstellung der GSMBA»
1956 Zürich, Graphische Sammlung der Eidg. Technischen Hochschule
 Basel, «Nationale Ausstellung der GSMBA»
 Bülach, «Zürcher Künstler»
1957 Thun, Kunstsammlung, «Zürcher und Graubündner Künstler»
1958 Zürich, Galerie Läubli
 Winterthur, Kunstmuseum, «Zürcher Künstler»
1959 Luzern, Kunstmuseum, «Moderne Wandmalerei in der Schweiz»
 Zürich, Kunsthaus, GSMBA, Sektion Zürich
 Olten, Atelhaus
 Uster, «Zürcher Künstler»
1961 Tunis, Tunesien, «Exposition internationale»
 Luzern, Kunstmuseum, «Sport in der Kunst»
 Winterthur, Kunstmuseum, «Zürcher Künstler»
1962 Solothurn, Kunstmuseum, Einladung als Gast mit Werkgruppe
 Saigon, «Eposition internationale de gravure»
 St. Moritz, «Exposition internationale de gravure»
 Männedorf, «Zürcher Künstler»
1963 Zürich, Galerie Orell Füssli
1964 Olten, Atelhaus
 Wien, «Internationale Ausstellung der Graphik»
 Santiago de Chile, «Exposition internationale de gravure»
 Winterthur, Kunstmuseum, «Zürcher Künstler»
1965 Zofingen, Galerie Zur alten Kanzlei
 Brüssel, «Les Arts en Europe»
1966 Chur, Kunsthaus, «Schweizer Graphik»
 Zürich, Galerie Läubli
 Zürich, Kunsthaus, GSMBA, Sektion Zürich
 Wetzikon, «Zürcher Künstler»
1967 Winterthur, Kunstmuseum, «Zürcher Künster»
1968 Aarau, Kunstmuseum, «Nationale Ausstellung der GSMBA»
1969 Bülach, «Zürcher Künstler»
 Zürich, Kunsthaus, GSMBA, Sektion Zürich
1970 Zürich, «Zürcher Künstler im Helmhaus»
 Strassburg, «Zürcher Künstler»
1971 Zürich, Kunstgesellschaft, Helmhaus, «Farbe als sinnliche Erfahrung», 15 Künstler
1972 Manoir de Martigny, «L'aquarelle en Suisse»

1973	Schaffhausen, Museum zu Allerheiligen, «Jubiläumsausstellung der Schaffhauser Kunstgesellschaft»		**Ausgewählte öffentliche Arbeiten** **Selected Public Projects**

1973 Schaffhausen, Museum zu Allerheiligen, «Jubiläumsausstellung der Schaffhauser Kunstgesellschaft»
Zürich, Kunsthaus, GSMBA, Sektion Zürich
1974 Winterthur, Kunstmuseum, «Zürcher Künstler»
Campione, Italia, «Biennale Internazionale d'Arte»
1975 Männedorf, «Zürcher Künstler»
1976 Winterthur, Kunstmuseum, «Zürcher Künstler»
1977 Thalwil, «Zürcher Künstler»
Manoir de Martigny, «La Lithographie»
1978 Zürich, Galerie Roswitha Haftmann, Modern Art
Küsnacht, «Zürcher Künstler»
1979 Winterthur, «Zürcher Künstler»
Zürich, Jubiläumsausstellung Orell Füssli
Zürich, Helmhaus, Alpine Kunst
1980 Wallisellen, Jubiläumsausstellung «Zürcher Künstler»
1981 Uster, «Zürcher Künstler»
Delsberg, Biennale Schweizer Kunst
1982 Winterthur, Kunstmuseum, «Zürcher Künstler»
Reinach, Radierungen
1983 Zürich, Galerie Roswitha Haftmann, Sommerausstellung mit Bissier, Kokoschka, Kirchner, Luginbühl
Opfikon, «Zürcher Künstler»
Zürich, Kunsthaus, «Arbeitskontakte»
1984 Uitikon, «Zürcher Künstler»
Wangen a. Aare, Galerie Steinke
Reinach, Originallithos Intérieur/Extérieur
1989 Zofingen, Kunsthaus zum alten Schützenhaus, zum Gedenken Richard Haller
1990 Köln, Galerie Baukunst, «Globale Künstler», zum 75. Geburtstag von Dr. Hans Gerling
Winterthur, Kunstmuseum, «50 Jahre Zürich-Land»
1991 Köln, Galerie Baukunst, «Künstler des Jahrhunderts», Gedächtnisausstellung für Irene Gerling
Zürich, Galerie Roswitha Haftmann
1993 Zürich, Galerie Wolfsberg
1996 Zürich, Galerie Roswitha Haftmann
1977 Bern, Schweiz. Landesbibliothek «Indien sehen»
New York, DC Moore-Gallery

Ausgewählte öffentliche Arbeiten
Selected Public Projects

Wandmalereien und Farbfenster
Murals and Stained-Glass Windows

1953 Kantonsspital Schaffhausen
State Hospital of Schaffhausen
1956 Stadttheater Schaffhausen
Schaffhausen-Theater, Schaffhausen
1957 Kantonsschule Wetzikon, Kanton Zürich
State School, Wetzikon, State of Zurich
1960 Kirche Oberhasli, Kanton Zürich
Church of Oberhasli, State of Zurich
1962 Kirche Männedorf, Kanton Zürich
Church of Männedorf, State of Zurich
1963 Kirche Sternenberg, Kanton Zürich
Church of Sternenberg, State of Zurich
1964 Stadtschule Zürich, Bülach
City of Zurich School, Bülach
1965 Kirche Ellikon a. d. Thur, Kanton Zürich
Church of Ellikon, State of Zurich
1967 Kirche Lichtensteig, Kanton St. Gallen
Church of Lichtensteig, State of St. Gall
1970 Pflegeheim Schaffhausen
State Nursing Home, Schaffhausen
Kapelle Limmattalspital, Urdorf
Limmattal Hospital, Chapel, Urdorf
1978 Kirche Freiburg/Church of Fribourg
1980 Kirche St. Peter und Paul, Zürich
Church of St. Peter and Paul, Zurich
1981 Universität Zürich/University of Zurich
1984 Kirche Niederhasli/Church of Niederhasli
1985 Kirche Freiburg/Church of Fribourg
1990 Hotel Zürich (Marriot), Zürich
Hotel Zurich (Marriot), Zurich
1993 Kirche Davos-Laret/Church of Davos-Laret
1996 Universitätsspital Zürich
University Hospital of Zurich

Radio und Television

1977 Television Schweiz
Erwin Leiser: «Film über H. A. Sigg»
1982 Radio Suisse Romande
«Portrait d'artiste: H. A. Sigg». Interview durch Michel Terrapon

Ausgewählte Bibliographie
Selected Bibliography

1950 Rüegg, Albert: Kunst und Volk
1953 Drack, Walter: «H. A. Sigg»: Arts, Paris, Juli
1954 Rüegg, Albert: Kunst und Volk
1958 Allgemeines Lexikon der bildenden Künstler des XX. Jahrhunderts, Bd. IV, Leipzig, Deutschland
1965 «Rencontre avec H. A. Sigg», L'Abeille, Paris, Frankreich
Freivogel, Max: Katalog, Museum zu Allerheiligen, Schaffhausen
1966 Swissair Gazette, L'artista degli ippodromi nivali
Christoffel, Ulrich: Neue Bündner Zeitung, H. A. Sigg
1967 Künstler-Lexikon der Schweiz XX. Jahrhundert, Frauenfeld
1969 Terrapon, Michael: H. A. Sigg. Ausstellungskatalog, Musée d'art et d'histoire, Freiburg
1976 Baumann, Felix: H. A. Sigg. Ausstellungskatalog, Zürcher Kunstgesellschaft, Helmhaus, Zürich
Hüttinger, Edouard; Bernet, Walter und Wehrli, René: H. A. Sigg, Bilder und Zeichnungen aus Südostasien, Orell Füssli Verlag, Zürich
1977 Billeter, Fritz: «Biblische Gehalte in ungegenständlicher Darstellung», Tages-Anzeiger, 6. Dezember
1978 Leiser, Erwin: «Bilder der Stille», Züri Leu, Oktober
1980 Leiser, Erwin: «Fenster zum Träumen», Züri Leu, Oktober
Billeter, Fritz: «Drei Fenster für Kirche St. Peter und Paul, Zürich»
Riesterer, Peter: «Der Maler H. A. Sigg», Südschweiz, 29. März
1984 Billeter, Fritz: «Urfigur des Flusses», zur Ausstellung in der Galerie Kornfeld, Zürich, DU, November
1985 Fasel, Pierre: H. A. Sigg, Musée Suisse du Vitrail, Romont
1988 Billeter, Fritz: H. A. Sigg, Galerie Baukunst Köln, Deutschland
Richter, Horst: Zur Ausstellung in der Galerie Baukunst Köln, Weltkunst, März
1989 Baukunst-Architektur und Skulpturen, Galerie Baukunst, Köln, Deutschland
1990 Globale Künstler, Galerie Baukunst, Köln, Deutschland
50 Jahre Zürich-Land, Kunstmuseum, Winterthur
1991 Billeter, Fritz: «Bilder zum Meditieren», Tages-Anzeiger, November
Künstler des Jahrhunderts, Galerie Baukunst, Köln, Deutschland
1994 Hahnloser, Margrit; Thurneysen, Matthias und Trümpler, Stefan: H. A. Sigg. Farbfenster und Malerei. Reformierte Kirche Freiburg, Benteli Verlag, Bern, Schweiz
1995 Billeter, Fritz: «H. A. Sigg. Farbfenster und Malerei. Reformierte Kirche Freiburg» Buchbesprechung
1997 Murdock, Robert M: «The Art of H. A. Sigg», Katalog Margaret Mathews-Berenson Fine Arts, New York

Zu den Autoren

Fritz Billeter

Geb. 1929 in Zürich; Jugend und Studien in Basel. Dissertation: «Das Dichterische bei Kafka und Kierkegaard». Seit 1960 in Zürich wohnhaft. Unterrichtete hier an verschiedenen Gymnasien. 1971–1995 Kulturredaktor am Tages-Anzeiger (Leiter der Abteilung Visuelle Kultur); seither freier Publizist. Verfasser zahlreicher Monographien vornehmlich Schweizer Künstlerinnen und Künstler.

Karl Ruhrberg

Prof., geb. 1924 in Wuppertal; 1945–48 Musikstudium in Oberstdorf, Düsseldorf, Duisburg; 1948–51 Sportredakteur; 1952–56 Studium der Theaterwissenschaft und Kunstgeschichte; 1956–62 Feuilletonredakteur; 1962–64 Chefdramaturg Deutsche Oper am Rhein; 1965–72 Gründungsdirektor Kunsthalle Düsseldorf; 1972–78 Direktor Berliner Künstlerprogramm/DAAD; 1978–84 Direktor Museum Köln; seither freier Autor.
Publikationen u.a.: Werner Gilles (Monographie) 1961; Der Schlüssel zur Malerei von heute 1965; Bernard Schultze 1984; Kunst im 20. Jahrhundert/Art of Twentieth Century 1986; Emil Schumacher, Zeichen und Farbe 1987; Die Malerei unseres Jahrhunderts 1987; Der streitbare Liebhaber (Festschrift, Hrsg. Eberhard Roters) 1994; Alfred Schmela (Hrsg.) 1996; Miotte 1998; Die Malerei unseres Jahrhunderts (dreisprachig) 1998.

Guido Magnaguagno

Geb. 1946, Studium der Kunstgeschichte an der Universität Zürich. Ab 1980 Ausstellungskonservator am Kunsthaus Zürich, seit 1988 Vizedirektor.
Ausstellungen und Publikationen u.a. zur klassischen Moderne (Hodler, Ensor, Munch, Segantini), «Böcklin – de Chirico – Max Ernst. Eine Reise ins Ungewisse» 1997/98, zur Dada-Bewegung und «Brasilien – Entdeckung und Selbstentdeckung» 1992, sowie zur Schweizer Kunst (Dreissiger Jahre – Ein Jahrzehnt im Widerspruch, Geiser, Aeschbacher, Moser, Tinguely) und Schweizer Photogeschichte (Senn, Staub, Bischof, Burri).

The Authors

Fritz Billeter

Born in Zurich in 1929, he grew up and studied in Basel. Dissertation on the poetic element in Kafka and Kierkegaard. Moved to Zurich in 1960, where he taught in various high schools. 1971–1995 editor of the arts section of the Tages-Anzeiger daily (head of the visual arts division). Currently a free-lance writer, he has published numerous monographs, mainly on Swiss artists.

Karl Ruhrberg

Professor Ruhrberg was born in Wuppertal in 1924; 1945–48 music studies in Oberstdorf, Düsseldorf, Duisburg; 1948–51 sports-journalist; 1952–56 theatre and art history studies; 1956–62 feuilleton editor; 1962–64 chief dramatic advisor of Deutsche Oper am Rhein; 1965–72 founding director of Kunsthalle Düsseldorf; 1972–78 director of Berlin art program of DAAD; 1978–84 director of Cologne Museum; now a free-lance writer.
Publications include: Werner Gilles (monograph) 1961; Der Schlüssel zur Malerei von heute (Key to Contemporary Art) 1965; Bernard Schultze 1984; Kunst in 20. Jahrhundert Art of the Twentieth Century 1986; Emil Schumacher, Zeichen und Farbe (Signs and Colours) 1987; Die Malerei unseres Jahrhunderts (20th-century Painting) 1987; Der streitbare Liebhaber: Festschrift, ed. Eberhard Roters 1994; Alfred Schmela (ed.) 1996; Miotte 1998; Die Malerei unseres Jahrhunderts (trilingual) 1998.

Guido Magnaguagno

Born in 1946; art history studies at University of Zurich. Exhibition conservator at Kunsthaus Zurich since 1980; vice-director from 1988 on. Exhibitions and publications on, among other subjects, classical modernism (Hodler, Ensor, Munch, Segantini), «Böcklin, de Chirico, Max Ernst: Eine Reise ins Ungewisse» (A Voyage into the Unknown) 1997–98, on Dada, and «Brasilien: Entdeckung und Selbstentdeckung» (Brasil: Discovery and Self-discovery) 1992, as well as on Swiss art («Dreissiger Jahre: Ein Jahrzehnt im Widerspruch» [The Thirties: a Decade of Contradiction], Geiser, Aeschbacher, Moser, Tinguely) and the history of Swiss photography (Senn, Staub, Bischof, Burri).

Photonachweis

Photocredits

Bruno und Eric Bührer
Gitty Darugar
Felix Eidenbenz
Peter Friedli
Jean-Pierre Gaechter
Rob Gnant
René Groebli

Urs Hegnauer
Giorgio Hoch
Jean-Pierre Kuhn
Endrik Lerch
Jean Mülhauser
Hilda Sigg

Diese Publikation erscheint auch in einer numerierten und signierten Vorzugsausgabe mit einer Collage des Künstlers in einer limitierten Auflage von 40 Exemplaren

This publication appears in a special numbered and signed version with a collage by the artist in a limited edition of 40 copies

Umschlagabbildung/Cover illustration: Im Zeichen des Flusses III/Under the
Sign of the River III, 1990/91, Acryl/acrylic, 162×116 cm

© H.A. Sigg und Benteli Verlags AG, Bern
© für die Textbeiträge bei den Autoren/authors as named for their contributions
Übersetzung/Translation: John M. King, Werkstatt P. Gillhofer, München
Satz, Gestaltung, Lektorat/Typesetting, Layout, Reading: Benteliteam
Photolithos/Photolithography: Repro Marti Digital AG, Hinterkappelen
Druck/Printing: Benteli Hallwag Druck AG, Wabern-Bern
Buchbinder/Binding: Schumacher AG, Schmitten

ISBN 3-7165-1123-4